Striking Eight Bells

An Uneasy Time for America

GEORGE TROWBRIDGE

Published by Richter Publishing LLC www.richterpublishing.com

Editors: Natalie Meyer, Margarita Martinez & Monica San Nicolas

Proofreader: Nastassia Clarke

ISBN-10: 1-945812-33-8
ISBN-13: 978-1-945812-33-0

DISCLAIMER

The stories in this book reflect the author's recollection of events. Some names, locations, and identifying characteristics have been changed to protect the privacy of those depicted. Dialogue has been recreated from memory. Dates, times, and locations were recreated from declassified U.S. Navy records and others. Photographs used are either public domain or owned by the author. Illustrations and maps used were either created by the author or in the public domain. The book is solely the opinion of the author and not the publisher.

CONTENTS

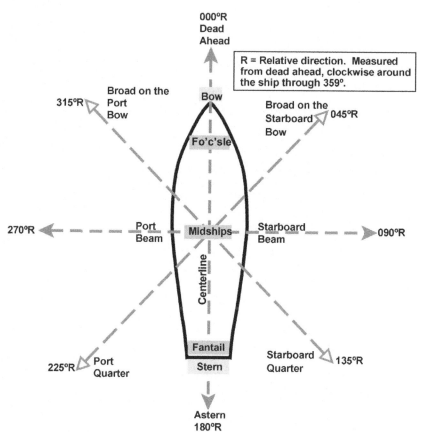

000°R
Dead
Ahead

R = Relative direction. Measured
from dead ahead, clockwise around
the ship through 359°.

315°R Broad on the
Port
Bow

Bow

Broad on the
Starboard 045°R
Bow

Fo'c'sle

270°R Port
Beam

Midships

Starboard
Beam 090°R

Centerline

Fantail

225°R Port
Quarter

Stern

Starboard
Quarter 135°R

Astern
180°R

Typical reference directions and commonly used terms on board ships.

PROLOGUE

Our Navy destroyer had just arrived off the coast of South Vietnam, close to the Demilitarized Zone (DMZ). Our ship had checked in by radio with our Marine Corps forward observer (FO) and artillery spotting team. One of my buddies, Jeff, and I were out on the ship's port bridge wing along with some of the other bridge crew when we spotted a Bell-Huey helicopter flying toward our ship. Listening over the bridge radio speaker, we learned that our Marine FO was aboard the helicopter and was outbound to do a fly over of the ship, as a way of welcoming us to Vietnam's infamous gun line. As the helicopter drew near flying overhead and around our ship, all of us out on deck waved at the helicopter pilot and the Marine FO. Several minutes later, the helicopter was headed back to shore and as it got over land, we all heard repeated *POP,POP,POP,POP* sounds of machine gun and small arms fire from ground enemy forces firing at the helicopter. The FO's helicopter appeared to increase in altitude and continued on, eventually disappearing over the tree-lined horizon. Jeff turned and said to no one in particular, "Welcome to Vietnam. This shit is for real."

Our war had begun. This place where I now found myself might as well have been another planet. Apparently, this place was now my world. I remember thinking that I had to make sure my stay here was temporary, not forever. My old world, home with my wife Janice and our baby boy, now seemed really, really far away.

In late November of 1972, I found myself as a bridge team member on a U.S. Navy destroyer stationed in the shallow water areas off the coast of Vietnam. Our ship was there to provide naval gun fire support to the Marine I Corps in South Vietnam near the DMZ, and to run strike attack missions on coastal targets in North Vietnam. It never had been my intent or purpose to be where I was. Like many young men of my generation after the age of 18, our choices were limited to being drafted into the U.S. Army, hopefully getting a college draft deferment, or enlisting in another branch of the armed forces to avoid being drafted into the Army. My choice ultimately ending up being the latter.

We were not unpatriotic by any means; serving in the military was still seen as an honorable thing to do. However, as products of the 1960s, my age group had already experienced the assassinations of our president and leaders like Martin Luther King Jr. and Robert F. "Bobby" Kennedy; our government's escalation of a war against communism that nobody really understood; Civil Rights protests and marches; the spread of rock 'n roll; a drug culture taking hold with our young people; and the best one of all, the spread of "Free Love." Around the fringe of all of this was the ever-growing antiwar sentiment about our country's involvement in the Vietnam War.

Vietnam aside, this was a great time to grow up. But by the end of 1960s and early 1970s, our continued involvement in the Vietnam War and the substantial losses of American lives brought a big question to America's consciousness: *Why are we fighting?* It seemed that for this particular question, there was no good answer.

In rural farming communities such as the one where I grew up in northeast Iowa, most young people were given adult responsibilities and treated as adults around the time they turned 16. For a young farm kid like me, it was expected that as I got older, I would take on more of the work on our family farm. I saw no future for me in farming. Once high school was finished, I would also be finished with farming. However, my friends and I were routinely warned by some adults, "Go to college and get your draft deferment. Otherwise, you may find yourself slogging through some rice paddy in Vietnam." The advice and warnings weren't wrong. Unless some alternative could be found, *slogging through rice paddies* might well be our future.

In 1970, after high school, I did leave the farm with the help from family, and began my working life. From my view, it seemed worth the risk to run the gauntlet of taking the chance of getting drafted. Youth often allows us to look at things in simple terms. My opinion was, "I'll worry about it when and if it happens." In the 15-month period after high school, I left home, met the girl who became my wife, found out my draft lottery number was one of the low ones, and joined the U.S. Navy.

Now a married man, when it came time to enlist in the Navy, I had two objectives in mind. First, to enlist in a technical field, because with that training and experience, I would find good employment opportunities after getting out. The second really wasn't an objective, it was just a hope that I wouldn't get sent to Vietnam. I achieved the first objective at least initially, but ultimately did not achieve the second. This book is the story of my four-year journey, beginning with my teenage years in Iowa through the completion of my ship's combat tour in Vietnam. Throughout the course of my journey, American culture and society evolved significantly. Sometimes these changes brought on a sense of uneasiness; other times, it was as if we as a people were becoming unhinged.

My journey was meant to go as I had mapped it, from points A to B. Well, as it turns out, forces in life often don't allow us to stick to the plan. Events or circumstances may come along that we never planned for, which skew us onto other unexpected paths, even if we've made contingency plans ahead of time. When we're young, we're generally more flexible in our thinking and can adapt more easily to change. If you're willing to take events as they come and make the best of them, this can sometimes end up fulfilling passions and needs you didn't know you had. That's what my journey taught me.

Alongside my journey, there is another story that also needs to be told about the accomplishments of the crews manning our U.S. Navy destroyers and cruisers operating off the coast of Vietnam out in the Gulf of Tonkin at an area called "Yankee Station" and more specifically near South and North Vietnamese shores and shallow coastal waters. Yankee Station was a designated point well away from the coast of Vietnam out in the Gulf of Tonkin. The open sea area was used by Task Force 77's Navy aircraft carriers to launch air strikes into Vietnam. While the point's official designation was "Point Yankee," generally everyone referred to it as Yankee Station.

During the close to shore naval gun fire support and combat strike attack missions targeting the North Vietnam Army (NVA). The crews of these ships performed superhuman feats in ensuring the missions were successful, as a matter of routine, all of them showed courage and resolve. Many of these ships underwent heavy counter-battery fire from NVA shore big-gun batteries.

Other ships were at times attacked by NVA MIG aircraft or fast patrol boats firing anti-ship missiles. By mid-1972, U.S. Navy destroyers were more frequently getting into fierce gun-to-gun battles with the NVA. Almost all ships that participated in strike missions received, at the least, damage from shrapnel. Other ships received direct hits from NVA gunners resulting in loss of lives and injuries.

Over the years, there have been many news and magazine articles as well as television shows about the Vietnam War. These stories rarely, if ever, tell of the Navy destroyers in Vietnam on the gun lines or the strike missions. Why? Your guess would be as good as mine. Maybe the stories aren't glamorous enough or don't fit the media's political narrative of showing only struggling operations in Vietnam, rather than successful ones.

The crews of these ships were all young men who had to adapt to the environment of combat operations fast. Why fast? Because everything there happened fast. You see, the crew of my ship was typical of all destroyer crews of the time. The enlisted men of all destroyer crews lived a meager, bare-bones existence. Once combat operations began, even the basics such as sleep, food, and other physiological necessities were now mostly gone for these crews. The top priorities for the crew now had to be keeping the ship's boilers producing steam, making the weapons systems operate, and having the guns always ready to fire.

1. WHAT HAPPENED TO MY WORLD?

It was early afternoon on December 1, 1972. Our 26-year-old U.S. Navy Gearing class destroyer was operating in the coastal waters of Vietnam, south of the Dong Hoi Gulf region, about 15 nautical miles out from the Demilitarized Zone (DMZ). The ship had gone to Watch Condition I, General Quarters (GQ), "battle stations" about 30 minutes earlier. I was at my assigned battle station as the GQ helmsman steering the ship. Just moments before, our ship had finished a shore bombardment attack against the gun batteries and radar sites on Hon Co Island.

The captain was in the Combat Information Center (CIC), located aft of the bridge. On the ship's bridge, the executive officer (XO) had the conn, and one of the ship's lieutenants was the officer of the deck (OOD). The GQ helmsman (me) and the lee helmsman stationed next to me manned the Engine Order Telegraph (EOT). The leading quartermaster and another quartermaster were on the Navigation Plot, and there was a Boatswain Mate of the Watch (BMOW). There are three sound-powered phone talkers for interior communications between the bridge and other on-board stations. One phone talker was on the JA circuit (with the Captain), the second talker on 1JL/1JS circuits (lookouts and CIC). The third talker was on the 1JV circuit (maneuvering and engineering). Everyone at GQ stations above the main deck wore flak jackets and steel battle helmets. Below decks, the crew, with the exception of the damage control parties, were in basic battle dress.

Hon Co Island had earned the name "Tiger Island" from U.S. Navy aviators. Navy aircraft were not allowed to return and land on their aircraft carriers while still carrying live ordnance. As such, for years, Navy bombers dropped any unused bombs over Vietnam on Tiger Island since the island was only inhabited by North Vietnamese troops. As a result, Tiger Island was loaded with anti-aircraft gun batteries and fire control radar sites to shoot down any U.S. aircraft flying over or nearby. Whenever anti-aircraft fire from Tiger Island became too much of a nuisance to naval aviators, a task unit usually comprising three Navy destroyers would be ordered to mount attack raids against the island.

We had engaged in this attack on Tiger Island with two other destroyers. After each ship completed its high-speed firing run on the shore batteries and radar sites, it turned away from the island. All three destroyers were now moving away from the island in a loose column formation on a base course of 125 degrees (heading southeast by east). We received a signal by tactical radiotelephone from the formation guide ship, slowing the formation speed to 15 knots.

The ship was about 10,500 yards (5.25 nautical miles) out from the island, when the bridge 1JL/1JS phone talker relayed from CIC that the electronic warfare (EW) station was reporting J-band fire control radar tracking and locked onto our ship. Just seconds later, the phone talker announced that EW was reporting a second locked-on J-band fire control radar track.

Most of us on the bridge team knew what this meant. The NVA had J-band fire control radars that could track the trajectory of our shells, and through a fire coordination center, could return accurate and sometimes deadly counterbattery. Next, the 1JL/1JS phone talker relayed the EW report, "Fire control radar bearing 015." Moments after this report, across a sector starting just aft of our port beam, the sounds of *BOOM..BOOM..BOOM..BOOM* from the NVA shore guns rapidly firing could be heard throughout the bridge.

The next 15 to 20 seconds were a tough time of waiting. We understood that somewhere up above us there was a lot of steel, lead, and explosives inbound and aimed at us. I readied myself for commands to helm that would be coming from the XO. The lee helmsman stationed to my left nudged me to stand by. I knew we would probably keep our course and speed until we could see a pattern or the fall of the shots, providing they didn't get us with a direct hit. The first incoming salvo was a four air-burst pattern that detonated directly ahead and above the ship at a range of less than 75 yards. Though it was daytime, white and orange-red light, much like lightning, flashed through the bridge, at the unmistakable loud *"KEERAACK"* sound of close high explosives. Then there was the distinct whining noise shrapnel sometimes made as it traveled through the air, hissing as it struck the water.

On the bridge, everything came alive with activity. Automatically, the BMOW began taking gyro compass bearings from the port bridge wing gyro compass repeater to the visible muzzle flashes and gun smoke on the island. The IJL/IJS circuit phone talker passed the BMOW's gyro compass bearings to the weapons officer in CIC. Sonar was reporting over the 21MC intercom close aboard splashes and underwater detonations. It seemed like one after another.

"KERUMPF" noises began as chaff was launched, spreading small metallic pieces overhead of our ship in an attempt to scatter the enemy's fire control radar signals. The forward lookout reported multiple splashes in the water, starting from 330 degrees on the port bow to 020 degrees on the starboard bow. We all could hear *"KEERAACKs"* repeatedly, one after the other, as the high explosive rounds in each incoming salvo detonated, giving off bright flashes of white-orange light. Through the front bridge windows, we could see some of the large geysers of seawater created by impacting rounds.

Now, the whining and hissing noises from flying shrapnel seemed to be coming from everywhere. Then the XO commanded, "Engines all ahead flank, make turns for 28 knots," followed by a command to the helmsman (me), "Left full rudder."

Immediately, I reacted to the command and repeated back the order, "Aye, left full rudder." At the same time, I was rapidly rotating the helm wheel to the left until the rudder angle indicator showed left 30 degrees. "My rudder is left full," I reported.

As the ship gathered speed and our heading was swinging to port, the XO ordered, "Rudder amidships, steady as you go on course 090 degrees (east)."

As I steadied the ship on the new ordered course, we could hear the whirring and grinding noise as our Mark 37 fire control director-radar mounted above the bridge rotated around. Then came the loud "KABOOM, KABOOM" from a salvo of two rounds from mount 52, the after guns.

Within moments, the mount 52 guns were firing again.

KABOOM, KABOOM ... KABOOM, KABOOM ... KABOOM, KABOOM ...

A salvo of six more rounds. As each round fired, the noise from each blast and percussion harmonic rippled through the ship. CIC relayed that another slug of chaff was being fired. We immediately heard the chaff launcher once more. Within the next several minutes, the North Vietnamese counterbattery began to slow and then fall off. The falling off of counterbattery fire probably indicated that their J-band radar might have acquired the chaff cloud (chaff can create false targets on radar).

We waited for detonations from more incoming salvos or reports from anyone seeing shell splashes. It grew relatively quiet on the bridge, except for the ever-present exhaust noise from the forward boiler stack located just aft of the bridge.

Within a short while, the captain called the XO on the 21MC intercom and told him that we had received orders to proceed away from the island and join up with the other ships in our unit. Task Unit, CTU 71.1.1 was comprised of three ships, the USS *Henry B. Wilson* (DDG

7), the destroyer USS *Rowan* (DD 782), and our ship. Upon arrival, we were to report in, then resume surveillance on Tiger Island. CIC called the bridge with the recommended course and speed to the station.

The XO gave the helm order, "Helmsman, come left and steady on new ordered course of 060 degrees," and I brought the ship around to the new ordered course.

Once we reached the surveillance station, I could see a change from erect and stiff body postures in some of the bridge team members as their minds shifted from the forced, but efficient, mechanical focus that combat reaction requires. However, through conditioning we had become disciplined to never show emotions while on watch or at GQ assignments. Any display of emotions could be seen as a sign of weakness and might be seen as a possible character flaw, which could cause others to lose trust and confidence in you. We could not allow that to happen to us.

As the helmsman, I couldn't just let go and relax; I had to keep my focus on steering the ship. This counterbattery attack we had just undergone from the NVA gunners on Tiger Island was not our first experience in receiving counterbattery from shore, but it was the first time our ship had come under NVA radar directed counterbattery fire. Though the NVA's J-band fire control radar directed gunfire had not resulted in any direct hits on our ship, they had gotten close, closer than any of us had experienced so far.

Strictly speaking, I don't recall ever being fearful during combat action. I may have internalized certain emotions that I guess could be called fear, but it was after the fact, not during. It could be that we had such a strong sense of confidence in our training, our team members, our leadership, and our ship that we felt we would make it through any situation that came at us. Don't get me wrong; you can bet your ass that I had concerns and worries about dying or getting wounded. One would be a total and utter fool to go into a combat zone and not have worries and concerns regarding their survival.

My ship, the USS *Rich* (DD 820), was on deployment from our home-port of Norfolk, Virginia to the Western Pacific (WESTPAC). We had originally been assigned to the gun line just south of the DMZ along the 17th parallel. The Dong Hoi Gulf is to the north of the DMZ. In 1972, this area, and areas further north to Vinh and Brandon Bay, were now the "hot" areas.

Part of my job required being wholly familiar with the combat grid and navigational charts for the land and sea areas. The Dong Hoi Gulf was a unique and active area. The coastline was mountainous and Highway 1 went through a pass very near to the Gulf of Tonkin. There was the point south of Brandon Bay where the highway could be attacked by naval forces and naval gunfire. It was in this place on April 19, where North Vietnamese MIG aircraft attacked U.S. Navy destroyers in what was known as the Battle of Dong Hoi Gulf. In that battle, one destroyer, the USS *Higbee* (DD 806), suffered damage from a bomb hit and the USS *Sterrett* (CG 31), a guided missile cruiser, shot down two MIGs with her Terrier missiles. Later on that day, the destroyers were attacked by high speed patrol craft and were successful in repelling the attack with enemy losses.

This story is meant for all readers, so a short overview of the U.S. Navy Gearing class destroyer is probably in order to help with some of the naval jargon and terms. Hopefully, the following information won't cause your eyes to glaze over.

The USS *Rich* was launched on October 5, 1945 and commissioned into service July 3, 1946. In the 1960s, *Rich* went through the Fleet Rehabilitation and Modernization (FRAM) program, which extended the lives of World War II-era destroyers by shifting their mission from a surface attack role to that of a submarine hunter. The FRAM conversion was also meant to update ships to be anti-submarine warfare (ASW) capable. During the FRAM I conversion in 1963, the ship retained two of her 5-inch/38 caliber twin gun mounts and the assigned crew size was about 14 officers and up to 260 enlisted personnel.

The forward 5-inch/38 caliber guns, Mount 51, was located forward on the main weather deck near the forecastle (fo'c'sle), and Mount 52 was located on the main weather deck aft of the superstructure and helicopter flight deck. The 5-inch guns had an effective range of about six miles.

The ship had a steam propulsion system, four boilers, and two General Electric geared steam turbines, which gave the ship 60,000 Shaft Horse Power. She had two propellers and twin rudders. The maximum speed was rated at 34 knots (about 39 mph). The ship's overall length was 391 feet (119.2 meters), with a beam/breadth of 41 feet (12.5 meters), and average draft of 18.7 feet (5.7 meters). She displaced approximately 3,400 salt water tons at full-load.

Upgraded systems from the FRAM I conversion included sonar, surface search radar, and two-dimensional, long-range air search radar. She was also equipped with two triple torpedo tubes, an eight-cell Anti-Submarine Rocket (ASROC) box launcher, and one DASH ASW helicopter drone with its own landing pad and hangar (the DASH ASW helicopter was removed in 1968). Both the torpedo tubes and ASROC launched homing ASW torpedoes. ASROC could also launch a nuclear depth charge.

USS Rich (DD 820) after FRAM I conversion.

The 5-inch/38 caliber guns were guided by a Gun Fire Control System with a fire control radar linked by the Fire Control Computer. This fire control system provided effective long-range anti-aircraft (AA) or anti-surface gunfire. The ship's Flag Hoist/Radio Call Sign was November-Alpha-Yankee-India (NAYI) and her Tactical Voice Radio Call Sign was BARLEYCORN.

In Vietnam, the ship systems we needed and relied upon the most were the surface search and air search radars, as well as the Gun Fire Control System, and obviously the 5-inch /38 caliber twin gun mounts. The ship carried about 400 rounds per gun mount in magazines, and 50 ready rounds per gun for a total magazine capacity of 900 rounds. We came to rely heavily upon the Electronic Counter Measures (ECM) and Electronic Support Measures (ESM) systems.

On the outer ends of the after secondary mast was ECM equipment that could be used to try and confuse the enemy by interfering with their communication systems. The ESM system allowed us to access enemy ship and aircraft radio, radar, and navigation transmissions. This information could reveal their location, type of enemy weapon systems, and potential threat. Additionally, .50 caliber and .30 caliber machine guns were installed at a number of locations for close in protection.

The Gearing class destroyers were relatively small ships, so they were fast and maneuverable. But they could also hand out substantial fire power to any potential enemy. Their shallow draft combined with the two 5-inch/38 caliber twin guns, they were well suited to provide near-shore naval gunfire support (NGFS). USS *Rich* mostly provided NGFS support to the U.S. Marine I Corps in the northern part of South Vietnam at an area we called MR1. The 5-inch/38 caliber guns were extremely reliable and very effective against medium range targets and coastal defense guns.

The newer destroyers DD and DDG (guided missile destroyers) had 5-inch/54 caliber guns, which were fully automatic, more complex, and though longer ranged, were often less reliable than the 5-inch/38 caliber gun. The Navy destroyers were sometimes called the "greyhounds of the sea," denoting their speed and maneuverability. Most just called them "tin cans." My understanding is that the expression "tin can" comes from the World War II sailors' perceptions that the thin armor of the destroyer was no thicker than a tin can.

Normal day-to-day life was a continuous cycle of four hours of watch standing, separated by eight hours, then four more hours of watch standing. In between watch standing, the crew also had to attend to the duties and responsibilities of their actual job. Normal work day lengths were upwards of 12 to 14 hours.

Upon our ship's arrival in the waters off the Vietnam coast, the normal underway routine just described went out the window. Now, it was endless hours at battle stations with the entire ship's crew at GQ. When the ship was not at GQ and performing NGFS fire missions, all watch standing stations were split into port and starboard watch sections, with six hours on watch and theoretically with six hours off watch. I say theoretically, because being "off watch" rarely meant you were off from other ship's work; you were just off watch.

Our ship was assigned to U.S. Navy Task Force 77. Operation Linebacker had begun earlier in 1972. The later Linebacker II, which began in late 1972, was a U.S. Seventh Air Force and U.S. Navy Task Force 77 aerial bombing campaign, conducted against targets in North Vietnam during the final period of U.S. involvement in the Vietnam War. According to published military records, Linebacker II was to be a "maximum effort" bombing campaign to "destroy major target complexes in the Hanoi and Haiphong areas, which could only be accomplished by B-52s." It saw the largest heavy bomber strikes launched by the U.S. Air Force since the end of World War II.

Linebacker II was a modified extension of the Operation Linebacker bombings conducted from May to October, when the emphasis of the new campaign shifted to attacks by B-52s rather than smaller tactical fighter aircraft. At the same time, Navy destroyers and cruisers acted as offshore artillery providing shore bombardment in support of ground forces ashore or attacking coastal defense installations north of the DMZ.

It seems that most military historians and archive records principally address and discuss the Linebacker Operations as strictly air and bombing campaigns. Rarely mentioned are the roles U.S. Navy destroyers took on in providing tactical support of ground forces in attempting to overcome and repel the NVA, now located both south

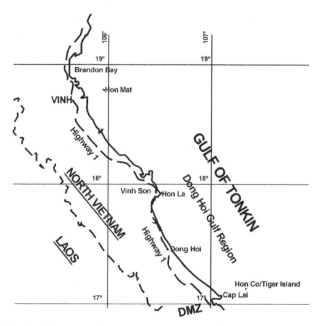

Coast of North Vietnam from the DMZ northward to the area of Brandon Bay.

and north of the DMZ.

By December 1972, a continuous flow of war material was being pushed southward along Highway 1, and NVA troops had penetrated to Quang Tri south of the DMZ. The task for ours and other ships when assigned to the Linebacker Task Force was to shut off that flow of war material.

Brandon Bay contained several small islands. The largest of these, Hon Me and Hon Mat, had large coastal defense guns protected by caves. In order for any ship to reach coastal targets, it had to close the North Vietnam coast inside of those islands. In addition to the big guns and radar sites on the islands, the entire coast was populated with heavy gun emplacements. It was this point along the coast where Highway 1 was most vulnerable to naval gunfire.

The coastlines of South and North Vietnam form the western shore of the Gulf of Tonkin. Along much of Vietnam's coastal areas the gulf waters remain fairly deep, even close to shore. This allowed Navy destroyers with their fairly shallow draft to work in very close to the Vietnam shoreline. Moving destroyers in close allowed their guns to reach targets even farther inland. However, moving the ships in close to shore further exposed them to attacks from shore batteries, aircraft, patrol gun boats, or missile boats.

In battle or gunfire missions, a destroyer crew's actions are orchestrated in carrying out a chain of events, or in war fighting jargon, they are following the kill-chain. The kill-chain actually starts with the engineers in keeping the steam flowing to the propulsion and electrical generator turbines. In other words, the engineers keep the ship's propellers turning and the lights on. The generated electricity powers everything, including steering, all radars, and the gun systems. Without the power supplied by the engineers, a ship is essentially defenseless. Next in the chain, up in CIC, the radar crews track each target's position relative to the ship in true bearing (direction), range, and then feed the target data to the weapons officer for evaluation.

During times when the ship is receiving counterbattery from shore guns, the bridge crew determines the true bearings to the shore batteries and provides that information to CIC. The weapons officer also in CIC works with the fire control director and fire control radar crews to acquire the target. The fire control solutions are used to direct the gun systems with the computed gun target line (bearing), range, and required gun elevation to accurately put the 5-inch projectiles on the target. Meanwhile, the bridge crew is maneuvering the ship to keep it in safe water (safe from risk of grounding or collision) and to keep the ship in the right aspect (angle with respect to the shore line) to unmask the fire control radars and guns allowing them to train onto the required gun target line. Finally, the captain or the tactical action officer in CIC orders, "Commence fire" or "Salvos release." Down in the bowels of the ship is a space called the "Gun Plot." One of the gunner's mates in the Gun Plot holds the firing trigger; he presses the fire control switch upon hearing the command "Commence Fire," shooting the gun or guns.

When firing from mount 51 (forward) if you're on deck, or on the bridge area, you plug your ears, as the loud *"KABOOM"* from each gun is deafening. As the guns fire each projectile, the entire ship momentarily jars with high velocity racking stress rippling through the ship's structure, accompanied with an indescribable noise that steel makes as it is suddenly and forcibly stressed. To give you an idea of the powerful recoil action of the 5-inch/38 caliber guns, when all guns in mounts 51 and 52 are fired broadside simultaneously, a destroyer's entire hull will actually move sideways in the water, moving away from the recoil force of the guns. After the guns fire, the smell of cordite and gun powder quickly permeates everything. There is no other smell like it in the world.

The ship arrived on the gun line at MR1 near the DMZ in late November. Two days before, we had departed from the Subic Bay Naval Station in the Philippines. Steaming in with fairly clear weather and good visibility, all hands were at General Quarters. Once we arrived at the area of the gun line, we were treated to quite the sight. Strung out all along the coast were up to a dozen Navy destroyers periodically belching fire and billowing smoke as their guns were raining down what had to be destruction on the coastal areas of Vietnam.

It wasn't long before we were assigned an actual station on the gun line. After the incident of where the first helicopter, which had come out from the beach with the Marine FO onboard but got fired on. This Marine FO instead called us on the tactical radio to welcome us to Vietnam. Later that day, we would begin to receive tactical radio calls from the Marine FO with our first gunfire support missions.

Destroyers deployed to the Gulf of Tonkin split their time between being escort ships with the Carrier Battle Groups, serving as Search and Rescue ships, or in the near-shore waters of Vietnam on the infamous "gun line," providing naval gunfire support to onshore ground troops. We are sometimes lumped into the category of "blue water veterans," which for me, more accurately describes the U.S. Naval fleet that stayed well offshore with the Carrier Battle Groups at Yankee Station.

My journey to becoming a sailor serving on board USS *Rich* while in

Vietnam happened over the course of approximately four years, from the ages of 16 to 20. Though I didn't join the Navy until the age of 19, this four-year period took me from boyhood to manhood. During this time, I began to understand that life beyond the cornfields of Iowa was much different, and on leaving at the age of 17, this was confirmed for me. It was about this time, when still only 17, that past and current events happening in our country and on the world stage began shaping my views and opinions. Many of my early views were carried with me into adult life; some of my other views and opinions changed as I gained more life experience.

During the years following the assassination of President John F. Kennedy, our country began going through sweeping changes. By 1966, people were paying more attention to our government's escalation of the war in Vietnam. The number of U.S. forces and troops in Vietnam was increasing every year until it peaked in 1969 at about 549,000 military members serving in Vietnam.

Within this same period, the struggles of those engaged in the Civil Rights movement were ongoing. More and more, we young people were picking up on the unrest at universities and on college campuses where discussions and protests focused on the message about the unjust war in Vietnam. We liked using the peace sign when greeting one another and using phrases like "Don't trust the man," "Down with the establishment," and my personal favorite, "Make love, not war." Except for the last phrase, most of us really didn't know what in the hell these things really meant, but we still liked them. The smell of rebellion was in the air. Rebellion is part of teenage DNA. These teens thought, *Hell, where do we sign up?*

There was one thing we teens did understand clearly. As we grew up, many of us became more aware that in just a few short years, we were going to be faced with some important decisions. Some of the impending decisions were going to be forced upon us, and other decisions we would make of our own choosing. Young men were compelled by law to register for the military draft with the Selective

Service System within 30 days of their 18th birthday. For many, the first major decisions would be regarding what to do if they were actually drafted into the military.

Our society now is much different than the one of my youth. The population in the United States has nearly doubled just in my lifetime. Our society's make up of people has become much more diverse in the past 45 years. Our current time is a little confusing for many; what was once considered acceptable is now considered unacceptable, what was once considered to be right is now considered to be wrong.

Early in the 1960s, it seemed so much easier for a person to identify acceptable expressions, words, behaviors, and actions. The difference between right and wrong was once clear. In the rural areas where I came from, it's a sure bet that people had disagreements about religious and political views. Nevertheless, people, no matter what their differences, always seemed to work together for the good of community. Maintaining a level of civility and respect for each other was the rule. A good argument could be made that as this decade wore on, it became ripe with forces that wrought many changes in society. The common thread throughout seemed to be the war in Vietnam, coupled with the antiwar sentiment that steadily grew in its strength and influence as the decade wore on.

Many factions of the antiwar movement were not just against the Vietnam War; some of them also truly hated our country and values. The Vietnam War also allowed many antiwar protesters on college campuses to ultimately become the educators of at least the last three generations of the children produced in this country. They took advantage of the draft deferral system by staying in college and gaining post-graduate degrees, which for many, led to education and careers in academia. In the vocation of being educators they believed they could be more effective in spreading their toxic views to the American youth. So far, I would say they have been effective, but fortunately for us, not totally efficient in warping all of the minds of young people.

It could be said the Vietnam War, combined with our lying political leaders, the antiwar activism, and racial unrest, created a petri dish that incubated the erosion of our societal values as a country. Some of our societal values probably did need to change. But, many of our core values as a society defined us as the greatest country on the planet. Key events did, however, result in bringing about changes of what we valued as a society.

One example would be the Tet Offensive in early 1968, launched by the North Vietnamese against South Vietnam and U.S. forces. We watched major television news broadcasters begin to openly question the U.S. government's optimism about the war. The news media and public began to openly challenge the need to continue the fight in Vietnam or our actual chances of winning the war. I recall overhearing adults start to speak with less optimism and begin to question our country's involvement in Vietnam.

In the ensuing years from 1968 through early 1973, the time frame for this story, antiwar sentiment kept growing. By 1971, even Vietnam veterans were adding their voices to the cause. In that same year, Americans began to learn that our current president and past presidents had not been honest with the country and had lied to us regarding how we had and were prosecuting the war in Vietnam.

I didn't allow any of the antiwar rhetoric or craziness in the news to influence me. The risk of ending up in Vietnam still lay ahead of me. I hoped that somehow I would get skipped. But at the same time, on some subconscious level, I was mentally preparing myself for the eventuality of going into the military. In 1968, no one could have foreseen that the Vietnam War was going to drag on for over five more years, just long enough for me, starting my adult life journey, to somehow arrive there, too.

"Baby Boomers" are generally described as the generation of Americans born during the mid-1940s through the early 1960s. The "frontal edge" of the Boomers, born between 1946 and 1953, came of age during the Vietnam War. This birth year parsing also identifies those who bore the brunt of the consequences stemming from the war in Vietnam.

This group can be divided further, into those who served in the war and those who avoided the war altogether. There were those who avoided the war but also actively or passively protested against it. Many who were able to avoid the war altogether did so by taking advantage of the various draft deferments or were found to be either physically or mentally disqualified for military service. Some in this same group just never got the call to report for the draft at all. The last remaining segment of this group are those who served either by allowing themselves to be drafted into the U.S. Army or by enlisting in another branch of the armed forces to avoid being drafted into the U.S. Army.

The segment many of us ultimately fell into was with those who fought or served during what became known as Vietnam's Cease-Fire Campaign in 1972 and 1973. By serving in this campaign, we ultimately and unwittingly in a sense became very much like *endlings*. By definition, an endling is an individual that is the last of its species or subspecies. Once the endling dies, the species becomes extinct.

The term endling also aptly describes those who sacrificed, fought hard, gave all they had, somehow survived, or somehow died throughout the final weeks and days of the Vietnam War. They were there fighting the war until the closing minutes and beyond the cease-fire agreement which went into effect in Vietnam at 0800 local time, January 28, 1973.

I've wanted to tell this story for decades, not necessarily just for me, but also for the men who worked, lived, and fought on the ships in the near coastal waters of Vietnam and the role of the U.S. Navy Destroyer. I think it's proper for the purposes of this story to still use the gender-specific terms "man or men," since the time period we are exploring is prior to gender integration in today's military and before our society slipped deeper into the insanity of political correctness.

The focal point is not necessarily about my experiences in Vietnam, though some of the engagements our ship was involved in will be recounted later. The main goal is to tell the tale of my unintended journey, which ultimately led me to becoming a member of USS *Rich*'s crew.

I went aboard USS *Rich* for the first time in May 1972, 19 years old, naïve, wide-eyed, and full of bullshit. I left this same ship at the age of 23, maybe in some respects still a little naïve, but the wide-eyed and full of bullshit stuff had long ago been wrung out of me. My time in the Navy began during the period when the quality of life aboard certain ships for enlisted sailors was generally poor. But at the same time, there were changes afoot as the Navy executed numerous initiatives in trying to improve enlisted sailors' life. Some of these changes were good. Others were failures that sometimes brought about unintended consequences.

We were not part of an all-volunteer armed forces such as we have today. Instead, we were just the remnants of the conscript armed forces era. Many in Vietnam, no matter their branch of service, weren't always there by choice. However, by far the vast majority of the sailors, Marines, soldiers, and airmen, in spite of their circumstances simply accepted the situation for what it was and forged ahead in doing their duty as Americans. You could say they played the hand dealt to them by our "friends and neighbors of the United States of America." Many won and survived, but too many didn't.

2. EVOLVING

It is worthwhile to emphasize the uniqueness of growing up in a Midwestern state during the 1960s. As a farm kid from Iowa, my perspective and view of the world evolved while coming of age. By 1967, even a farm kid like myself had a level of awareness that the country beyond the bounds of our isolated farming community was changing. Lyndon B. Johnson had successfully won reelection as president the previous year. Since the assassination of John F. Kennedy in November 1963, things were no longer status quo. We were beginning to realize that the world maybe wasn't such a stable place after all.

On television, we could receive three TV broadcasts: ABC, CBS, and NBC. Broadcasters like Walter Cronkite daily discussed the escalation of the war in Vietnam. They spoke of young people called hippies, the antiwar protests, and the Civil Rights movement. In between that kind of news reporting, the TV broadcasts also constantly reminded us about the ever-present threat of a nuclear holocaust between the United States and the Soviet Union (Russia). If you think about it, what a scary-ass time.

Even though I was a poor student in school, I began reading the newspaper every day from a fairly young age. My initial reading was probably limited to the comic pages, my horoscope, the sports section, and reading about other people's problems in the "Dear Abby" column. But over time, I started reading almost everything printed in the paper; it became my daily ritual. My reading was combined with watching the news on television as much as possible to get an idea of what was happening beyond the cornfields of Iowa.

From the news, I learned some things about politics and politicians and formed a basic understanding of some of the differences between conservative and liberal views. I also began to recognize that some reporters and editors would slant their stories or editorials to fit their political views. As a result of reading the newspaper and watching news programs, sometimes I was much better informed about what was going on than many of my friends.

During the late 1970s, a person whom I respected and admired confirmed my suspicions regarding newspaper reporters slanting their stories to fit their personal political biases. I had the pleasure to attend a presentation made by then Captain Richard "Dick" Stratton, U.S. Navy. In January 1967, his A-4 Skyhawk went down and crashed in the north-central coast region of North Vietnam. Captain Stratton was captured by the North Vietnamese and was a POW for six years in North Vietnam.

Captain Stratton said two things that evening that struck home hard and fast with me. First, he expressed that from his POW experience, he had learned what it meant not to be free. Second, he held up two newspapers from different news outlets, but with headlines for the same story, and said, "I have also learned, you can read any two articles on the same story, and somewhere in the middle you might find the truth." This second statement is not a direct word-for-word quote, but it captures what I learned from the captain's comment.

My dad farmed in northeast Iowa in Mitchell and Howard Counties. For the most part, I was raised in the country on our family farms. I grew up in a so-called traditional family with two parents, five sisters, and one older brother. Since I was the youngest, my older siblings were marrying and starting families of their own while I was growing up.

My dad was hardcore all the way. I believe he was an honest man, but as a father to me he was nearly impossible to live with. Dad was overbearing, never praised or thanked you for anything, and he demanded respect and hard work. As a farm boy, you are expected to take on the work of caring for livestock and working in the fields, and my specialty became removing one or two tons of manure from the cow and pig barns every day with a pitchfork and/or shovel. No matter what the task, even tasks I knew I was good at, it was never done quite right for my dad. What riled me most was occasions where Dad hired men or other boys to help during haying or harvest season and he was patient, soft-spoken, kind, and cordial to them.

My older brother Jon enlisted in the Navy when I was very young. I never really knew what his relationship had been with our dad growing up; Jon and I never really talked much about it. After his enlistment was up in the Navy, Jon moved back to the farm for a while before getting married and moving on. When he wasn't working at some job, usually construction, he worked with Dad and me on the farm. Over time, I do think Jon must have observed some similarities to his own boyhood experiences with how our dad treated me.

Years later, just hours before our dad passed away from cancer, I was somewhat surprised to hear Jon ask our dad the following question: "Dad, why were you so hard on us boys?"

Dad simply replied, "It's a tough world, and I wanted you boys to be able to take care of yourselves." That's about the last coherent thing I remember my dad saying before he passed away.

Needless to say, by the time I was in high school, I had some self-esteem and confidence issues. To be fair, a lot of other people probably did, too. I compensated for my issues by having as much fun as I could. My fun was partying, working on cars, more partying, generally finding like-minded friends, and raising as much hell as possible. Fortunately, the small town of Riceville, Iowa, where I went to high school, and which was the epicenter of my social sphere, was loaded with young people that generally liked to do what I did.

The downside of that time for me was my attitude. Around the age of 15, my general attitude was simple. I really didn't give a shit about much of anything and that applied to studying and my grades in school. Even today I can't say why, but I do know that back then I really could not have cared less.

I think kids living and growing up on farms had some advantages over town kids. For one, most farms had a machine shed with generally well-stocked workshops full of tools and welding and cutting equipment. Many of us became fairly decent self-taught motor and automobile mechanics. As our mechanical knowledge and skills grew, our fathers were more than happy to turn over the chore of maintaining and doing the basic repairs on the farm tractors, implements, and other mechanical farming equipment. We didn't just work on cars; we built machines. Until we were old enough to legally drive cars on the road, many of us started by building or rebuilding go-carts, motor scooters, or other contraptions with engines, transmissions, and wheels that we could drive around on the back-country roads.

Usually, I was able to earn enough of my own money to fund my recreational activities, from working on our farm or for other farmers. Generally, once the daily chores of caring for the livestock or other work was done, I was free to go fishing, hunting, horseback riding, shooting, or engage in my favorite activity of working on my car or on one of my friend's cars.

A lot of young people like me were still filled with hope and wonder about our futures. Some of us were just marking time to the day when we would be able to leave our families and go out into the world. On the other hand, when I sometimes let my mind wander back to those days, I don't think there was ever a better time period for a young person to grow up. Our parents allowed us a lot of freedom to discover life on our own. There was very little sense of any danger associated with allowing us to drive cars and to go essentially wherever we wanted to go, within reason. At least where I grew up, young people in high school were for the most part treated as adults. We were free to make most of our own decisions, but at the same time, our parents and other adults also made sure we were held accountable for our actions. I'm not sure that is the case today.

During late summer 1968, as my 16th birthday approached, my plans and preparations for being able to drive legally were in motion. In the state of Iowa, at 14 years of age, you were eligible to get a driver's learner's permit. The learner's permit allowed you to drive a motor vehicle during daylight hours only and an adult licensed driver had to be with you in the vehicle. I had completed the driver's education course at school the year before. Using money from my savings, I bought a 1959 Ford Galaxy two-door hardtop sedan for $150. The engine was a V-8, 352 cubic-inch, with a three-speed manual transmission.

The Ford's exterior color was a somewhat faded teal blue, with white trim. To me, it was great. The engine used about one quart of motor oil every hundred miles or so because of a leaky rear main bearing and seal. A quick trip to the auto part store, about two nights of work, and the rear main bearing and seal were replaced, solving the problem.

The end of the first week of September, on my 16th birthday, coupled with now having my own car, represented a big milestone to me in achieving more freedom. The only rule my parents imposed on car ownership was that I carry my own automobile insurance and paid the premiums.

Being able to drive our own cars also meant that we farm kids could drive ourselves and our buddies to and from school and no longer had to ride the school bus. We lived about eight miles from my high school. Rural school buses follow planned pick-up and drop-off routes. The morning bus route from our farm to school usually took about 45 minutes. The afternoon bus route was reversed, with our farm on the later part of the route, so it often took more than an hour to get home from school. The bus trip could be even longer in the wintertime, depending on snow and ice on the roads. By car, I could get home in about 10 minutes, which allowed more time for me to do the afternoon and evening chores around the farm.

The summer between my sophomore and junior years, another event occurred in my life. I went from a somewhat chunky kid, about 5 foot 8 inches tall, to a somewhat muscular kid standing about 6 foot 3 inches tall. My growth spurt actually started near the end of my sophomore year and lasted throughout the summer. I remember it as a painful time, particularly in my back and legs. My mother was constantly trying to help me find clothes and shoes that would fit me, because my shoe size also went from about size 9 to 13.

At that time, hayfields were cut and raked into windrows much as they are today. Most farmers baled their hay and put it up for storage in barn hay mounds or other buildings to protect the hay from weather. The process was labor-intensive, unlike today where hay is rolled into big bundles and left in the field. That summer, I got a job working with a guy who did custom hay baling. My job, after each bale of hay was formed and tied by the machine, was to pull each bale off the discharge chute and stack the bales on a flatbed hay rack/trailer, which was towed behind the baling machine.

Bales of hay vary in weight depending upon moisture content between 90 and 120 pounds. My pay was one cent per bale. On good days, the average was 2,000 bales of hay, which paid $20 for the day, four to six days per week, so I earned between $80 and $120 per week. I lasted all summer doing custom hay baling, plus the normal farm work. Along with my rapid physical growth and weight lifting all day on most days, I had a considerable growth of muscle. Most importantly, the hard work helped with maintaining or learning the physical coordination I needed as my body continued to grow.

Returning to high school that fall for my junior year, other dramatic changes also transpired. Now with my own car, a new bigger body, and a little more confidence, it was easier to talk to girls. Some girls, even those I had known for some time but who'd never had much to do with me, now would talk to me. The other change was that the school bullies and jerks that had given me a hard time in past years now were much friendlier and the threats of "kicking my ass" came to an end. Who would have thunk it? An increase of seven inches in height and about 20 pounds of added weight and muscle brought about much change. However, still being basically a dumbass and an introverted personality type, I often squandered opportunities for more social interaction. Unless around friends I was comfortable with, and bolstered with three or four beers, my social skills were generally poor.

Later that fall, I met the girl that would become my steady girl for a while. My new girlfriend was really cute. She had a great body; she was hot. She was actually a senior in high school from a neighboring town and a year older.

So far, the fall months of my junior year in high school were turning out to be pretty good. However, what I wasn't counting on were the things life can sometimes throw at you. Several major events, starting on Christmas Eve, changed everything for me for some months ahead.

At the closest neighboring farm lived my friends and buddies, all brothers from the same family. The oldest brother, Tom, was two years older, and his twin brothers were my age. Tom had introduced me to my girlfriend. We all went to the same school and became fast friends. All of us had varying levels of mechanical skill. Their dad's workshop was fully equipped and had a pit in the garage floor for working under machinery and cars. Tom was by far the best and most knowledgeable mechanic among us. Together, we often built machines or rebuilt all kinds of cars and engines. Most weeknight evenings and on Sunday afternoons, we'd gather in the workshop.

During the Christmas and New Year holiday vacation from school, we all gathered in the workshop on Christmas Eve. I wanted to get out of my house as most of my older sisters and their families were home for Christmas, so our house was full. There was no reason to go out or to town since everything in town was closed for Christmas Eve and there was a bad snowstorm blowing that night. We had been working on a project building weights for lifting and exercise. The materials we were using for the project, of all things, were sections of old steel railroad rails we had gotten from a scrap pile.

We cut a longer section of rail about five feet long and built two spaced steel handholds into it. Next, we cut four sections of rail each about two feet in length and then welded two sections of short rails on each end of the long middle rail. Lying on the workshop floor, the finished project looked sort of like a big capital letter "I." The ends of the short sections still had jagged edges from where they had been cut with the cutting torch. The idea was to grind and smooth the end edges later.

On the floor weight scale, our project weighed somewhere around 175 pounds. Instead of finishing the weight though, the brothers began taking turns deadlifting it from the floor. Next, the brothers tried to press the entire weight above their heads, but none of them could do it. Then came my turn to make the attempt.

As is often said, but too late, "Hindsight is 20/20." This axiom definitely ending up applying here. I didn't really want to try, but someone bet I couldn't lift it, then press it up over my head. A young man's pride is powerful and can make for stupid decisions. Walking over and straddling the weight, I deadlifted it to shoulder height, then rebalanced and made the rest of the lift overhead. With the weight over my head, apparently my center of gravity became too high, because the weight quickly caused me to fall backward. I tried to push the weight away from me as I let it go and fell to the floor.

Lying on the floor, I immediately knew that my right hand was under the weight's end section. Someone pulled the weight away and I pulled out my right hand and looked. It was a mess. The jagged steel end of the rail had hit in the palm area just above the fingers. Starting at just above the right index finger, then diagonally across the palm area it was smashed meat and skin and I could see some of the bones in my hand. My right index finger was nearly cut off and both my index and middle fingers were dangling at strange angles.

I remember taking both of those fingers with my left hand and trying to put them back where they belonged. That obviously didn't work, so I let them go back to dangling. My hand was bleeding badly, and then the pain began. I remember thinking, *Shit, this may not be good.* On the other hand, my thoughts were that with some bandages and maybe some stitches, my hand would be fine.

Someone went to the house to tell their parents what happened. The brothers took me into the kitchen and sat me down in a chair. Their mother began to wrap my hand in towels and applied direct pressure to see if she could slow or stop the bleeding. Everyone seemed to understand how serious my injury was except me.

Soon an older brother-in-law of mine arrived, looked at the injury, and asked to use the telephone to call my parents. It was decided that he would take me to the closest doctor in Elma, Iowa. We went outside to Dad's pickup truck; my brother-in-law drove, and Tom came with us. It was snowing hard and the country gravel roads had more than a foot of snow cover. Our farm truck was only rear-wheel drive, but earlier that week, we had put snow chains on the rear tires and about 200 pounds of full feedbags in the truck bed for traction, so it was the best vehicle we had for driving in the snow.

The distance to Elma was only about nine miles, but the going was slow because of the heavy snow drifts on the roads. We finally got to the doctor's office in Elma and he examined my hand, did some cleaning, and dressed it. He told us that was all he could do without an x-ray, and he didn't have an x-ray machine. The closest hospital with x-ray capabilities was in Osage, Iowa, about 35 miles west. The doctor insisted that I must go there. My brother-in-law used the doctor's phone to call home and let my family know we were now headed to Osage.

The drive was a long one. It was snowing heavily and the roads were filling with more snow by the hour. When we arrived at the Osage hospital, I was surprised to see the time on the emergency room clock was close to 12:30 a.m. I know it had been about 9:00 p.m. when we'd left Elma. The only doctor who had been able to get to the hospital through the heavy snowfall was actually an eye and ear specialist, but our family knew this doctor. Plus, he was all we had.

The x-rays showed that luckily there were no broken bones in my hand. After some numbing shots, the doctor set about putting my hand back together, a procedure that took several hours. The doctor asked my brother-in-law to help hold my lower arm and hand steady. At one point, he asked my brother-in-law if he was okay. I looked up at his face; he was pale and sweating a lot. Finally, it was over. I have no memory after that until waking up the next afternoon in a hospital room and realizing it was now Christmas Day.

Later that afternoon, the doctor came by my hospital room to examine my hand. He seemed satisfied with his work from the night before, but then he told me an infection had developed in my wound and that they were watching for the onset of gangrene. He added that if the infection didn't clear quickly or if gangrene developed, it was likely that most, if not all, of my right hand would have to be amputated. His news about the possible amputation of my hand was a bit disturbing.

Then he gave me some more news: my dad was in the hospital, too. He had been brought in early that morning. My whole life, Dad had suffered from asthma, and particularly in the winter months the cold weather often caused him to have a lot of difficulty breathing, which in turn sometimes made him weak and sick. The many years of asthma attacks also seemed to have added heart problems to his health issues. I asked the doctor if Dad had been brought in because of his asthma. He replied yes, and added that there were some other complications, too. As the doctor was about to leave, he suggested that if I felt up to it, I should go see him, and gave me Dad's room number.

After the doctor left my room, I attempted to get out of bed. I stood up and generally felt okay. Trying to tie the back of the hospital gown closed with only one hand was futile. A nurse happened by the doorway of my room; she told me to wait a minute and returned with a robe. After getting to Dad's room, I saw he was lying in bed but was awake. Dad looked weak and smaller somehow; I could see he was really sick. His voice was weak, and he talked in an extremely calm manner, which was odd for him. We talked for a while, then he told me that he would be headed to a major hospital in Rochester, Minnesota the next day to see some specialists and he didn't know when he would be going home. He also told me that I wouldn't be going home right away. It had already been decided for me to stay with my brother Jon and his family in Cedar Falls, Iowa until it was time to go back to school.

A couple of days later, the doctors believed the immediate danger of infection in my hand was over. They released me from the hospital later that day.

My sister-in-law and Jon were at the hospital to pick me up, and someone had packed some of my clothes for me. That afternoon, we made the drive to their home in Cedar Falls. I liked my sister-in-law and generally got along with my brother most of the time, so I really didn't mind going home with them. I was tired and really just wanted some sleep. The next week at my brother's home went well. I was still weak and experiencing some dizziness and nausea. Jon did take me to see a doctor that week to make sure my hand was still doing well. I don't know how anybody other than a medical professional could have looked at my wound and not immediately vomited on the spot; it still looked awful. My sister-in-law was a trooper, helping me clean and redress the injury every day.

Jon and my sister-in-law wanted to go out on New Year's Eve, but they knew that with my bum hand, I probably couldn't take care of their kids. They hired a babysitter for the night to help me with the kids, which I felt a little weird about. That night, I got over that feeling of weirdness real fast once the babysitter arrived. She was my age, had long, dark hair, was cute with a great body, and really friendly. My brother let it be known that they planned to be out well past midnight.

That evening, once the kids were in bed, with a really cute and friendly babysitter as company, turned out to be a very good New Year's Eve. The year 1968 was done and over. Some historians say it was the year that changed history. Besides the events that were occurring in my life, on the national and world stage an awful lot of things were boiling on the proverbial stove:

- Starting on January 23, North Korean patrol boats captured USS *Pueblo* (AGER-2), a Banner-class environmental research ship attached to Navy intelligence as a spy ship. The 83 members of the ship's crew were arrested on charges of violating North Korea's 12-mile territorial limit. The ship's crew was held until December.

- On January 30, North Vietnam launched the Tet Offensive against the United States and South Vietnam. In February, a South Vietnamese security official was photographed executing a Viet Cong prisoner. This photograph was published around the world and quickly became another hot point of contention for the antiwar protestors.

- In February, the U.S. State Department announced the highest casualty toll of the Vietnam War. The country learned that 543 Americans had been killed in action, and that over 2,500 had been wounded in a period of one week. Walter Cronkite visited Vietnam to view the aftermath of the Tet Offensive. His report was highly critical of U.S. officials and directly contradicted the official statements regarding the progress of the war. After listing Tet and several other military operations in Vietnam as "draws," Cronkite advised that the U.S. should negotiate with North Vietnam.

- On April 4, Martin Luther King Jr. was assassinated in Memphis, Tennessee, and on June 5, Robert F. Kennedy was assassinated in Los Angeles by a Jordanian-born Palestinian named Sirhan Sirhan.

- In July, at a music festival in Rhode Island, folk singer Arlo Guthrie performed his 20-minute ballad, "Alice's Restaurant."

- During late August at the Democratic National Convention in Chicago, police took action against crowds of demonstrators without provocation. The police beat some marchers unconscious, sent at least 100 demonstrators to emergency rooms, and arrested 175. The next day at a press conference, the mayor of Chicago famously tried to explain the police action by stating, "The policeman isn't there to create disorder; the policeman is there to preserve disorder."

- During September, McDonald's sold the first Big Mac sandwich for 49 cents. In November, Richard Nixon won the presidential election, and on the TV show "Laugh-In," said, "Sock it to me!"

- In December, Elvis made his comeback on a nationally televised show. On December 24, 1968, Christmas Eve, also the night my right hand got smashed to hell, Apollo 8 became the first manned spacecraft to orbit the moon with three astronauts on board, circling the moon 10 times.

The year 1969 started with me heading back home to the farm. School was restarting the first week of January. Dad was still in the hospital in Rochester; Mom had been trying to take care of the livestock and daily chores with the help of neighbors. In between, she was making the hour-long drive each way nearly every day to see Dad in Rochester. I felt strongly that I could take over the care of the livestock and did so, but it was really hard with just one hand. Certain tasks simply couldn't get done without re-injuring my hand. On returning to school the following week, I was able to do the morning and evening chores before and after school hours.

The next weekend, Jon and some of my older sisters were at the farm. My brother found me working out in the barn, and he came to tell me that they had decided to auction off all of Dad's livestock. Immediately I was opposed to the idea, mainly because no one had asked me. In the strongest possible language, I expressed my disagreement. My belief was that I could take care of everything until Dad came home, and I told my brother so. In our family, as the youngest child and still a teenager, my opinions didn't matter to anyone. I knew this and understood it, but it still pissed me off.

About a week or so later, the auction was held, and there was a pretty decent turnout from local farmers and livestock buyers. By the end of the week, the only remaining animals were our farm dog, some cats, and my horse, Fred. Getting rid of the livestock was a big load off of my mom, but I still didn't agree with the decision, nor did I think it was right. What didn't help in the middle of all of this was finding out that my girlfriend had apparently moved on as well. I tried calling her several times, but her mother always answered the phone and told me that she wasn't home. After a couple of tries, I knew it was over and confirmed it a week or so later by seeing her in Riceville riding around in a car with some other guy. Oh well! That was over. At that age, my heartbroken status probably lasted for about two days or so, then it was time to move on.

Dad finally came home after five or six weeks in the hospital. He did seem much better and recovered. He never said anything, at least not to me, but you could see his disappointment about all his livestock being gone. Within weeks, he began buying feeder pigs, sows, a boar, and beef cattle, so by early spring, the feed and cattle lots held livestock again. It was like starting the farm over, in a way.

As time moved into the spring months and spring planting, life seemed to normalize again. Dad essentially had the farming operation back to what it had been before he became sick. I never knew what my mother thought about all of this, because my folks were the type of parents who did not share much adult information with the younger kids. My right hand healed as well as could be expected. It was still sore and painful much of time, but I could use it pretty much for everything again. My right index finger, however, was always numb and had no dexterity, so I learned to work around it.

That spring, my old Ford had to be laid to rest, since both the engine and transmission were shot and the body was rusting badly. At a car lot in Osage, I bought a 1958 Chevrolet for $235. The Chevy was a two-door post sedan and unbelievably, it only had about 35,000 miles on it. It turned out to be a good car. Its engine would start every time, no problem, a big change from the old Ford.

Soon, summer break from school came and like the summer before, my days were spent working on ours or other farms, and when the season for haying began, I worked with the same custom hay baling operation from the year before. My summer nights were consumed with the normal stuff, driving around, drinking a lot of beer, looking for girls, and having as much fun with my buddies and friends as could be had. That summer held good luck in meeting quite a few girls. Happily, none of the girls that summer wanted to get into steady dating or stuff like that. It was a great summer, and way too soon it became time to go back to school.

Over the summer, I started to pal around with a neighboring farm kid named Allyn. Allyn had started going to school in Riceville the year before when a school district change put his farm in my school district. He had a husky build and was a good guy. Allyn kept bringing up the idea that the two of us and another friend, James, should go out for football in our senior year. I hadn't played football since junior high.

Finally, Allyn convinced us to sign up to play football for Riceville High School. Football practice began during the last two weeks of August. Except for the pain and sore muscles from practice and workouts, I had forgotten how much I really enjoyed football. It was surprising how accepting of us both the coaches and the players were, because for many of the players, it was their fourth high school season. Riceville football was close a religion for some people in town. Though a small school, Riceville was known for fielding good football teams.

Allyn, James, and I were all fairly big guys, and at least Allyn and James were somewhat athletic. The team saw all three of us as adding more depth to the offensive and defensive lines. Throughout the season, Allyn got a lot more playing time than me or James. I played the defensive tackle position and mainly was sent into games as a substitution or just to confuse the opposing team's offense. It seemed the coaches would play me until I started getting penetration into the offensive backfield, then in most cases, the offense would start double-teaming me in the line. Once the double-teaming began, I was usually pulled from the game and the first string tackle would go back in.

All in all, it was an enjoyable season, and I actually lettered, getting my Riceville "R" at the end of the season. Looking back to my high school years, I probably should have played more sports; maybe my grades in school would have been better. While playing football for most of the first semester of my senior year, my grades came up. To participate in sports, students were required to maintain at least a "C" average grade in all subjects. After the football season was over, I allowed my school grades to go down to about the same level they had been during prior school years.

The remainder of my senior year in high school was focused on partying, having fun, and counting the days until it came time to leave home. Until that day, we filled our time by listening to rock bands, the Beatles, The Who, and the Rolling Stones; working on cars, more cars; drinking beer (lots of beer); trying to get laid; and generally raising hell to the best of our abilities without ending up in the county jail.

At the same time, we were anxiously looking forward. Guys, at least, knew that as their 18th birthday approached, by law they had to register with the United States Selective Service System. They would be issued a Selective Service (draft) card. After high school, if you couldn't get your butt into college with a draft deferment or get into the Army National Guard, it was going to be just a matter of time before you received your notice to report for processing.

During processing at the Armed Forces Examination and Entrance Stations (AFEES), unless you could convince some doctor you were crazy or could find a way to not pass the physical examination, you would most likely end up doing at least a two-year active duty enlistment in the U.S. Army.

The general view that many of us held regarding going into the military was that it was not a bad thing as long as you didn't wind up finding yourself in Vietnam. There were also many who wanted to avoid being drafted altogether. Males without a draft deferment were often at some point notified to report for processing. Some would develop a plan to avoid being drafted or inducted into the Army.

Jumping ahead a little in time here, during my processing for enlistment in the Navy at the AFEES in Fort Des Moines, Iowa, I witnessed a couple of poor or lame plans executed by guys trying to avoid getting inducted. The first event happened during the mental testing and examination. Two guys sitting near me openly discussed how they were going to do everything they could to fail the test. They had heard that if they could get a low enough mental score, they would get sent home. I had been told by the recruiter and other people that if you did well on the test, you might be offered a spot in a technical school for engineering or electronics, which could keep you out of Vietnam.

After the test, the Army proctor gave each person their test score. One of the two guys got a score of something like 22 and the other one got a score a bit higher. They both were quite happy with themselves until their names were called to go out in the hallway and follow the red line for the Army. They both protested to the proctor that they had failed the test.

The proctor smiled and said, "You both are high school graduates. Even with your low mental scores, you both are qualified for the Army, probably infantry; now, go follow the red line."

The second event occurred during the physical examination. They had a bunch of us standing in a long line. We were all told to drop our underwear, bend over, and spread our butt cheeks for rectal inspection by a person I assumed was the doctor. As the doctor finished inspecting each person in line, the medic with the doctor would tell each guy to stand up straight and pull up their underwear. Just seconds after my inspection, the doctor and the medic were examining a fellow about three guys down the line. I heard the medic loudly say, "Boy, what in the hell is that stuff packed in your ass?"

The guy, who looked like a long-haired hippie type, smiled, took his forefinger and wiped it through his butt crack, then licked his finger and said "Well, it's shit, doc. Don't you know what shit looks like?" What happened next was surprising.

The medic told the guy to bend over again and he wiped his finger through the guy's butt crack. He brought up his finger covered with what looked to me like shit. He took a long sniff of the stuff that was on his finger. Then the medic turned to the doctor and said, "It's just peanut butter." The medic said to the guy, "Good try, but not good enough. Welcome to the United States Army, asshole."

Most of the guys from the Riceville area that got drafted, it seemed, after basic and other training, were being sent to places like Germany or South Korea, but some got a tour in Vietnam. The alternative of waiting to be drafted into the Army was to just go and enlist in the Navy or Air Force and hope you might not get a trip to Vietnam. I'm not sure, but I don't remember many from the area around Riceville who enlisted in the Marine Corps.

A person not familiar with this time in our country might ask, "What was the big deal?" The big deal was the draft. We all tended to pay a lot of attention to what was going on. We all knew someone in the military, so our conversations about the Vietnam War generally were informed.

Obviously, many important events from that era have changed over time and new events have occurred. The Vietnam War eventually came to an end. The draft went away in 1975, and the Cold War with the Soviet Union ended. The United States was attacked on 9/11, and the global war on terror began, starting with the wars in Afghanistan and Iraq. Russia didn't disappear and go away; China doesn't want to stay home anymore; and North Korea isn't happy with anyone. I have read where experts state that with today's all-volunteer armed services, more than 95 percent of Americans are opting out of military service. Today, most people do not know anyone in the military, and very few people are informed enough to intelligently discuss military topics.

For young men coming of age during the Vietnam era, though, there was a certain thrill and excitement that existed. However, at the same time, the era was also about the looming, ever-present shadow of possible doom that existed as we grew into adults. If we got drafted and did end up in the war, there was the possibility of getting killed or maimed for life. Young people from our area were already attending the funeral services of friends and upper classmen from high school who were killed in Vietnam. In our small farming community, everyone knew everyone else. The young men from our area who were killed or wounded in Vietnam had an impact on everyone. It was obviously a sad time; not just for the affected families, but for the community as a whole.

We tried to renew friendships with the guys that did come home from the military. Some had been wounded or disabled as a result of their service. Some didn't appear to have suffered any physical injury or damage. What we did find was that almost all of them were now different people from who they had been. The change we observed in these guys was difficult for a teenaged farm kid's mind to understand. This was all happening to young people of a relatively small and sparsely populated farming community. What we were coming to realize was that the same events we were experiencing due to the impact of the Vietnam War were happening at a holistic level throughout the entire country.

After high school, I did not go to college or get into the Army National Guard. With my poor high school grades, I wouldn't have gotten into college, anyway. About 15 months later, I found myself enlisting in the Navy as an alternative to getting drafted into the Army. However, this 15-month period was eventful. Several pivotal events occurred that would change my life forever.

Even though my high school years were now done, I was still only 17 years old, and wouldn't turn 18 until September. During my job hunting, it became clear right away that no one could hire someone full-time under the age of 18. Apparently, someone else had been counting the days for my leaving too: my dad. Dad began applying pressure about my future plans. Finally, I just told him straight out about my total lack of any desire to become a farmer. I recall telling him, which some years later I realized was really stupid, "I just want to get a job working from eight to five." Going further in my explanation to him, I added that in no way did I want to keep working long hours, seven days a week, pitching manure, freezing in the winter, and dying of heat in the summer.

He seemed to have already anticipated what my position would be as he immediately informed me that I was leaving that day. He let me know that one of my older sisters (who was married and lived in Illinois) could get me a job. Though I owned my own car, he told me, "In Iowa, you are still a minor. If you take your car, I will call the sheriff." He added that my mother would give me a ride to Riceville. He told me there was $100 on the kitchen table to buy my bus ticket and some money for traveling.

The axiom my dad had followed was "to break my plate," which as a rule meant that there was no longer a seat at the dinner table for me in his house. I can only guess, but Dad probably had planned the time of day of when to have our discussion. He must have known the bus schedule. So, later that afternoon I was on a bus leaving Riceville bound for Illinois. I actually didn't mind leaving home; I had just thought it would be of my own design, not my dad's. But by then, after all the years of turmoil with him, I was close to not caring about it, or about my relationship with him, anymore.

I arrived at the bus station in Clinton, Iowa, the next morning. Clinton is located on the Mississippi River. Just across the river and downstream from Clinton is the town of Albany, Illinois. My sister met me at the bus station. She and my brother-in-law had a nice acreage property about a mile outside of Albany. My sister offered to let me rent their spare bedroom; I took her up on the offer. The next day, she took me to where she worked at Bunge Grain Corporation in Albany. She introduced me to her boss, who was one of the managers. The manager explained to me that if I worked out, they could cover my only being a 17-year-old until my 18th birthday in September.

He explained that my job was to offload the barn river barges delivering oats for government storage until the fall harvest season.

They would start me on the night shift, 4:00 p.m. to midnight. My pay was $2.50 per hour, but any week that we worked more than 40 hours would be overtime. The next day I, started at my new job.

Working for Bunge Grain actually turned out to be good deal. Being raised on the farm, one thing I knew how to do well was hard physical labor and work. Bunge Grain had plenty of that to offer. The facility was located on the Illinois side of the Mississippi River, with a waterfront and offshore barge mooring system. There was a huge grain conveyor structure that was nearly a quarter of a mile long. The conveyor structure spanned from the shore facility to a point high over the barge mooring area and had an installed vacuum-piping hose assembly with a hose and nozzle that could be lowered down into barge holds to essentially suck the grain out of the barge and transfer it via the piping system to the huge million-bushel capacity grain bins on shore.

River barge work required that the barges be routinely unmoored and moored and repositioned for loading or offloading, which required working with large fiber mooring lines, wire ropes, and winches. Besides spending hours on end during each shift shoveling grain to level the barge load or pushing grain to the vacuum nozzle when offloading, I was also beginning to learn seamanship skills.

One of my first weekends off from work, my brother visited. He and his family now lived near Cordova, Illinois, about 25 miles down the river. Jon offered to sell me his old car at a good price, a 1959 Chevrolet Impala, four-door sedan. I bought the Chevy from him. To my thinking, I was in great shape, had a job, some money, a place to stay and now a car to get around in.

We worked through the summer into the fall. By the fall season, two things had changed. I was now an experienced, heavily relied-upon hand, and the Midwest harvest season had begun. Semi-tractor trailer grain trucks were waiting in lines around the clock to offload their grain cargo at the terminal. Sometimes the line of waiting trucks and trailers grew to a mile or longer. The grain cargo consisted of oats, then corn and soybeans that were transferred from the terminal to temporary storage bins until they could be loaded on the barges for transport down the river.

Fleet river tugboats arrived every day, delivering empty barges and to make up the loaded barges into fleets headed downstream. Further down the river, the big line-haul tugboats would make up the large barge tows and take them downriver to Baton Rouge or New Orleans.

During this period, we worked 16 plus hours a day, seven days a week. Our workweek for pay started on Sunday, and most weeks we had 40 hours in by midday on Tuesday. The rest of the week was usually 45 to 55 or more hours, all on overtime pay. I put most of my paychecks aside in a bed-stand drawer in my bedroom. Since I was always working during banking hours, my sister would cash some of my paychecks for me so I had some cash for rent, gas, and food. I kept a running tally of how much money had accumulated in uncashed paychecks and it was adding up. I felt like I was rolling in the dough.

By mid-November, work at Bunge Grain had slowed after the crazy harvest season ended. Now we were working just 40 hours per week. Believe it or not, I felt it was time to move on. I was now 18 years old and had what I thought was a lot of money saved. I had found time to upgrade cars to a 1967 Pontiac Lemans, a two-door hardtop. I bought the car from one of the Bunge corporate executives, who gave me a good deal on the car for $750. I liked the car because it was the same body style as the Pontiac GTO. I gave Bunge Grain two weeks' notice that I was quitting. My plan after my last day of work was to pack my stuff in my car and head back to Riceville for a short visit before I moved onto whatever would come next. But first, I had to cash all of my saved paychecks.

The day after quitting my job, with my stack of paychecks in hand, I went to the local bank in Albany. There was about $3,500 worth in uncashed paychecks, a small king's ransom for an 18-year-old in 1970. At the bank, the teller asked to see some identification. At that time, Iowa driver's licenses did not have your photo on them. The only other identification documents with my name on them were my draft card and social security card. The teller checked with the bank manager.

The bank manager came out and explained to me that they would not cash my checks because they didn't know me. I called my sister, who agreed to call the bank to vouch for me. Once my sister called the teller, they cashed my checks. Walking out of the Albany bank with an envelope stuffed with $100 and $50 bills, I was good to go.

After arriving back in Riceville, I first visited with my parents on the farm for a while. Though my leaving home the previous spring had not been on the best of terms, I still had a sense of family. This short visit with my parents made me realize that there was no longer a place for me under their roof. While home, I did start doing some of the farm work and chores, but I made it clear to Dad that my work was only temporary.

After several weeks at home, I felt deserving of some R & R, so after looking up some old high school buddies, the partying began. After several weeks of good fun every night, one of my buddies wanted me to go to Mason City, Iowa, with him. A girl he had been dating went to school at Hamilton Business College. His girlfriend had a friend he thought I would really like. In other words, he needed a wingman.

I figured, why not? So, the next afternoon, in early December 1970, we drove to Mason City, which is about 50 miles from Riceville. We met up with his girlfriend and they introduced me to a great girl named Jan (Janice). Who knew? I was actually meeting my future wife and life partner. Jan was also a student at the business college. We double-dated several times with my buddy and his girlfriend.

Finally, I asked Jan out on a date, just the two of us. I remember we went to see some movie at the theater in Osage, and we had a great time together. At the end of the evening, I asked if she would like to go out again. She said yes. The rest you could say, is history. Jan and I quickly became a couple. It wasn't long before we were spending time together every day and every night. It didn't take long before realizing I was in love. I had been with other girls before, but this was different and I knew it. We both eventually admitted that we loved each other and were crazy about each other.

It was about the middle of March of 1971, when Jan let me know she might be pregnant. A visit to the doctor confirmed it. Having been raised with the concept that we are all responsible for our own actions, coupled with the strong conviction to do the right thing, I knew what my course of action had to be. Without any doubt or reservation before that day was through, I asked Jan to marry me and she accepted. Within several weeks, we set our wedding date for late June. The prospect of getting married along with a baby on the way at first was a little overwhelming to think about, but the relationship we had quickly built between us seemed right for me. This gave me the confidence that I needed to move ahead.

Between working at different odd jobs, I had essentially been living off the money saved from working in Illinois, which was just about gone. Now that I was going to get married, there was a need to find a steady job and fast. Luckily, within a couple of weeks a company called Kayot Forester in Forest City, Iowa, hired me. Kayot Forester manufactured travel trailers and pontoon houseboats; their factory sat in the shadow of the recreational vehicle giant at the time, Winnebago Industries.

Kayot Forester put me to work in the cabinet shop and as a cabinet installer. I think they hired me because on my high school transcripts, my best grades beside physical education were in wood shop and industrial arts. By this time, Jan had quit college, and for a while, we stayed with her older sister and brother-in-law in Forest City until we found our own apartment. As I saw it, there were now three hurdles to contend with.

Hurdle number one: In Iowa, males under the age of 21 are legally minors. That meant at 18 years of age, I would need my parents' permission to get married.

Hurdle number two: Jan insisted that I ask her father for his permission to marry her.

Hurdle number three: With a baby on the way, the question became, how would I be able to pay the doctor and hospital bills? At the time, the average cost to have a baby with a hospital stay cost at least $300 to $400, providing there were no complications. Four hundred dollars. Doesn't seem like much money, does it? But when you were only making $2.85 an hour ($91 a week after taxes), have very little money in savings, and no medical insurance, $400 in 1971 was a huge sum of money.

Back to hurdle number one. This one was dreaded and it needed to be knocked off first. As you may have surmised by now, my relationship with my dad was, at its best, volatile. Any conversation with him always involved a high risk of becoming an argument, sometimes an out and out fight. The only thing in my favor was that I too could be a stubborn S.O.B., a trait probably inherited from him. Mom and Dad had met Jan several times by this point. Mom told me that she liked Janice and thought she was a very nice girl.

I picked an evening to go out to the farm alone to meet with Dad and Mom. As soon as possible, I brought up my intention to marry Jan. As anticipated, Dad immediately said, "No way. You're too young, and I will not give my permission." Mom just sat quietly, not saying anything.

I simply told Dad, "I have to get married." The look on his face told me he understood my meaning. I added a final thought on the subject: He would give his permission. If he didn't, I was done with him for good.

To my surprise, he simply replied, "Okay, but you're making a big mistake." I left and went outside to my car. I remember getting into the car. My hands were shaking and my breathing was fast and hard. But at the same time, there was a sense of relief. If Dad would have stood firm in not giving his permission, I would have washed my hands of him for good. Part of my relief was in not having to go to that extreme with him yet. Since I had made my mind up to marry Janice, no one, not even my dad, was going to stand in my way. This hurdle could now be checked off the list. Next, it was on to hurdle number two.

Janice was from Stacyville, Iowa. She was from a big family of eight kids, four boys and four girls. I had been raised as a Protestant in the

Methodist church and her family was Catholic. Janice's family and many people from Stacyville were often referred to as "German Catholics." Growing up in the 1950s and 1960s in northeast Iowa, there were generally three groups of people, divided by religion. There were the Protestants, Catholics, and the Lutherans. The Lutherans were considered by some to be essentially the same thing as Catholics. In that era, a Protestant male marrying a Catholic female or vice-versa might be an issue.

Janice wanted to be married at her church, the Catholic Church in Stacyville, with the ceremony officiated by the local priest. This meant attending Pre-Cana marriage preparation classes and promising to raise our children in the Catholic faith. I arranged the Pre-Cana sessions with a Catholic priest in Forest City and attended in the evenings after work.

The next part to this hurdle was the actual act of asking my future father-in-law, Bill, for his permission and blessing to marry his daughter. From the very first, Bill had always been friendly and kind toward me. But now that Jan and I had reached this point in our relationship, I wasn't sure how he would react to the idea of me being his son-in-law. One thing that concerned me was that Bill was a devout Catholic. He went to mass on Wednesday evenings and Sunday mornings and confession on Saturday nights. Even with his large family, he faithfully tithed to the Catholic Church. He was a carpenter and ran a construction crew; he also often did any carpentry or construction work the church required.

We had spent a good number of weekends at Jan's home with her family. Ann, Jan's mom, was somewhat lukewarm toward me at first. But over time, she seemed to come around and became friendlier. When the time came, it was actually Ann who encouraged me and set the scene of when I should approach Bill. I was a bit afraid to approach Bill on this subject. Being aware of his strong convictions regarding his Catholic faith, I didn't know how he would react. Would he give me his permission to marry Jan, or just throw me out of his house?

One weekend evening, Bill was working in his basement shop. Ann let me know where he was and that I should go down and talk with him. I recall going down to the basement to meet with him. But for the longest time, I just couldn't bring up the topic. We talked about work, carpentry, camping, fishing, and a bunch of other stuff for over an hour. No moment seemed like the right one. Finally, I just said it. "Janice and I intend to get married. We would like your permission and blessing."

As I recall, he stopped whatever he was doing, turned to look at me, and said, "Well, sure." Then he held out his hand and we shook hands. It was like a ton of bricks had just been lifted off of me. It wasn't long after Jan and I were married that on occasion I would overhear Bill refer to me as his pagan son-in-law, and then he would always laugh. I realized he was using the term "pagan" in reference to me simply as a noun, not an adjective, but it did reflect his special sense of humor.

Janice and I were married on June 26, 1971. As planned, we were married at the Catholic Church in Stacyville. Waiting in a side room before the ceremony, suddenly I wanted to bolt and run. Mike, my best man, picked up on my nervousness and he was able to talk me down, if you will. Finally, we made our way to the church altar and the music began. At the back of the church, I could see Jan along with my soon to be father-in-law. For whatever reason, just seeing Jan caused me to calm down. She looked beautiful, and as she started down the aisle with her father, that was all I needed.

We only had time for a long weekend honeymoon, which we spent in Mason City, Iowa. I had to get back to work at Kayot Forester, since I hadn't worked there long enough to have any vacation days. Most summer weekends we spent at Jan's parents' home in Stacyville. We also spent some weekends at my parents' farm. Jan was okay with it, but the weekend visits to my parents on the farm often entailed me falling back into farm-boy mode doing work around the farm and helping during haying.

Summer nights on the farm are very quiet. There is noise, but for farm families many sounds are no longer noticed. The major livestock my dad raised were feeder pigs, which are raised until they reach

48

market weight and then are sold for slaughter. Feeder pigs eat like, well, pigs; they eat constantly. Most feedlots are equipped with automatic pig feeders. Each individual feeder bin is covered with a hinged steel door. Young pigs quickly learn to lift the feeder bin doors with their snouts to gain access to the feed in the bin, and as they back away after feeding, the steel door slams shut. Our farmhouse was not air conditioned, so at night, all of the windows would be opened for ventilation.

Jan was a town girl, and I don't believe she had ever slept in a farmhouse before. After several weekends at my parents' farm, she told me that she couldn't sleep very well because of all the noise. I remember asking her, "What noise?" She said, "You don't hear the constant slamming noises from the pig lots all night long?"

The summer of 1971 went by quickly. Now as a married couple, we quickly fell into the routine of life. I worked at the factory Monday through Friday on the day shift. Jan was a good cook and made us both dinner each night. Later in the summer, it became more apparent that Jan was pregnant as our baby grew inside her. I would say generally we were happy and content. The only thing we both still worried about was that we hadn't yet solved was our hurdle number three and the question of how to pay for the birth of our baby.

I think I learned something else over that summer. For young newly married couples, spending too much time with in-laws might not be the best idea. It's the weekend visits and the discussions (for lack of a better term) about whose turn is it, her parents or mine?

During this same time, through the summer of 1971, America was learning something else about our past presidents and leaders through the *New York Times* as they published their stories on what became known as the Pentagon Papers. The official title for the papers was, "History of the U.S. Decision-Making Process on Vietnam." The Pentagon Papers were actually a report that had been leaked to the press, their contents revealing secret communiques, decisions concerning our country's role in Vietnam, and recommendations from

John F. Kennedy and Lyndon Johnson's presidencies. Probably what surprised most was that the Pentagon Papers revealed that in 1963, John F. Kennedy's administration had actively helped overthrow and assassinate the South Vietnamese President. The report also discussed that the intensive bombings of North Vietnam had no real impact or effect on the North Vietnamese "will to fight," contradicting the official U.S. government's pronouncements about the impact of the bombing.

I would say the most significant impact from the release of the Pentagon Papers came from finding out that all of the presidential administrations, all the way back to Harry S. Truman and Dwight D. Eisenhower, had misled the U.S. public about the degree of our country's involvement in Vietnam. For that time period, it was astonishing to publicly learn that our last four presidents and leaders in their administrations had knowingly misled and lied to the American public. It begged the question, if they all lied about our involvement in Vietnam, what else had they lied to us about?

The fact that our government had been lying to us for this long was a pretty big deal. Some might dispute my view, but I would say that we were probably the last generation in the history of our country that was raised and educated to believe that our governments—local, state, and federal—would never lie to us. The release of the Pentagon Papers gave many the evidence that served to further confirm their suspicions that our U.S. government was not honest and had been dishonest for a long time. As young adults, these types of news events shattered many of our beliefs and values. It also served to make some suspicious of any member of the government. Reading and hearing about the Pentagon Papers during the summer of 1971, to a degree, validated what I thought I already knew about politicians.

On December 1, 1969, the Selective Service System reinstated the draft lottery system, of what became known as the Vietnam Draft Lottery. The lottery was changed from the "draft the oldest man first" method, which had been the determining method for deciding order of call. There were 366 blue plastic capsules containing birthdates placed in a large glass container and drawn by hand to assign order-of-call numbers to all men of the age specified in Selective Service law.

On August 5, 1971, the Vietnam draft lottery was held for those born in the year 1952. The lottery number for my birthdate was 43. It was announced in the news that lottery numbers up to 50 would be called for physical examinations by October 31, 1971. The Administrative Processing Number (APN) for that year was stated as 125, which meant lottery numbers 1 through 125 would be called for at least the physical examination. The highest number called that year actually ended up being 95.

From my view, it was either the choice of getting drafted into the Army or enlisting in another branch of the Armed Forces. It wasn't in me to try to snivel my way out of the military obligation. Even at my age then, I didn't hold our government in very high esteem. However, I did then, and still do care, a great deal about my country. And I was not about to dishonor myself in attempting to avoid military service.

Now as a married man, any decisions had to include my wife. I leaned toward joining the Navy. My brother Jon had done four years in the Navy as an aircraft mechanic. Two of Jan's older brothers were already in the Navy. Jan's oldest brother, Jim, was a first class petty officer in the "Seabees" and her other brother Joe was a data systems technician stationed at Dam Neck, Virginia.

Jan's brothers had not been sent to Vietnam, so that seemed to be a positive factor. My father-in-law, Bill, had spent four years in the Navy during World War II. Based on my preference for the Navy, we ultimately decided to make an appointment with the nearest Navy Recruiting Office in Mason City.

3. THE NEXT STEP

During the last week of August, Janice and I visited the Navy Recruiting Office. The visit went well. The recruiter was a chief petty officer (E-7)/chief commissaryman who had me take a short written test first. After the test, the chief explained that my scores looked very good and it looked like I had an especially high mechanical aptitude. He told us all about the differences between the four- and six-year enlistments and the benefits for married Navy personnel. The chief reemphasized to us that because of my initial testing results, I should qualify for training in one of the advanced technical programs. But because of the necessary amount and length of training in these programs, it required a six-year versus a four-year enlistment. There was an incentive attached to the six-year enlistment in that it included what he called "accelerated advancement." That meant enlisting in paygrade E-3 versus paygrade E-2; in other words, more pay.

When the chief started talking about the medical benefits, he struck a chord with both of us when he said that the cost for a military family to have a baby, even at a civilian hospital, was only $25. The caveat was that in order for "Champus" (military healthcare) benefits to apply for new births, the service member must have at least 60 days of service before the date of birth. My thoughts leapt to the final problem on my list: *Oh shit, this takes care of hurdle number three.* Remember my hurdle number three, how would I be able to pay the doctor and hospital bills? My mind raced. Our baby was due in December! *Oh shit, I'm going to have to join up really soon.*

By the end of the visit, we decided for me to go through the full processing to see what I could qualify for. Then, after knowing what the Navy offered, we would make our decision. We agreed to a date in early September to take the physical examination, the entrance examination, and go through the classification processing.

During the second week of September, I made the bus trip to the AFEES at Fort Des Moines, Iowa. It was during this trip to the AFEES that the earlier described events occurred, which demonstrated the extent that some would go to in trying to avoid being drafted. I arrived early in the evening, so after reporting in at the main gate to the Fort, they directed me to go to an area where there were two large buildings.

The larger building was a huge open-bay barracks; the other building next to it was the cafeteria (chow hall). I signed in at the main desk in the barracks and was issued some bedding (a pillowcase, two sheets, and blanket) and was told to go claim an empty bunk and make it up. The guy at the desk told me that if I had money or valuables with me, I should keep a close watch on my stuff. He added that they were not responsible for the loss of personal effects.

In the big open-bay area of the barracks, there must have been 250 to 300 bunks. There were a couple of areas with a bunch of chairs, piles of magazines, and a television mounted on the wall. Near the back of the barracks, there was a big restroom and shower room. There were signs posted all around on the walls and stanchions with information about the processing day. The signs informed us that 0500 was the time of reveille that all bunks were to be stripped with bedding turned in, and applicants (us) had to be dressed and at the muster area at the front of the building no later than 0530.

By around 1930 that evening, there must have been more than 200 guys checked into the barracks. For the most part, everyone pretty much kept to themselves. Many spent the evening just watching television or reading magazines. Others hung around outside the barracks by the vending machines, smoking. At about 2100, an announcement came over intercom speakers that the shower room would be closed at 2130 and lights out would be at 2200.

The next morning promptly at 0500, a loud booming voice came over the intercom speakers. "Now everyone get up and turn out; you have 30 minutes to report to the designated area in accordance with the posted instructions." The intercom announcement was repeated at least four or five more times.

At 0530, several guys in army uniforms showed up. They were eventually able to get everyone to fall into a line, and single file we began the walk along a path crossing a large field with freshly mowed grass. Shortly, we came to a large three- or four-story building (the AFEES building). Outside of the entrance there was a big paved asphalt lot, with areas marked out as large painted squares.

The Army guys began shouting instructions; those processing for the Army, or who were just there for initial examination for the Selective Service, went to the red square; Air Force went to the green square; Navy went to the blue square; and Marines went to the yellow square.

Some guys were grumbling that they hadn't gotten any breakfast. Others were bitching, "They have a chow hall, but we don't get to use it." One of the Army guys commented that the reason there had been no breakfast was because the physical exam included blood and urine tests.

I went to my assigned area marked by the big painted blue square. There were maybe a dozen or so of us there for the Navy. There were about 8 to 10 guys at the Air Force area, and about 20 or so at the Marine Corps area. Everyone else was standing in the red square. I had noticed as we approached that the painted red square was a lot bigger than the other squares; now I knew why.

My processing day at AFEES had some high points and some not so great ones as well. Once the Navy group was gathered up from our blue square outside, we were escorted into the building and taken to a large room filled with rows of student-type desks. A soldier came in and announced that he would be administering and proctoring the Armed Forces Qualification Test (AFQT). He ran through what was clearly a memorized speech: "The Armed Forces Qualification Test will be used to measure your general ability to absorb training in the military within a reasonable length of time, and provide a uniform measure of your potential usefulness in the military." Then he continued in a more instructional tone, telling us that everyone should do their best on the test, because the score would be used to determine our mental group category and potential for an occupation in each respective military service.

We were allowed about two hours to take the written test. I recall finishing with all sections of the test in a little over an hour. After rechecking a number of my answers, I turned in my test for scoring. I really, really had to pee, so I asked the test proctor about using the restroom. He answered that yes, I could go, but reminded me to come back right away. I went to the restroom and returned to the testing room and waited. After everyone had turned in their tests, the testing proctor came around the room and handed us each a piece of paper.

Each person's name and social security number was printed at the top of the paper. We were asked to verify that our name and social security number were correct. Then the proctor explained that on the paper was our AFQT score and mental group category, followed by our scores on each subsection of the test. On my paper, there was the Roman numeral II filled in the mental group box. I generally knew what the AFQT score meant, but no idea what the II meant.

Next, we were told to exit the testing room and out in the hallway there would be a white line painted on the floor. We were instructed to follow the white line to the first station where our physical examinations would begin. At the first window in the physical exam line, a medic handed each of us a small plastic cup and directed us to the restroom across the hall. He instructed us to fill the cups with urine up to the mark on the side of the cup. Once we had filled our urine cups, he directed that we place the cups at the next window to his right.

Well, hell, I had just pissed less than a half hour before. There was no way I was going to be able to pee right then and there. I told the one of the medics that I didn't have to pee. He directed me to a nearby water fountain and told me to drink water until I did have to go, and said that I would be there until I could fill the cup. In the next 15 to 25 minutes, I'm sure I drank more than a gallon of water. Then, numerous trips to the restroom to try, and nothing. I must have repeated this cycle three or four more times and still nothing. The whole thing was getting embarrassing. Groups of guys came in, filled their cups with no problem, and were on their way.

I was standing at one of the urinals for what had to be my umpteenth attempt, and by then I was getting desperate. A blond-haired guy with a beard walked up to the urinal next to mine. Smiling, he asked me, "You having some trouble? Want to borrow some of mine?"

I answered, "Hell yes." So, he filled his urine cup, then filled mine too, and handed my cup back to me. I followed him out of the restroom across the hall to the window where we turned in our cups. I placed my cup on the counter right after his.

This next part is the absolute truth, or in the Navy we would say, "This is a no shitter." The medic came up and put a small white strip in the blond guy's urine cup. The part of the strip submerged in the urine turned pink. The medic said to him, "You need to go over to the red line next; you seem to have high sugar in your urine and you'll need to get it checked out." I was thinking, "Shit, now I've screwed up."

Next, the medic put a strip in my urine cup. The part of the strip submerged in the urine didn't turn pink; it turned kind of a purple-bluish color. The medic looked at the strip for several seconds. Then he said, "You're good. Follow the yellow line."

I still remember asking myself, "How in the hell did that just happen?" The rest of the physical examination went well. The only other event was the peanut butter in the butt crack incident mentioned earlier. I had to use the restroom about five times throughout the rest of the morning to get rid of all the damn water I drank earlier.

After the physical examination, they told me to report to the Navy processing office and check in. Once checked in at the Navy office, they gave me a lunch ticket for the chow hall and sent me to lunch. As I was given a time to be back, I ate my lunch quickly and spent the remaining time nervously chain smoking outside before going back inside to the Navy office.

After arriving back at the Navy processing office, my name was called within a few minutes by the "classifier." Once I was seated at the classifier's desk, he introduced himself and began to go over my AFQT scores and the fact that my scores had placed me at the high end of the Mental Category Group II. He pointed out that my scores were very high for the sections on arithmetic reasoning, tool knowledge, mechanical comprehension, and automotive information. He indicated that my AFQT scores qualified me for the Navy's Nuclear Power Program. He believed that the Machinists Mate (MM) rating in the Nuclear Power Program would be the best fit for me. Then he went on to explain that it required the six-year enlistment and the added benefits of the training and education.

Everything the classifier said about the Navy's nuclear power training rang true. While working in Illinois the year before, there had been a café I ate at regularly. A lot of the customers there worked at the nuclear power plant near Cordova, Illinois. I had struck up conversations with a number of the power plant workers and quite a few had told me they had received their nuclear power training and plant operating experience while in the Navy. In that part of the country, some of the best jobs around were those at nuclear power plants. So, I believed what the classifier told me.

Next came the deal. The classifier explained that because of quotas, there were a limited number of nuclear power Machinists Mate seats available that month. He made it clear that if I wanted to take advantage of the availability, he would need a commitment from me very soon. I asked him about taking some time to think about it. He indicated that of course I could go home and think about, but said he couldn't guarantee there'd be an opening if I decided to come back later.

Next, he cast out the bait. The classifier was looking at my paperwork and began talking as he looked through the forms. "I see you're married, and I have a note here from your recruiter that you and your wife are expecting a baby. Congratulations." He made the suggestion that I could enlist now and then delay my boot camp report date for a month. He went on to add that by committing that day, he would guarantee me the MM seat in the Nuclear Power program. More importantly, it would start the clock of when my wife would be eligible for Navy medical benefits. Then the kicker came when he said, "You know, Navy Nukes don't get sent to Vietnam." The hook was set.

Considering my low draft lottery number, I realized that my options were few. Everything did sound like a good deal. I really wasn't that hyped up about signing up for a six-year enlistment, but my hurdle number three issue would be solved. The nuclear power training and experience would probably help me get a good job after my enlistment was up. I guess you could say, now as a married man, I was thinking for the first time about the future and how to make it a better one. I made the big decision, and said to the classifier, "Yes, I will commit and enlist today."

I took the oath of enlistment later that afternoon. As part of a fairly large group of enlistees, we were assembled and shown into a large room. At the front of the room behind some tables there were flag stands with the U.S. flag and the service flags for all branches of the military. We were lined up into ranks and rows. An Army officer came in and began to address us by congratulating us on our decision to become members of the United States Armed Forces.

The officer told us he was there to administer the enlistment oath. He asked all of us to raise our right hand; then he instructed us that after he said the first word of the oath, "I," we were to repeat "I," then state our full name, then repeat after him each phrase of the oath. For those who have never served in the military, the following is the enlistment oath:

"I, (state name of enlistee), do solemnly swear (or affirm) that I will support and defend the Constitution of the United States against all enemies, foreign and domestic; that I will bear true faith and allegiance to the same; and that I will obey the orders of the President of the United States and the orders of the officers appointed over me, according to regulations and the Uniform Code of Military Justice. So help me God."

After the enlistment oath had been administered, our names were called one at a time to come forward to a table at the front of the room. Each of us was presented with our enlistment contract. An administrative staff person instructed us to ensure our names and all other information stated in the contract were accurate. Once we confirmed the accuracy of information contained in our contract, we were shown where to sign. After signing our enlistment contract, the Army officer who had administered the oath shook each person's hand and congratulated them on becoming a member of the U.S. Armed Forces.

That was it. I had just committed myself to an enlistment in the U.S. Navy. I wasn't sure how Jan would feel about me making the commitment to an enlistment; our agreement had been that the purpose of completing the processing was to explore and confirm what options the Navy could offer me. Now that I had obligated myself, I would have to break the news to Jan and see what her reaction would be.

Later, we were given large envelopes, which contained copies of our enlistment contracts and other paperwork. My envelope also had my official orders for when to report back to Fort Des Moines for final processing and then transport to Naval Training Center, at Great Lakes, Illinois, for recruit training.

There were passenger vans waiting outside the AFEES building that were going to the Des Moines Airport and to the downtown bus stations. I caught one of the vans to the bus station. While waiting for the bus, I found a phone booth and made a collect call home to talk with Jan. I told her that I had enlisted in the Navy and didn't need to report to boot camp until October 20. I was excited to tell her about the Nuclear Power program training guarantee. The only thing I distinctly remember her saying was that she was surprised that I had actually enlisted. She said she'd thought that I was going to check it out first before I made a decision. By the end of our phone conversation, though, I believe she was okay with my decision.

After arriving back in Forest City with my enlistment in the Navy a done deal, we had to make some fast decisions. We had 30 days to prepare for my departure to Navy boot camp on October 20. I went back to work. We had decided that I would work until the last week before leaving. We needed the money. Secondly, it was decided that Jan would live with her parents in Stacyville while I was away. Our baby was due in mid-December, when I would still be in boot camp. I felt comforted in the knowledge that Jan would be with her mother and family for our baby's birth. The week before I was to leave, we moved out of our apartment in Forest City and moved our few belongings to Stacyville.

Several weeks before, I had called my parents to let them know I had joined the Navy and when I was leaving. Dad made it clear that he was not happy with my decision. The last weekend before my departure, we visited them to say goodbye. When we arrived, Mom was at the house and Dad was out working in one the fields. I walked out to the field where Dad was working. Once I found him, we talked for a bit. He asked if I was sure about joining the Navy. I told him it didn't matter; I was already obligated.

As usual, Dad was not going to make this easy. He told me that if I would have come to him and agreed to come back to farming, he was pretty sure I could have gotten an exemption from military service. I was never quite sure how he figured that one. Dad mentioned that my brother had gotten into some trouble while he was in the Navy, which I knew was true. I can only guess, but Dad was probably already assuming that I would screw up worse than my brother.

Finally, I told him I'd just come out to say goodbye and I walked away, heading back to the farmhouse. Back at the house, we talked with my mom for a while. Before we left, Mom insisted on taking pictures. She took several pictures of me and Jan together on the south side of the farmhouse. Then we said goodbye to Mom and drove back to Stacyville.

On Wednesday, October 20, I took the bus from Mason City back to Fort Des Moines. I spent that night in the same barracks as the previous month during processing. The next morning, we reported to the AFEES Navy office for final processing and by that afternoon I was waiting at the Des Moines Airport for my flight to Chicago O'Hare Airport. All the airport workers knew that when guys like me were walking around with a big brown envelope, we were headed into the military. While waiting for my flight, my thoughts were focused on the fact that this was my first separation from Jan. I didn't really want to go. However, my gut told me that based on our circumstances going into the Navy was the best thing I could do for Jan and our baby's welfare.

My flight out of Des Moines was during the late afternoon and we landed at O'Hare Airport probably about 6:00 p.m. At Fort Des Moines, they had told me that upon my arrival at the O'Hare airport I should find the military check-in desk near the ticket counters. Once I got to the desk and checked in, the person at the desk pointed to an open common area and told me where to go. The instructions were to wait and to not leave the common area.

After several hours of waiting, there were probably more than 50 of us at the waiting area. A sailor in a dress blue uniform finally showed up around 8:30 p.m. He had a list with him and had us answer when our names were called out. Once he was sure everyone was there, he escorted us out of the air terminal to a waiting Greyhound bus outside. About an hour later the bus pulled into Camp Barry at the Great Lakes Naval Station. Camp Barry was the Navy recruit training center in World War II and was used until the mid-1970s as the recruit check-in and processing facility.

The check-in process began quickly. As soon as the bus stopped, uniformed sailors boarded the bus and immediately began yelling at us to get off the bus and line up outside. Once we were all off the bus, we were rushed into a large building nearby, then shown to a big open room and directed to wait until our names were called. There were rows of chairs in the room, but we were told to sit on the deck along the bulkhead. I knew the term "deck" was the floor and quickly figured out the "bulkhead" was the wall.

It seemed like we waited for hours. Then, as usual, I had to use the restroom. We had been told not to leave the waiting area at the airport, then we'd had the hour-long ride from the airport, and now I was sitting there. I had been watching guys going in and out of a door near the far corner of the room with a stenciled sign above it that read "HEAD." I remember wondering what the heck could be the purpose of a room marked "HEAD." By this point, none of us wanted to ask any questions. I had already watched a couple of guys try to ask questions—what they got in reply was someone screaming at them to shut up!

Finally, I asked one of the guys sitting next to me on the deck (floor), if he had any idea if they had restrooms here. He pointed at the door with the sign. I got up to go use the head. Just as I got to the door, a short red-haired guy in uniform ran up to me, yelling, "No one told you that you could get up; get back to your spot!"

At 6 foot 3 inches and weighing around 205 pounds, I wasn't used to taking much shit off of anybody. I think I told him, "Well, I can either piss on you or I can piss in there, but I am going to piss." I think I got my point across, because after he gave me a nasty look, he turned and went back to wherever he had come from. So far my bladder and the military were not faring too well.

Sometime after the "head" incident, my name was finally called to come to the front counter. At the counter, the sailor there directed me toward a side doorway. He told me to go outside and form up with the rest of the *slugs*, and then we would be taken to our barracks for the night.

It was well after midnight when we got to the barracks. The building was an old two-story, probably built during World War II. Our barracks was on the second floor (I mean deck). We were told by the sailors who'd escorted us to find a bunk and get settled in for the night. I found a bunk at the end of a row of bunks near one of the end windows. The barracks were dark, hot, stuffy, and of course, none of the windows would open. I don't believe any of us slept much that night. I can only guess, but I imagine most of us were going through a bit of initial culture shock. So far our first several hours in the Navy had consisted of someone yelling and screaming at us or being looked at as though we were invisible.

It seemed that I had barely fallen asleep when suddenly the lights came on and there were four or five sailors banging on steel trash can lids yelling for us to get up and get dressed. They were yelling, "It's 0500, and it's Reveille; you have 15 minutes to use the head, get dressed, and fall in outside. Let's go, let's go, let's go!"

Once outside, our group stood around in the same general area. One of the sailors had a list of our names, and he yelled out, "When I call your last name, answer up and get in line in the same order." We were lined up single-file alphabetically by our last name, A through Z. Once our line was formed, we were escorted to the galley (chow hall) several blocks away for breakfast. There were other groups ahead of us waiting in line. While we were waiting, a sailor walked up and down along our line, letting us know that we would get 15 minutes to eat breakfast. He kept restating, "In the Navy, you take all you want to eat, but you must eat all that you take."

Once in the chow hall, we picked up our trays, and eventually made it to the serving line. In the serving line, the servers slopped what I guessed were powdered eggs, some type of breakfast meat, and two slices of what looked like toasted bread on my tray. I was able to get a small carton of milk and sat down at a table. I was starving; my last meal had been lunch the day before.

We had just started eating when a sailor came to our table and said we had three minutes to finish and to muster back outside. Apparently because we had entered the galley in alphabetical order, the guys with last names starting with the letters A through P had gotten served first. Now group A through P had finished with its breakfast, so those with last names starting with letters Q through Z were screwed. My last name starts with the letter T, so of course I was in the screwed-over Q through Z group. However, the rule was that you must eat everything on your tray before leaving. So we all ate our food as fast as we could.

As we walked over to turn in our trays at the scullery, there were two sailors checking the trays for any food left. So, breakfast was sort of a bust. It seemed that day one in the Navy was not going much better than the night before.

Next, we were marched (if you want to call it that) to a building which looked somewhat like a large gymnasium; there we continued the check-in. We filled out shipping tags for returning our civilian clothing and other personal effects home. From there, we went to another area for clothing and uniform issue. Everyone stood in line with nothing on except our underwear (called "skivvies" in the Navy). People measured our waist and inseam for trousers and our feet for shoe size. Next, they measured our chest, head, and hand size and for uniform shirts, hats, and gloves. Things moved quickly; it was very much like a factory assembly line.

The check-in process continued until the following Thursday. By that time, I had been in Camp Barry for one whole week. The prior days had been spent getting haircuts, more physical examinations, dental examinations, dental hygiene classes, and on and on. Then came the vaccinations and shots. We were given a long series of shots over several days; two doses of triple typhoid, tetanus, influenza, diphtheria, two doses of typhus, and a trivalent polio vaccine. The shots were given using a jet gun (air gun). For the shots, you had to stay very still and not flinch, or the jet gun could cut you.

My line was manned by two hospital corpsman administering the shots with the jet guns. One of the corpsmen seemed to take a lot of pleasure yelling in each person's ear trying to startle them

RTC tunnel leading into and out of Camp Dewey. Raisins to the left, white hats to the right.

just as the jet gun trigger was pulled. If the person receiving the shot moved and was cut by the jet gun, he would say with a nasty laugh, "We told you not move; what's wrong with you?" Apparently, we were just a source of entertainment for him.

We were provided with stenciling kits and had to punch out stencil lettering, spelling out our last name and our service number (my service number was B67-90-17). Next, all of our clothing and uniform items from skivvies, T-shirts, to dress uniforms had to be stenciled with our last name and service number using either white or black laundry markers with our stencils. In between the other activities, we spent time out on the grinder (concrete or asphalt paved areas for marching and drilling, etc.), learning how to form up into a unit and receiving some basic instruction on how to march as a unit. Finally, on Friday, we were ready to make the move to Camp Dewey, where Recruit Training Command (RTC) was located across the main road and actually begin our recruit training.

We were told to form up outside of our barracks on the grinder, with our sea bags fully packed. Waiting on the grinder was a first class petty officer wearing the undress blue uniform and white hat. His uniform was different because he also wore a red braided epaulette around his left shoulder. The petty officer introduced himself and explained that he was our company commander (CC) and we all now belonged to him.

Our sea bags, which weighed about 65 pounds, were loaded up onto a Navy truck. We formed up to march as a unit, three-abreast per row and three columns in line, and prepared to leave Camp Barry headed for the Recruit Training Center (RTC). Our company, with a total of about 80 men, made the march across the street to the entrance of Camp Dewey. The entrance to Camp Dewey was made via an under-the-street tunnel. Whenever they entered the tunnel, recruit units had to sing "Anchors Aweigh." The echo from our singing reverberated inside the tunnel. A lot of us still didn't know all the words to "Anchors Aweigh." I don't think it mattered, because no one could tell the difference anyway.

The other side of the tunnel brought our company up and into Camp Dewey's RTC complex of modern barracks and other facilities that would be our home for the next nine weeks. Informally, we now would be called "raisins" by senior recruits who had completed their fourth week of training. They had earned the right to wear the Navy white hat cover (the Dixie cup). Until completion of training week four, recruits had to wear the navy blue knit watch cap, or the "raisin."

It had been a little over a week since getting off the plane at O'Hare Airport, and most of us had reached the point of settling down and were becoming more accustomed to the life of a recruit. The unit had been formed into Company 383 of the 2nd Regiment and 26th Battalion. Our CC would spend his next nine weeks training the recruits of Company 383. Our company commander was a first class petty officer, aviation ordnanceman (AO) rating. Company commanders are noncommissioned officers, but we were required to salute them and address them as "company commander" or "sir." The CC was now our leader and he had the responsibility to make us into sailors.

Our barracks was not just a place to sleep, it was also our most important classroom. Here, we learned by doing. The cleaning and the constant inspections all served just one purpose—to prepare you for a

successful life during your time in the Navy. One of the mor
lessons was how to live with others in a military organizatio
and living conditions were now so different from anythir
known as civilians. I think learning to live in close quarters as
of a group is one of the major functions of recruit training. Early in
training, no one had really gotten to know the names of the other
company members, only their faces. Gradually, during each morning's
muster, everyone learned to identify a name with each person.

Life in the barracks was a constant challenge to keep everything
spotless. We scrubbed the decks every morning and night. The head and
showers were kept immaculately clean. We washed clothes and
uniforms in metal buckets by hand and hung them up in a drying room
each night. The clothes were hung using short braided lines called
"clothes stops" instead of clothespins. The clothes stops had to be tied
to the article of clothing and the clothesline with square knots, and each
article of clothing had to be hung and spaced exactly three inches (the
length of a military I.D. card) apart. We learned how to fold all our
clothes the Navy way and the importance of stowing them in our
lockers only one way; no alternative was acceptable. We would spit-
polish our shoes to an immaculate shine that would last until the next
round of pushups.

Our company marched everywhere we went. After a few days at
Camp Dewey, we were issued our Springfield 1903 bolt action rifle (our
piece) to carry and march with everywhere we went. Outside of each
building there were rifle racks where we stowed them until we left for
the next location. Other than going to the galley for meals or while in
the barracks, your piece was with you at all times.

With our piece, a lot of our time was spent learning the
fundamentals of military drill, the manual of arms, marching, and
physical drill under arms. We all had to perfect the 15-count manual of
arms. We had to memorize the *Eleven General Orders of the Sentry* from
our copy of the Bluejacket's Manual. When standing a security or fire
watch, any CC or other staff might approach your post day or night and

demand you recite for them the *Eleven General Orders of the Sentry*. Sometimes you would be asked to recite just one or two of the general orders, such as, "What is general order number five?" Other times it would be demanded that you recite all 11 general orders, word for word from the Bluejacket's Manual as follows:

1. *To take charge of this post and all government property in view.*

2. *To walk my post in a military manner, keeping always on the alert, and observing everything that takes place within sight or hearing.*

3. *To report all violations of orders I am instructed to enforce.*

4. *To repeat all calls from posts more distant from the guard house than my own.*

5. *To quit my post only when properly relieved.*

6. *To receive, obey and pass on to the sentry who relieves me, all orders from the Commanding Officer, Command Duty Officer, Officer of the Deck, and Officers and Petty Officers of the Watch only.*

7. *To talk to no one except in the line of duty.*

8. *To give the alarm in case of fire or disorder.*

9. *To call the Officer of the Deck in any case not covered by instructions.*

10. *To salute all officers and all colors and standards not cased.*

11. *To be especially watchful at night, and, during the time for challenging, to challenge all persons on or near my post and to allow no one to pass without proper authority.*

If our company didn't march together to classes or some other location, everyone had to double-time it, which meant we ran everywhere. Daily inspections became normal routine.

By the time we started our actual recruit training, most of us had become proficient in two physical activities. One was running long distances wearing the working uniform shoes (boondockers); the other was doing a lot of pushups. Anytime a recruit didn't do something fast enough or didn't do something precisely as directed, they were ordered to, "Assume the position," meaning to drop to the deck and assume the pushup position. Then the order would come, "give me twenty" or "give me thirty." The number of ordered pushups could increase depending upon the category of the offense.

In between everything else, we attended classes or orientation sessions nearly every day. There were instruction and classes for water safety, ordnance and gunnery, seamanship, damage control, and shipboard firefighting. I'm sure anyone who has ever attended boot camp remembers the gas mask training. Every recruit had to learn how to properly don a gas mask. More importantly, once you had mastered the donning of the gas mask, into the gas chamber you went. Once the recruits were in the gas chamber with gas masks on, the chamber was filled with tear gas.

After a set period of time, recruits were ordered to remove their gas masks, then hold their gas masks over their head and sing "Anchors Aweigh." The escape door would not be opened until the instructors made sure everyone had removed their gas masks and was singing. Once the escape door was opened, we were required to calmly exit one by one with our gas masks held over our heads. If anyone panicked or did not follow instructions, that could get them a second trip through the gas chamber.

Recruits learned to fear a number of things in boot camp, but what they feared the most was something called the Assignment Memorandum Orders (ASMOs). One way to get ASMO-ed was if a recruit got too sick or injured to continue training. Other reasons for an ASMO could be failing tests or needing remedial reading work. Getting ASMO-ed meant the recruit would be removed from his company and placed in a holding company. His training would be suspended pending resolution of the issue.

When a recruit was able to overcome the cause of the ASMO, they would be assigned to a later formed company. None of us wanted to go to "Sick Call" unless we absolutely had to or had been ordered by the CC. In the first week of training we lost several company members who went to sick call and were ASMO-ed. Even after just a couple of days in training, a high level of comradeship and friendship already existed between company members. It was not easy for a recruit to have to leave his original company. For me, I saw getting ASMO-ed as unacceptable, because my goal was to get through boot camp in the shortest possible time.

I missed not being home with Jan terribly. Except for one phone call home the first week at Camp Barry, the only other communications up to this point had been by letter. Each person had been issued a stationary kit, with postage stamps and envelopes. Most nights after all company work was done, I would write short letters to Jan and mail them the next morning. It was while in boot camp, I learned the importance of "Mail Call." Jan had been sending me letters almost every day. Every other day, when the time for mail call came, everyone would anxiously wait to see if there name was called as having received mail.

I believe it's worth mentioning that Company 383 was made up of young men from varied and diverse backgrounds, ethnicities, races, and religions. They were from urban and suburban areas. Some like myself came from rural areas. Others came from inner city environments. We were a group of Caucasians, Hispanics, African-Americans, Latinos, and Polish-Americans. In Company 383, we had guys that were Protestant, Southern Baptist, Lutheran, Catholic, Jewish, and one atheist. For many of us, this was our first exposure to people of other races or ethnicities. You know what? None of that mattered to any of us. All of us realized very quickly that we needed each other to make it through.

We all learned fast that we had to pull together as one for the good of everyone, and we did that. I have no recollection of anyone, even when angry, ever insulting another guy's race, religion, ethnicity, or background. We had too much respect for each other to ever say anything hurtful or insulting to one of our comrades. Don't get me wrong; we joked and poked fun at each other all the time, but no one ever crossed the line. That would have been unacceptable to all of us.

Sometimes, especially at night, I would really get down about being away from home and Jan. It felt better knowing she was safe at home with her family while I was away, but as the days of separation turned into weeks it wasn't getting any easier. Fortunately, I had made a friend with one person who was empathetic and often helpful in making me feel better. Walter, who went by the nickname "French Fry", turned out to be my best friend while in boot camp. At night when I was sometimes a bit down, it was French Fry who always recognized my mood and would talk and joke with me, always making me feel better. French Fry was an African-American kid from north Philadelphia, the "hood" as he called it. He often spoke of lying up in his "crib" with his lady and what his life had been like in the tough inner city neighborhoods where he came from. For whatever reason, French Fry and I had become fast friends. Who would think two people from such different backgrounds and cultures could become friends, but we did. French Fry was about a year younger than me, but he was wise about life beyond his years. More importantly he was able to communicate his life wisdom in highly effective ways. If not for my friend French Fry, I know boot camp would have been a lot tougher for me than it was. Like most people in the military, the last time I spoke with my friend was as we said goodbye to each other on the last day of boot camp as we all departed for our next destinations in the Navy.

The initial goal for Company 383 was to make it through the fourth week of recruit training. Week five was called Ship's Work Training or Service Week. The official line on Service Week was that it was supposed to be devoted to instruction and practical experience in Ship's Work Training. One perk of reaching Service Week as we saw it was that we now had earned the right to wear the coveted white hat. Going back to day one and our arrival at Camp Barry, all the sailors who had herded us around, yelled at us, and in some cases abused new recruits, had been in their Service Week.

There were a lot of different jobs recruits were assigned for Service Week. Most were assigned jobs at the galley, and some got to shovel snow all week or perform sentry duty. My assignment was in the galley, and of course I got the worse damn job anyone could be assigned, working in the scullery. The scullery was hot, wet, and could be overwhelming. There were piles and piles of steel pans and pots that had to be scrubbed clean by hand after every meal. Some of the burned-on or baked-in food was like chipping away at concrete, and of course, each pan and pot had to be made spotless or it was unacceptable.

I worked in the scullery from 0400 in the morning until we were done after dinner service in the evening. Some evenings I wouldn't make it back to the barracks until after Taps at 2200. Since we wore only one uniform set for the week, I had to wash my uniform shirt and trousers every night. More than once when dressing at 0330, I put on a still-wet uniform and headed out in the late November cold for my run to the galley.

On the fourth day of Service Week, I caught a break. Due to my constant exposure to the hot water, detergents, scouring powder, and pads, I had developed a bad rash all over my fingers, hands, and lower arms. That morning, after reporting to the scullery, one of the galley supervisors saw my hands and ordered me to go to sick call at 0800 that morning. I worked through breakfast and reported to the medical dispensary building in time for sick call. I was really worried about getting ASMO-ed.

The hospital corpsman during sick call took one look at my rashes and asked me what I had been doing. I explained my assignment to the scullery for Service Week and that the rashes had started after the first day. He said, "Well, I can fix that." He wrote me out a "medical chit" to take to the galley supervisor. The medical chit contained instructions to remove me from the scullery and to assign me to a job not requiring contact with detergents.

I got assigned to the galley storeroom unloading supply trucks and organizing food supplies in the warehouse. It was easy work, and seemed like a vacation after being in the scullery. The rest of my Service Week was all smooth sailing and my rashes had all but disappeared by the end of the week.

By week six of recruit training, we all started to see the light at the end of the tunnel. Each Saturday during recruit training, we were allowed time to go to the Navy Exchange store and near the Exchange was the Recreation Hall. The Recreation Hall had about 25 phone booths in the lobby area. This was where I would make what had become the weekly collect phone call home to talk with Jan. As the weeks went by, we were getting closer to her delivery due date.

Early evening on Saturday, December 11, my mother-in-law, Ann, answered the phone when I called, instead of Jan. Ann let me know that she had just gotten home from the Osage Community Hospital and that I was the father of a healthy baby boy. Our son had been born that afternoon and weighed 7 pounds, 10 ounces. Ann told me that Janice and the baby were doing fine and that everything had gone well.

I don't recall ever having the same feelings as those that came over me after getting off the phone. First, there was a huge sense of relief that both Jan and the baby were okay, and doing fine. Next, the reality of it sank in, thinking, *Holy crap, you're really a father.* Jan and I had already agreed that if our baby was a girl, we would name her Elieth Ann, after her mother. If the baby was a boy, believe it or not, we had decided to name him Mitchell Thomas, after my dad. My theory was that if I raised a boy carrying my dad's name, it would always remind me to do things differently with him from how Dad had raised me. Crazy idea, right? At the Navy Exchange store, I found two big boxes of (cheap) cigars and bought them.

The next morning before the company departed for breakfast, the message arrived from the American Red Cross with notification of my son's birth. Within minutes, the whole company knew about my new son. That afternoon during the company "smoke and coke" break in the barracks lounge, I handed out my cigars. Soon there was a really thick haze of cigar smoke throughout the lounge, along with some hacking and coughing. The cigars were pretty bad, but no one seemed to care; it was a celebration.

Going to boot camp during the last three months of year had an upside and a downside to it. The upside was that we would all be able to take two weeks of Christmas leave; the downside was that we would have to come back to boot camp after the leave period to finish the last 10 days of recruit training. Our graduation date was set for Friday, January 14, 1972.

Our last day of training before Christmas was on December 22, but the CC ended the training day early at noon. We all were granted liberty for the rest of the day until 2000 that night. Wearing our dress blue uniforms with liberty passes in hand, a group of us walked out of Camp Dewey's main gate for the first time in over seven weeks. Most of us walked over to the main side (Great Lakes Naval Training Station) of the base. There, many of us went to the Navy Exchange store to buy Christmas presents. The Navy Exchange complex also had a gift shop, restaurant, and a recreation section. After a couple of hours of relative freedom, we began to feel almost like normal people. Later, we went for some beers at a bar outside the main gate before returning to the barracks. Walking back into Camp Dewey that night wasn't easy.

The next day, we all donned our Navy dress blue uniforms and packed our duffel bags. A lot of us noticed that our dress uniform jumpers (tops) and our trousers fit more loosely, as if they had gotten larger, but we didn't care; we were getting out. You could tell many of us had a sense of pride in being able to wear our dress blue uniforms for the first time off-base. Those of us who were taking leave had been allowed to go to the base travel office and buy our plane tickets the week before. My flight was set for early evening on December 23, from Chicago to Mason City.

The next morning, as we all were preparing to depart the barracks and start Christmas leave, almost all of the guys from the company gathered around my bunk area. I asked them what was up. One of my best buddies stepped forward with a fat white envelope in his hand. He told me that the company had decided that my son was the company's son, and since we were all brothers, they had decided they should help. Then he handed me the envelope and said, "We took up a collection to help you with our son." The envelope was stuffed with $5, $10 and $20 bills.

I was speechless, but stammered something about not accepting the money and how much I appreciated it. A reply came from someone (I don't remember who): *"You're taking the money, and we really don't want to beat the shit out of you before you go home."* After I thanked all of them, each guy stepped forward and shook my hand. Later, when thinking over what my friends had done, I realized they had demonstrated to me what brotherhood was all about. I don't remember the exact amount of money in the envelope from my friends; I believe it was close to $400.

That evening after my flight had landed in Mason City, to my surprise, one of Jan's sisters and her husband were at the airport to meet me. They explained that Jan hadn't wanted to take our baby out in the cold winter weather and that they were going to drive me to Stacyville. Walking to their car outside the airport, I understood why Jan didn't come to meet me; it must have been 20 degrees below zero and was windy as hell. On the way through Mason City, we stopped at a restaurant and bar. They had something to eat and I had a beer. I nursed my beer, waiting as patiently as I could for them to finish eating so we could make the drive of 45 miles to Stacyville.

Once we got to Jan's parents' home in Stacyville, I rushed from the car to the house. After opening the door and stepping in, Jan was there to meet me. I've never forgotten the long, hard hug she gave me that night. After we kissed and hugged some more, Jan stepped back, took me by the hand, and walked me over to where my mother-in-law was holding our son. She said to me, "Meet your son."

My mother-in-law handed our son to me to hold for the first time; it was almost like a dream. Just hours earlier, I had been on another planet called "boot camp" and now I was home with my wife, holding our beautiful baby boy. It was as if I had made the leap from that other planet where I had been marooned back to my familiar home planet.

The next day was Christmas Eve. That morning, I gave Jan the money given to me by the guys of Company 383 and explained how they felt about the birth of our son. We decided between us that the men of Company 383 were our son's informal godfathers. That morning, we deposited the money in our account at the local bank. Earlier that morning while in the bathroom, I stepped on the bathroom scale; it read about 170 pounds. I had lost close to 35 pounds while in boot camp. That explained why my dress uniform was somewhat loose-fitting, as I knew we had been measured for our uniforms on the first day of in-processing. There is a statement often said in boot camp: "Big guys get smaller and little guys get bigger." Apparently this saying was not without basis, or at least it seemed to be true in my case.

The week between Christmas Day and New Year's Day, we spent a lot of our time in an upstairs bedroom with our baby. I'm sure all new fathers go through much of what I did that week, for every time I looked at or held my son, I couldn't help but have a sense of disbelief that we had really created another small, delicate, perfect human being. As for other events that occurred over the next week, they're just a blur.

Jan wanted our son to be baptized before my return back to boot camp. Though we had been married in the Catholic Church, we had decided that we did not want to raise our children in the Catholic faith. We talked to my mom about having our son baptized. My mother was able to arrange for the Methodist minister from Riceville to perform the baptism ceremony on Sunday, January 2, at the farm. We went to my parents' for Sunday dinner and later that afternoon, the minister arrived from Riceville and our son was baptized.

For Jan, I know having our baby son baptized as soon as possible was a big deal. She believes if one has not been baptized and should die, their soul may not be allowed into heaven. One kind of weird thing about that afternoon happened after someone took a Polaroid photo of our baby son. Later my mother brought out an old black and white photograph taken of my dad as a baby on his baptism day in 1912. On lying the pictures of my son and dad side by side, it was almost eerie how similar their facial features were when compared to each other. My thought was that maybe we had done the right thing in naming our son after my dad.

Before we knew it, my leave was over and it was time to go back to Great Lakes to complete the last ten days of boot camp. I had a morning return flight from Mason City to Chicago on January 4. Boot camp was to resume the next day on January 5. Once boot camp was over, I would be going into the next convening class for Machinist Mate (MM) "A" school, which was also located at the Great Lakes Naval Training Center.

During the early afternoon, I arrived back at Camp Dewey and checked in off leave. On arriving at the barracks, about half of the guys from the company were already there. For the rest of the afternoon, most of us shot the breeze talking about what we had done while on leave. The relaxed atmosphere in the barracks seemed almost unusual. By evening, all 72 members of Company 383 had returned. After evening chow, and for the remainder of the evening, most of us spent our time getting ready for the next day, the restart of recruit training. For anyone that wanted, I made sure they got a chance to see the pictures of our new baby son.

The next day, Company 383 was back in stride with the routine in short order. One of the drawbacks to the Christmas leave break was that it hadn't changed the schedule for several examinations that everyone needed to pass in order to graduate the following week. Every evening after barracks cleaning and doing laundry was spent studying. There were several guys in the company that had difficulty reading, so some guys worked with them to make sure they knew their stuff.

The next Monday began week nine, the last week of recruit training. Besides examinations, much of our time was spent marching and rehearsing for the formal graduation ceremony that Friday. The CC drilled us and drilled us some more in preparation for our company to march for graduation's "passing in review." Graduation from boot camp is an opportunity for each company under the leadership of fellow recruits to display their learned abilities in military drill and ceremony, not only to the reviewing officials, but also to their families and friends who are able to attend. The graduation passing in review is the climax of recruit training. None of us wanted to screw it up and embarrass our company.

Company 383 graduation, "passing in review." It's just about over.

During the graduation ceremony, special recruit units—the State's Flags Company, the Drum and Bugle Corps, the Drill Team, and the Bluejackets Choir, composed of and commanded by only recruits in training, helped to create a vivid and exciting picture. For graduation, we wore dress blue uniforms, outfitted with traditional white canvas leggings. Leggings date back to World Wars I and II. In order to conserve leather, only low-cut boots were issued; when worn with leggings, they kept debris, snow, and mud out. We also wore the white four-inch guard belt around our waists. Each company displayed and marched with all the competitive flags we had earned during the past eight weeks.

Company 383 had earned all three Star flags for cleanliness in the barracks, lockers, and personnel inspections conducted by a staff unit known as "Brigade Inspectors." We also had earned the "S" flag for being the company in our battalion scoring the highest on scholastic examinations. Our company had not earned any Drill flags, which are awarded to the recruit company for proficiency in close order drill, manual of arms, and physical drill. We were a good company, but as a whole we'd achieved only the satisfactory level in our marching and drill abilities.

Graduation went off without any problems. At the end of the graduation ceremony, each company marched out of the drill hall returning to their respective barracks. At that moment anyone would be hard pressed to find 72 people that were that happy at the same time; we had as a collective team made it through recruit training. It was a bittersweet experience; all of us were happy that very soon we would be leaving boot camp behind. But at the same time, it meant saying goodbye to people that had become both friends and brothers.

That afternoon when our company returned to the barracks, the CC was there waiting for us. He didn't say much, except that everyone had off-base liberty passes for the weekend. Our liberty expired on Monday morning at 0500. I spent part of my time off that weekend scanning through a local housing rental list from the base housing office. My intent was to rent an apartment somewhere in the area and then move Jan and our son to the area before starting MM "A" school.

Over the weekend during the evening, a number of us went to some of the local bars near the base. Everyone kept it low-key; no one wanted to get in trouble at this point and jeopardize getting the hell out of there. We now just had to mark time for a couple of days before leaving Camp Dewey forever.

When reflecting back on my time in boot camp, one person always comes to mind immediately—our Company Commander. During the first week of recruit training, we feared the CC, who consistently got into everyone's shit for what often seemed to us was over nothing in most cases. The climate in recruit training, coupled with the CC's constant berating, belittling, and aggression would shake anyone's confidence.

The goal was to tear down individuality and will. Once that process was complete, the goal then shifted to teaching each person how to work and contribute to the collective well-being of the team. Each success, failure, reward, or punishment were experienced together. Next, the orchestration of a steady progressive process of building each recruit's confidence was undertaken. I believe the objective here was to push each recruit into becoming a meaningful and contributing member of their team.

The CC initially was feared by all, especially after several demonstrations of what happens if the CC became displeased. No one wanted to be the one who provoked the CC by making a mistake or committing an error. However, at the same time, the CC served as the primary teacher and coach.

Over time, our view of the CC started to evolve. We began to recognize that he was really a human being, too. But recruits also gained the understanding that the company commander was the person who has set very high standards for the team, and would never relent in his insistence that every recruit must meet those standards. I can't help but think that anyone who served in any branch of the military remembers their Company Commander or Drill Instructor for the rest of their lives.

4. CRUMBLING OF THE DEAL

Finally, on January 19, I checked out of Camp Dewey RTC with Official Orders in hand to report to the Service School Command (SSC), Great Lakes Naval Training Center (NTC) on the same day. My orders directed me to report in by 1500 to the SSC Administrative Office. After reporting in, I was given a check-in sheet and told to report to building 230. Building 230 also the SSC barracks for the engineering "A" school ratings, was a huge complex. This particular barracks was informally called Snipe's Castle. The term "snipe" in the Navy, like a lot of terms in the Navy, has some history and a story. A snipe is anyone working in one of the Navy's engineering or hull ratings.

Life at Snipe's Castle was like a vacation compared to boot camp. I was assigned a billet on the third deck. Each deck was subdivided using lockers to create sleeping cubicles with four bunks per cubicle. My instructions were to muster every morning at 0730 with the Master at Arms (MAA) at the building's quarterdeck. The MAA was a first class petty officer, who assigned us to working parties, security duty, or fire watches for the day. This was to be our daily routine until MM "A" school class started in about two and half weeks on February 7. The days were easy, especially if you were assigned to working parties doing odd jobs, cleaning, painting, or some other assignment around the base.

81

On most days, working party assignments were completed by lunchtime. After lunch, we would report back to the MAA; much of the time, he would just tell us to knock off for the rest of the day. This meant freedom to go on liberty and spend my time looking for an off-base apartment to rent.

During my apartment hunting, I looked at a number of one-bedroom apartments, most of which were beyond my budget. Eventually after several days of searching, I found a furnished apartment, if you want to call it that, in the town of Waukegan about four miles from the base. The place was actually a finished full attic of a large three-story house. To get to the apartment required climbing three flights of stairs located at the rear of the house. At the top of the third flight of stairs was the only entrance into the apartment.

After entering, across from the doorway was a small bathroom, then three in-line rooms starting with the kitchen with a small dining area, then onto the living room which was only large enough for a small split couch, coffee table, and one small table. The bedroom was last, which was actually decent-sized, big enough for the full bed, dresser, and our son's crib. There were vaulted ceilings on one side throughout.

Being over six feet tall required me to stay on one side of the living room or I had to bend over to walk from one room to the next. It was cheap and fully furnished for $85 per month on a month-to-month basis with no lease required, plus one month's security deposit. I immediately took the place. Now all that was left was getting the time off to go to Iowa, then moving Jan and our son in before starting MM "A" school.

A major event for all military members became effective on January 1, 1972, mainly to the benefit of junior enlisted pay grades E-4 and below, with less than two years of service. In 1971, Congress passed a bill raising military pay, which as I understand it, President Nixon signed into law with some reluctance. My pay grade of E-3 in 1971 provided base pay of $180.90 per month, and being married also made me eligible to collect the Basic Allowance for Quarters (BAQ), which was an additional $105 per month. However, at that time, service members had to contribute to the BAQ amount. My BAQ contribution was about $40, which was deducted from my base pay. That gave me a total gross pay amount per month of $245.90.

The pay raise increased the base pay for an E-3 to $333.60 per month and we were no longer required to contribute to the BAQ amount, which for me stayed the same at $105 per month. Now, my total monthly gross pay was $438.60, equaling about a 44 percent raise. Can you imagine anyone today getting a pay increase of that size? For married junior enlisted, this pay raise was huge and for many represented a tremendous relief of their financial stress.

The next day, my "request chit" was submitted, requesting permission to take a 96-hour weekend liberty, January 28 through 31. Once my liberty request was approved, I arranged for an evening flight to Mason City on Thursday, January 27. This time, Jan met me at the airport, leaving our son at home with her mother. It was a busy weekend; however, Jan had been working on getting packed and was nearly ready to go. By midday on Saturday, we had our 1966 Pontiac Tempest, which I had bought before we got married, packed as full as we could get it. I was surprised how many more belongings we had accumulated since the birth of our son. We left that afternoon and started the drive of 365 miles to Waukegan.

I've never forgotten the long hug and goodbye my father-in-law, Bill, gave Jan just as we were leaving. What struck me was that he told her how much he loved her and to be careful. Hearing a parent say the words "I love you" out loud was a little strange and foreign to me. In my family, I don't remember my parents ever saying those words to me or any of my siblings. Hearing those words coming from a parent always made me feel a little uncomfortable.

As it was still wintertime and much of the highway in Iowa and Wisconsin was covered with snow and ice, at night driving became even more dangerous. We stopped somewhere in southern Wisconsin that night to stay at a roadside motel until morning. The next morning it was only about two more hours of driving before we reached our apartment in Waukegan.

I was anxious as we went up the stairs, wondering what Jan would think or have to say about the tiny third-floor apartment, but upon taking her up to see it, she seemed happy and okay with it. We quickly moved in our belongings and settled in. The only thing we lacked was a television, so we went to the local Sears & Roebuck store that afternoon. We found a small portable black-and-white TV we liked and could afford. Jan got somewhat embarrassed when I haggled with the salesman over the price of the TV, but in the end, the price got reduced. I had watched my dad haggle over prices even in retail stores my whole life. He often said, "Try to never pay the sticker price." So, I probably picked up a bit of the art of negotiating from him.

One week later, Machinist Mate "A" school commenced. At that time the MM "A" school course curriculum was eleven weeks. Machinist Mates in the Navy are trained to maintain, operate, and repair steam turbines used to propel ships and power auxiliary machinery, as well as other equipment and systems such as turbo-generators, pumps, valves, piping, condensers, oil purification, air compressors, evaporators, air conditioning systems, and refrigeration plants.

After boot camp, it became apparent that not only had I enlisted in the United States Navy, but now I was also part of Zumwalt's Navy as well. In July of 1970, Admiral Elmo R. Zumwalt, at age 49, became the youngest man to serve as the Navy's top-ranking officer as the Chief of Naval Operations (CNO). He was selected by President Nixon over 33 more senior admirals. It has been written that what probably prompted his selection was his advocacy for making rapid and drastic changes in the way the Navy treated its uniformed men and women. Once selected, he made his advocacy a reality. According to the Naval History and Heritage Command records, Admiral Zumwalt made many changes that included:

- Improving living conditions in the Navy.

- Promoting the first female and first African-American officers to flag rank.

- Allowing females to become naval aviators.

- Opening up ratings for Filipino sailors whose service had long been limited to a Steward's rating.

- Eliminating demeaning and abrasive U.S. Navy regulations that negatively impacted sailors' attitudes without providing a corresponding positive enhancement of professional performance; and many more.

During the Vietnam War, reenlistments in the Navy had plunged. Hoping to again make naval service an appealing career, Admiral Zumwalt over the next 4 years issued 121 directives known as Z-Grams, which sought to change the way the Navy had done things for almost two centuries.

The positive impact of his changes was tremendous, as evidenced by the effect on reenlistment rates. According to an article in the Naval History and Heritage Command, written by Marine Col. (Ret.) James "Jim" G. Zumwalt, "Enlistment rates were at an all-time low when Admiral Zumwalt took command of the Navy in 1970; when he retired four years later, reenlistment rates had tripled."

One change made by Zumwalt was a major morale booster. Prior to Zumwalt's regime as CNO, enlisted sailors were not allowed to leave a ship, naval base, or station unless they wore the dress uniform. This also meant that enlisted sailors were not allowed to have or keep civilian clothing on ships or at their barracks on shore side bases. Before departing at the end of the day, a married sailor living off-base would have to change out of their working uniform into their dress uniform before leaving the ship or the naval base itself. Most often on "The Strip," the bars located immediately outside the main gate of every single naval base in the U.S. and around the world, also hosted "Locker Clubs." Sailors rented lockers at the club, where they then kept their civilian clothing.

The Locker Club was where the sailor would stop and change out of their dress uniforms into civilian clothing. The management of the

Locker Clubs hoped to entice the sailors to fuel up on alcoholic beverages before they made the rest of their trip home. Many of these Locker Clubs also offered topless female dancers, strippers, and other sources of recreation. For some sailors, it wasn't uncommon to get no further than the Locker Club. To report back to work on their ship or the naval base in the morning, the sailor had to reverse the order. First, arriving at the Locker Club to change out of civilian clothing into their dress uniform and then for the shipboard sailor changing out of their dress uniform into their working uniform once they arrived on board. What a royal pain in the ass, but that's what Navy regulations required.

One of Zumwalt's Z-Grams changed all of that. This particular Z-Gram changed the policies so enlisted sailors could keep civilian clothing on board or at their barracks. Sailors also were now allowed to have and wear civilian clothing when departing the ship or naval base. Additionally, sailors driving or as passengers in a motor vehicle were allowed to leave and enter naval bases wearing just their working uniforms. Sailors that were just going home for the night had the option of either changing into "civvies" or just departing the ship in their working uniform. If you chose to just leave in your working uniform, the new policy simply required that no stops were allowed where a sailor would be seen in public view in their working uniform.

May sound simple, but this was highly favored by everyone, or at least by the enlisted sailors. I recall very little or no abuse by sailors of this new privilege. This did cause the Locker Clubs to eventually close up, since there was no longer a clientele. The demise of the Locker Clubs probably saved a good number of sailors from getting arrested while driving under the influence, and/or may have helped in preventing their relationships or marriages from crashing and burning, too.

Once "A" school began, Jan and I settled into a routine. We only had the one car, which I used to drive back and forth to school each week day. This left Jan and our son marooned while I was gone, but Jan was always a trooper and made due with the circumstances and never complained. For me, school was tough. The classes were fast-paced and very comprehensive. Every Friday, we took written examinations covering the topics and subjects that had been presented throughout the week.

Passing every weekly written examination was mandatory. If a student failed an examination, they would be placed on academic study (supervised night remedial study at the school) for the next week. On the next Friday, they would take two examinations. One written examination would be on the current week's curriculum, the other was the retake of the written examination from the prior failed week. If a student failed either of the two written examinations, they were immediately academically dropped from MM "A" school and would be sent to the fleet as undesignated strikers, but would retain their general Fireman Apprentice (E-2) or Fireman (E-3) status. Upon reporting on board their ship, old or new, undesignated strikers could be assigned to any division in the ship's engineering department based on the department's manning needs. I had no intention of letting that happen to me.

Each weeknight after getting home, eating dinner, and playing with our son, it was study time until I no longer could stay awake. This was the routine from Monday through Thursday. Jan would wait for me to get home every Friday afternoon with my news about the examination. Because of the Nuclear Power Program, it was necessary for me to maintain a minimum class standing. A nuclear candidate who slipped into one of the lower class standing tiers in his class could be dropped from the program. For the first six weeks of training, I managed to stay out of the lower class standing tiers.

During my time in school, Jan and I actually had some of our first real fights of our marriage. I understood that she was stuck in a strange city in a cramped apartment, and we hadn't made any friends yet. She had to depend on me for transportation since I had the car each day, and she essentially had to care for our son all of the time. Because of the feeling of being under the gun to do well in school, I didn't know what else to do. Looking back, I did try to understand her position. In reality, we were two young 19-year-old kids with a small baby, trying to tough out our first real challenges of married life. For Jan's sake, I had to remind myself that she was much closer to her family and missed them.

During the first week of "A" school in the classroom during break time, there was a guy sitting at the desk in front of mine. Unheard of today, but smoking was allowed in the classroom. I was fiddling with a Zippo cigarette lighter, lighting and shutting it. The guy in the seat in front of me started to lean back in his chair to stretch and extended his arms upward, leaning even back farther. Not meaning to, I had just lit the Zippo lighter as he leaned back when suddenly the hair on the back of his head caught fire. I began slapping the back of his head with my hands, trying to put out the fire. He leapt out of his seat, stood up, and turned with his fist raised.

I was laughing while at the same time trying to explain to him how I had accidentally caught his hair on fire and was trying to put it out. We both now could smell that unmistakable smell of singed hair. I apologized to him and explained it was an accident. He relaxed, smiled, and extended his hand to shake. We shook hands and introduced ourselves to each other. This was how I met my friend, Al. Fortunately, the damage to Al's hair was minimal, thanks to my rapid firefighting response.

We began to hang out during lunch and breaks. Al was just one of those people we all come across from time to time and can't help but take a liking to. Al was from upstate New York, so we had a lot of discussions about whether the Midwest or upstate New York had the worst winter weather and snow. Al had spent a year on special detail right out of boot camp as a crew member on the Navy's first warship, now a museum ship, USS *Constitution* in Boston, Massachusetts. In return for doing the special detail on USS Constitution, the Navy offered each sailor the "A" school of their choice, if qualified.

Al had picked the Machinist Mate rating, so here he was in my class. Al was married as well and lived in Waukegan. We decided that we should start getting together on weekends, because as we talked, we learned that our wives were in the same predicament, except Al and his wife did not have any children. We set a date to get together at his place that Friday evening. On our first visit, both Al and his wife were taken with our son. I was surprised to see how both of them were happy to hold and play with our baby. They were great people, and having some friends to get together with outside of school and our apartment was good for all of us.

On most Saturday mornings, Jan and I spent our time shopping for the groceries at the Commissary or spending time at the Navy Exchange stores on base. Then in the afternoon, we went to a nearby laundromat in North Chicago to do the weekly laundry. The amount of clothes and diapers our son went through in one week seemed unreal. The rest of our time on weekends was either spending time with Al and his wife or just taking drives along the shore of Lake Michigan. Just north of the naval base was a small park called Foss Park, located on the bluffs above Lake Michigan. We often just sat in the car, enjoying the view. Life seemed good, and I was content.

As "A" school continued, other than the constant studying, the overall experience was very different from boot camp. Instructors and staff spoke to you like a human being, which was a big change. Everyone was expected to do what they were supposed to be doing and doing it when they were supposed to. All students were assigned to duty sections each day. A duty day essentially consisted of policing classrooms after hours or being assigned to stand evening building security watches. If assigned an evening watch, you simply had to show up on time, relieve the watchstander, follow the written standing orders, make the patrol rounds of the facility, and make the required entries in the logbook. At the end of the four-hour watch, your watch relief would show up on time and then you could go back home. Pretty simple life in some respects.

Starting in week seven, some troubles of my own began. I was having an awful time with some topics such as boiler water chemistry, thermodynamics, and heat exchangers. I passed the weekly examination, but just barely. At the end of week eight, I passed the weekly examination, but again, just barely. After the week eight examination, the instructor told me to report to the director's office.

The meeting with the school director was short. He let me know that my lower examination scores for two weeks in a row had affected my class standing. If my recollection is correct, he told me that my class standing had slipped to 46 out of 88 students. He also let me know that he was filing the paperwork to drop me from the Nuclear Power Program. He was having none of my attempts to persuade him to give me another week, but he was right. He pointed out that it would be necessary for me to achieve near, if not perfect, examination scores to get back up in the class standing, which as he pointed out would be impossible with less than three weeks of "A" school remaining.

The director then informed me that I would not be advanced to petty officer third class (MM3, paygrade E-4) during week 10 (the accelerated advancement to E-4 was part of the deal for Nuclear Power candidates upon completion of "A" school), and that my enlistment obligation would be reduced from six years to four years. He had all the paperwork ready for my signature, acknowledging that I understood the new terms of my enlistment. He let me know that my Duty Preference Sheet had been submitted to the Machinist Mate Rating Detailer in Washington, and I would receive orders to a ship in about 10 days. His parting words were, "I'm sure you'll do fine in the fleet as a conventional MM."

That was it; my deal with the Navy had changed. I was disappointed about not advancing to E-4 (I was thinking about the pay), but on the other hand, I was okay with the reduction of my enlistment period from six years to four years. I had learned from guys in my class who had already spent time in the fleet as undesignated strikers in the MM rating. They had explained that once you had six months as an E-3 (Fireman) in the engine room, passing the MM3 advancement examination and getting advanced to E-4 was no big deal. Most of these guys thought a six-year enlistment in return for accelerated advancement to E-4 was dumb. That heartened me a bit.

Now, I had to go home and break the news to Jan. I don't believe any husband ever wants to have to tell his wife that he has failed at something. As always, Jan took the news well, as if it was no big deal. I believe she even expressed that she was actually glad that we were now doing a four-year instead of the six-year enlistment.

The end of week 11 and graduation from "A" school came quickly. I finished with a barely respectable class standing of 55 of the 82 students that actually made it to the finish. I believe the class size started out with about 95 total students, so we lost around 13 along the way. The week before, my orders had come in for my assigned ship, USS *Rich* (DD 820), homeported in Norfolk, Virginia. Al received orders to USS *Cone* (DD 866), homeported in Charleston, South Carolina. I had been hoping that Al and I would get ship assignments in the same home port, but that was not to be.

However, I was happy about having graduated from Machinist Mate "A" school and was now at least a Fireman (FN, paygrade E-3) designated MM, or an MMFN. On Friday afternoon, April 28, I checked out from the Service School Command. I had my Permanent Change of Station (PCS) Orders, papers for 30 days of leave, and two government checks. One check was for one month advanced pay and the other was for the travel allowance from NTC Great Lakes to Norfolk, Virginia. We had all of our belongings packed up at the apartment and we were ready to hit the road the next morning. Our plan was to go back to Iowa for a couple of weeks to see family, then onto Virginia to find an apartment and get settled in before reporting on board the ship at the Norfolk Naval Station. I was excited about taking the next step.

While back in Iowa, we spent much of our time at Jan's home in Stacyville. We decided that our 1966 Pontiac Tempest might be too tired and old to safely make the trip to Virginia, so we immediately began searching for another car. My dad had a nice low mileage 1970 Chevrolet Impala he indicated that he might sell to me. Dad's price for his Impala was too high and in my opinion, unreasonable. The next day at a car lot in Osage, we found a 1970 Chevrolet Biscayne, four-door sedan. We made a deal to trade in the Pontiac plus some cash for the Biscayne.

The Biscayne was a pretty basic car, but it was clean with low mileage, a six-cylinder engine, and a three-speed manual transmission with an on-the-column shifter, and most importantly, it was affordable. Back then, we would not even have considered getting bank financing or a car loan. In our opinion, it was foolish to go in debt just to own a

car. My idea was to buy a car that we could afford and could pay for upfront. We were also fortunate that Jan knew how to drive a manual transmission vehicle.

After the purchase of the car, we also realized that we would need to rent a small U-Haul trailer to move all of our belongings. The car itself would not be able to hold everything and us. It seemed that we were accumulating more and more stuff. After

The picture my mother took of me on our farm, May 1972, the day before I left for Norfolk, VA.

carefully weighing our finances, we believed we had just enough money to comfortably make the trip, to rent an apartment, and cover other expenses in Norfolk until getting my next paycheck. Both of us were highly cognizant that we were about to make a long road trip with our six-month-old baby. We figured that we should have an extra cushion of $125 to $150, just in case.

The question was, where to get the money? We really didn't want to ask Jan's parents for any money, since she had stayed there during my time in boot camp and they had helped so much already. So, I decided to ask my dad for a $150 loan. We were planning on visiting my parents for a couple of days on the farm; I decided to ask Dad for the loan sometime during our visit.

My thinking was that because Dad had sold my car after I left home in 1970 and kept the money, there was somewhere between $1,500 and $2,000 of mine which he had supposedly invested. I had earned most of the money while growing up from 4-H projects and from working for other farmers. So, from my position, if he was going to be fair, I didn't see how he could turn me down.

The first evening after dinner, I asked Dad about loaning me the money. I should have known better; he turned me down flat. He expressed that he felt I had gotten myself into my situation, so it was my problem, not his. I was so taken aback by his response, I couldn't even get pissed off. I didn't push the topic any further with him as the end result would have just been a verbal fight. Also, I didn't push it out of respect for Jan, she previously had made it clear to me that it made her very uncomfortable being around when I had conflicts with my family members. For these reasons I decided to drop the subject and let it go. I made a resolution right then and there that I would never ask him for anything ever again, and I never have. The next day, we left and went back to Jan's home in Stacyville to finish our preparations for the trip.

As for the money situation, we didn't have to worry about it after all. I'm not completely sure, but I think Jan may have confided in her mom about what happened between me and Dad. The next afternoon when Bill got home from work, he pulled me aside and handed me his weekly paycheck, already signed over. He told me all that had to be done with the check was to take it to the bank in town and they would cash it. We thanked him and told him we would repay him as soon as we could. He just replied, "Pay it back when you can." If I remember correctly, the check was for $184. Jan and I walked downtown to the Stacyville Bank and cashed the check. Now, we both felt better about the money situation.

The next morning, we got an early start on the drive to Norfolk. I had estimated the trip would take at least two full days of driving. Both of Jan's parents had gotten up early to see us off. Once again, I was left watching as her parents delivered the hugs, kisses, and long goodbyes with Jan and our son. I was wanting to get going because we had already learned that when traveling with a baby in the vehicle, more frequent stops were inevitable.

We stopped somewhere in eastern Ohio that night and late the next afternoon we made it to Virginia Beach, VA. The plan was to stay with Jan's brother Joe and his wife until we found an apartment. The next morning Joe showed us a number of apartment listings he had collected for us. We began our search for a place to live that day. By the end of the day, we settled on a two-bedroom furnished apartment at Robin Hood Apartments.

Years ago, just about anyone who had ever been stationed in Norfolk at one time or another had either lived at or knew someone that lived at Robin Hood Apartments. The apartment buildings themselves might have been converted from military barracks from the World War II era. Each two-story building typically had two apartments at each end, one apartment on the ground floor the other on the second floor for a total of four two-bedroom apartments in each building. Many military people lived there for two reasons: the rent was cheap and the apartments were centrally located in Norfolk. It was an easy commute from just about every Navy or military base in the area. The going rent for a two-bedroom apartment in Robin Hood was $95 per month for an unfurnished unit and $105 per month for a furnished unit.

We rented one of the furnished units, which was located, of course, on Robin Hood Road. We moved in the next day. I still had almost 10 days of leave remaining before reporting to the ship. We spent that time basically setting up house, shopping, and becoming familiar with the area. Generally, we were just enjoying our time until my leave was up and it was time to report in.

On Saturday morning, May 27, I reported on board USS Rich wearing my dress white uniform. Reporting to the ship during the weekend was on the advice I had gotten from some of the fleet guys back at "A" school. They had explained that by reporting on board over a weekend, no one would be on board except the crew in the duty section. There would be no one to assign you to a duty section, so once the quarterdeck watch checked you in off of leave, they would take a copy of your orders and just tell you to come back on Monday morning by 0730. The advice was good. Everything happened as the guys back at "A" school said it would, and I still got the rest of the weekend off.

Monday morning, once again wearing my dress white uniform, with my fully packed sea bag in hand, I arrived back onboard at 0700. I reported to the officer of the watch (OOW) on the quarterdeck and handed him a copy of my orders. The OOW called over the 1MC intercom for the duty engineer to report to the quarterdeck. Once the duty engineer arrived on the quarterdeck, he introduced himself as Ray, then he instructed me to follow him down to the M&B division berthing compartment. Once in the berthing compartment, Ray showed me an empty bunk and a locker where I could stow my gear. He told me to get changed into my working uniform (dungarees) and go to the Ships Office after 0730 and they would start my check-in.

Ray asked if I knew how to get to the Ships Office. I told him that I did (I had been shown on Saturday morning). He then said that he was going to go finish breakfast before morning quarters. He headed up the ladder and out of the compartment saying, "I'll see you later." That was my unofficial "welcome aboard" on my very first seagoing ship.

My morning was spent going through the check-in process. Upon reporting to the Ships Office, one of the personnelmen (PN) said he would start my check-in. I waited a while in the passageway outside the Ships Office while he began typing up some other paperwork. Finally, the PN came to the door with my check-in sheet. During the check-in process you basically wandered around the ship looking for the location of the person or officer you needed to check-in with. The PN reiterated several times that when entering the Officer's Wardroom, Captain's

Cabin, any other officer's stateroom, or the Chiefs Mess, I should first knock on the door, enter the space, then request permission to enter. I told the PN that I understood and headed off.

Check-in was at the sickbay first with the chief corpsman and then the Disbursing office, simply because they were both located on the same passageway near the Ships Office. It didn't take long to complete the check-in with the main propulsion assistant (the MPA was also the division officer for "M" division), the chief engineer, then the executive officer (XO), and finally the captain. The meetings with the chief engineer, XO, and the captain were fast and brief, each meeting ended with the same statement from each of them, "Welcome aboard." Eventually, I got to the "M" division chief petty officer, an MMC (chief machinist mate). The chief let me know he had assigned me to In-Port Duty Section 3, and told me that since the In-Port Duty Section 4 had duty that day, I wouldn't have to stand duty for two more days. Next, the chief gave me my assignment to B-4, the after-engine room, and then told me the name of the second class petty officer, machinist mate (MM2) to report to after lunch.

After lunch, I located the entrance to B-4 engine room on the main deck in the interior after passageway. To enter the B-4 engine room, you went down through a deck hatch via the open 18-inch diameter emergency escape scuttle, then climbed straight down the vertical ladder to the upper level of the after-engine room. I quickly found the MM2, who was friendly and informed me that my first day or two would be spent doing a physical tracing out (line drawings) of the entire engine room. My tasking was to find and draw the identity of every pipe, valve, strainer, pump, and gauge along with each equipment item and piece of machinery.

While still smiling, he handed me a pad of notebook paper and a pencil and recommended starting under the lower level plating in the bilge area and working up to the lower level and then to the upper level of the engine room. He said to come find him if I had any questions. I'd expected this; several instructors at "A" school had mentioned on more than one occasion that a good engineer would require all new engineers to trace out the entire propulsion plant, including all auxiliary equipment and machinery first. The concept was simple and effective. After any new engineer completed a full and thorough trace-out of the plant system, they became wholly familiar with the layout and learned where everything was located in their engine room.

I quickly set to work, starting in the bilge area. It wasn't long after starting on my task that parts of my nice clean uniform already had oil, grease, and bilge water on it from crawling around. I didn't care; I was finally working toward becoming a full-fledged snipe. It took about two days for me to complete the line drawings of all the systems and equipment in the B-4 engine room. The MM2 checked with me every several hours each day to monitor my progress.

The "hot plant" experience week back at MM "A" school was really helpful in completing this assignment. During hot plant week, we had gotten the chance to work with fully operational steam 600 pound per square inch propulsion and auxiliary plants, but in a building. My confidence grew a bit throughout the process. I could now at least recognize on sight all of the engine room piping, valve systems, equipment, and machinery.

The next day was my first full day of working in the engine room. I was assigned to work with an MM3 everyone called Ski, and one of the other firemen whose name was Matt, changing the oil in the sump of the turbo-generator and performing some basic valve maintenance. What astounded me was the lack of available hand tools in the engine room. Finding the right size or type of wrench, or even a decent screwdriver, was difficult. When I mentioned this to the MM2, all he could say was that hand tools tended to have a way of disappearing. His only suggestion was to go to the other engineering spaces and see what could be borrowed.

The better part of my day was spent just chasing down the tools we needed. It was also my first duty day as a member of the engineering department. For a fireman, the duty day mainly required staying on board for the night. My assignment was to one of the evening engineering monitoring watches (under instruction) with one of the other fireman in the section. The four-hour monitoring watch essentially was just making hourly rounds of all the engineering spaces and checking the main electrical switchboard, the bilge, and fire pumps. The ship was in "cold iron" status, which meant the entire steam plant was shut down and the ship was on "Hotel services," meaning it was receiving electrical shore power and potable freshwater from the pier. With the ship in cold iron status at night at least, there was little to no activity in the main engineering spaces.

The ship was scheduled to be in port until mid-July for upkeep, maintenance, and repairs. I had learned on my first day on board that the ship was scheduled to get underway in July for six to eight weeks of operations in the Caribbean, and at least five of those weeks would be spent operating out of the naval base at Guantanamo Bay (GITMO), Cuba. The naval base at GITMO was also home to the Fleet Training Center for the Atlantic Fleet. The job of the Fleet Training Center was to help prepare ships and their crews through intensive training for the ship's next overseas deployment.

I also learned that the ship was scheduled to depart in October 1972 for a nine-month deployment to the Western Pacific (WESTPAC), which would include operations off the coast of Vietnam. When I learned about the impending deployment to WESTPAC, all I can remember thinking was *Damn, damn, and damn!* One of my objectives in joining the Navy was to hopefully not find myself in Vietnam. Navy destroyers deploying to WESTPAC inevitably included some, if not all, of the deployment period conducting combat operations in Vietnam. Obviously, there was nothing I could do about the ship's scheduled deployment but to accept it as my fate. Both Jan and I well understood that being stationed on board a ship meant separations and deployments; after all, that's what Navy ships are supposed to do.

I buckled down to start my life as a snipe. One aspect of the military life of a snipe had to come quickly, and that was changing uniforms fast.

For morning quarters and musters we were expected to fall in wearing clean working uniforms, ready for personnel inspection. After morning quarters, before starting the work day, we would all go to the berthing compartment to change into our real working uniforms for the day. For snipes, our real working uniforms generally had permanent grease and oil stains on them, but this was acceptable for working in the engineering spaces.

Each main engineering space was referred to as the "hole." Entry into the fire rooms and engine rooms was through deck hatches, then climbing straight down a vertical ladder to the space below—much the same as climbing down into a hole. Our days were spent tearing down machinery and equipment for maintenance or repair. Some machinery parts had to be delivered to a repair ship called Destroyer Tenders (AD) docked nearby. The ADs were large ships filled with repair shops, foundries, and machine shops.

As an example, the process of taking a major turbine part to the AD went something like this: After removing the part from the turbine housing, it had to be moved to the ladder. Then the part had to be hoisted out of the hole using rigged chain falls to haul it up to the main deck through the deck hatch. At least two snipes were required to carry the heavy turbine part to a staging location near the ship's quarterdeck area and gangway.

Next, we snipes got the repair paperwork and work order forms from the engineering log room. Then we went to the berthing compartment to change into clean working uniforms. We returned to where we had left the turbine part up on the deck, made our way to the gangway, set down the part, saluted the ship's flag, and requested permission from the OOW to depart the ship. Then we'd pick up the part and carry it down the gangway to the pier. Once on the pier, the turbine part had to be carried to the AD. While carrying the part, every effort was made to keep our uniforms clean.

At the AD, we made our way up the gangway to the AD's quarterdeck, stopping to put down the part in order to salute the ship's flag and request permission to come aboard from the OOW. The officers of the watch onboard ADs were well known for giving snipes delivering parts from other ships a hard time, usually about dirty uniforms, shoes not being shined, or for needing a haircut.

Once onboard the AD, after any obligatory hassling by the OOW, the quarterdeck personnel would call for the right repair or machine shop personnel. We had to wait for the right person from the right shop to come take possession of the turbine part and the paperwork. After departing the AD, we walked back to the ship. The first stop back on board was to the berthing compartment to change back into our dirty uniforms, then we reported back to the hole to resume work. To get a finished or repaired part back on board from the AD, these steps were carried out in reverse order. Even while the ship was in port, we snipes were usually tired at the end the day, no mystery as to why.

During the next week or so, I settled into becoming a member of "M" division. Those assigned to the B-4 engine room were a good group of guys and all were hard workers. I was getting along fine with just about everyone in B-4. Many of the guys showed a lot of patience when working with me in learning the different jobs. Matt and Ray, an MM3, both helped me a lot by answering my questions. The other MM3, Ski, was generally a good guy, but sometimes could be a bit of a jerk when he lost his patience. Ski made sure that since I was the junior guy in the hole, that also meant getting assigned the hottest and dirtiest jobs. I took on every job without complaint. After a couple of days, I noticed that everyone was becoming much friendlier. It was Ray who let me know I had passed their test and everyone liked how I had handled myself in dealing with Ski. In other words I had gained their acceptance. Even in port with the cold iron plant status, it was still always hot down in the hole. Each day was a learning experience about the layout, operation, and maintenance of the main turbine and auxiliary machinery in the engine room.

After about a week of working in the hole, skin rashes were beginning to develop between my fingers on both hands. Over the next several days, the rash worsened and began to spread all over my fingers and also appeared on the insides of both forearms. Each day, the rashes on my hands and arms grew worse, until there was constant oozing of fluid and sometimes blood. I bought rolls of medical gauze to wrap up my fingers and forearms before work each morning. I wasn't sure what to do about this problem except to just keep working while hoping my rashes would improve or just go away.

About a week later, when cleaning oil out of the turbo-generator oil sump, the chief engineer officer happened by. He must have seen the blood coming through the oil-soaked gauze on my fingers. The chief engineer inquired what was wrong with my hands. I replied, "Sir, I don't know, but it's getting worse every day."

He said, "You need to get out of here and go see the corpsman in sickbay, now."

I left the engine room and made my way to sickbay and knocked on the door. The chief corpsman opened the door and asked me what I wanted. I tried to go in and started to explain about the rashes on my hands and arms. The chief blocked me from entering and said with a disgusted look on his face, "Get your dirty, oily ass out of my sickbay. Go get cleaned up, put on a clean uniform, then come back." A navy chief is the chief; sailors never talk back to a chief. I backed out of the chief's sick bay, telling him I would come back.

I went to the after head to clean the oil and grease off of my hands, arms, and face in one of the sinks. Next, I went to the berthing compartment and donned a clean uniform, then returned to sickbay. Once again, I knocked on the sickbay door and the chief opened the door; this time he allowed me to enter. On showing the chief the rashes on my hands and forearms, he still had the same disgusted look as he did during my first visit. All he said was, "I don't even want to touch that shit."

He tossed me some rolls of gauze and medical tape and told me to wrap my hands up. Then the chief told me that there was nothing he could do and that he would call and make a dermatology appointment for me. He told me to check back in an hour for the appointment time, wrote a medical chit, and told me to give it to the "M" division chief. The medical chit basically read that I was to be kept out of the engineering spaces until medically cleared to return.

An hour or so later I went back to sickbay, and the chief gave me a form with an appointment time to go to the dermatology clinic in Portsmouth the next day. On talking with the "M" division chief about my appointment, he told me to go home, go to my medical appointment, and report back to him on board after the appointment.

The next morning, I reported to the dermatology clinic at the Portsmouth Naval Hospital. After the initial examination, the doctor told me that it would take several days of testing to find out the cause of my rashes. I called the "M" division chief on the ship to let him know that the clinic would have me there for several days of testing. Over the course of the next several days, I was given a myriad of different allergy and other tests. After the tests, the dermatologists concluded that I had chronic eczema and dermatitis, with allergic reactions caused by contact with nickel, brass, bronze, turbine oils, JP-5 (aviation fuel), and the list went on, naming several more materials or substances. After looking at the full list, I realized it included just about everything found in a ship's engine room.

The next afternoon, I went before a medical review board made up of three Navy doctors. The doctors told me that their purpose was to decide if I should be medically discharged from the Navy. I wasn't sure how I felt about that, and said so to the doctors. The doctors had some sort of lengthy discussion amongst themselves. Finally, one of the doctors asked me if my ship was due to deploy soon. I answered that the ship was leaving for a WESTPAC deployment in several months.

One of the doctors told me that rather than deciding on a medical discharge now, that I should return back to my ship and see if the ship could move me to out of engineering to "a cleaner rating." They added that if it was possible for me to move to a cleaner rating, there would be a reevaluation of my condition after six months. One of the doctors handed me several prescriptions to have filled for some creams and salves to treat my rashes. The board told me they would be sending my medical paperwork to the ship, then they dismissed me. They allowed me to leave and go home for the rest of the day, with orders to report back on board the ship the next morning.

After leaving the hospital and while driving home, my thoughts went to the questions of what could be a cleaner rating, but still allow me to stay in the engineering department. My brain couldn't grasp thinking beyond the scope of somehow still being a snipe, but in some other engineering rating. When the doctors had first mentioned the possibility of a medical discharge, my initial reaction to the idea had been favorable. Then the rational side of me had taken over with the question. What the hell would I do otherwise?

One factor weighing in was that I had made the determination that there was nothing for me back in Iowa, so that was out. On getting home, I discussed everything with Jan and we agreed that all we could do was wait and see what happened after going back on board the ship in the morning. It was a somewhat restless night for both us, now not knowing what our immediate future might be.

5. A NEW LIFE

The next morning, I reported back on board the ship as instructed. After attending morning quarters with "M" division, the chief told me to report to the engineering log room. When I got to the log room, the chief and the division officer were there looking at some paperwork. Once in the log room, the chief said, "Well, Trowbridge, it looks like your MM days are over."

The division officer then told me that he and the chief engineer had spoken with the XO about my medical situation. The XO decided there was the possibility for me to strike for the Quartermaster (QM) rating since the Navigation "N" division was short of Quartermasters. I recall asking the chief, did they mean up on the ship's bridge? The chief replied, "Yep, that's them." The chief gave me the name of the first class petty officer, QM1 Janson, and told me to go see him on the bridge.

That was it. I was no longer going to be an engineer! I wasn't sure how I felt about it, other than being disappointed. It seemed my whole plan for joining the Navy was now all blown away. What confused me was why I was now having problems with allergies when I had been a motor-head since about the age of 12; I was always getting grease and oil on me. Skin contact with grease and petroleum oil had never caused any bad effects before.

I kept mulling over the question of why my body was different now compared to the years before. I've never found the answer to that question. A dermatologist once told me our bodies go through roughly seven-year cycles. He stated that many people with allergies to certain substances will have reactions for a period of years, then over time, contact with the same substance may not cause any issues at all. Huh, who knew?

Making my way up to the bridge, I found QM1 Janson out on the starboard bridge wing drinking a cup of coffee. I introduced myself to him and started to explain why I was there; he stopped me and said he knew why I was there. We talked for a while as he explained the job of a QM in general terms. Then Janson said, "Before I make my decision, we need to find out if you are smart enough to be a QM." That statement took me back a bit.

I replied, "Okay. What is it that I have to do?"

Janson explained that one of the other QMs would show me how to complete three tasks: (1) taking an Azimuth of the sun bearing, then computing the Azimuth to determine gyro compass error; (2) calculating the local height of the tide; (3) calculating the velocity and direction of the local tidal current. Janson added that I would be shown how to do each of the tasks only one time. After each of the three demonstrations were completed, he instructed me to come back the next morning.

Janson then said, "If you can successfully complete each of the tasks, there might be potential for you to be a QM." He handed me a hardcover book about three inches thick titled *American Practical Navigator*, by Nathaniel Bowditch. Janson instructed me to read the first chapter titled, "The History of Marine Navigation" and told me he would have questions for me from the reading.

I believe all I said to him was, "Okay."

That afternoon one of the third class petty officers, a QM3 who everyone called Chip, was assigned to work with me. Chip showed me how to complete each of the three assigned tasks. He was a good teacher and showed a lot of patience. He walked me through the step-by-step procedure on how to observe and take an accurate Azimuth bearing to the sun, then the mathematical process of computing what the actual Azimuth (true bearing) to the sun was from the ship's actual position for the time of the observation.

Next, Chip walked me through the steps of computing the height of the tide and the velocity/direction of the tidal current for a given locality. Chip also allowed me to borrow the navigation work books and other publications, explaining that I should practice that night by working out past observations and solutions in the workbooks.

That night, I followed Chip's advice and guidance. I worked and reworked a good number of the different Azimuth observations. Then I worked out about a dozen tide and current problems and solutions. Next, I read the chapter in *American Practical Navigator* as directed by Janson. In reading about the history of marine navigation, I found that, surprisingly, the information was very interesting and informative. I ended up reading late into the night. On going to bed that night, I felt confident in my ability to show Janson I was smart enough to be a Quartermaster.

The next morning was my first morning quarters with "N" division on the forward torpedo deck. After quarters, I, along with all of the quartermasters, went up to the bridge. Janson gave everyone work assignments for the day. My assignments were to complete the three tasks. Chip was assigned to work each solution with me as a check of my results. I observed the Azimuth of the sun from the starboard gyro compass repeater, computed the true Azimuth and determined the gyro compass error. Chip's solution matched mine; one task down.

Then Chip gave me two localities to compute the tides and currents for that day. Once again, Chip's solutions matched mine, so all three tasks were done successfully. Chip notified Janson that I had done everything correctly. Then Janson began to quiz me about Nathaniel

Bowditch and marine navigation history. My answers to his questions seemed to be satisfactory. Finally he said, "I think you might do; welcome to the QM gang."

The ship sent off a message to the Chief of Naval Personnel, requesting that my MM Fireman striker identification be removed and re-designated as a QM striker with the Seaman identification on June 21. I had been working with the QM gang in "N" division for several weeks as a QM striker when the ship received approval of the request from the Chief of Naval Personnel on July 5. The XO actually came to the bridge to let me know and gave me a copy of the approval letter.

During my time working on the bridge, my rashes had begun to clear up and were healing. The only thing that did irritate my skin a bit was when using a product called Never Dull to clean and polish brass. The bridges on Navy ships are loaded with brass and brass fittings, including the helm wheel, voice tubes, phone, and alarm covers. Every day before knock-off, one of the many jobs given to the junior QM, now me, was shining all the brass work and fittings.

The next week, in between painting and cleaning assignments, the other QMs showed me how to apply the Notice to Mariners corrections to navigation charts and publications. The Notice to Mariners is a weekly publication distributed by the national hydrographic office, detailing the latest changes, revisions or corrections to navigation charts and navigation publications. By U.S. and International Maritime Law, as well as Navy regulations, all navigation charts and publications that will be used for a ship's voyage or passage must be corrected up to the date of the latest Notice to Mariners. Additionally, there were a myriad of other navigation and administrative duties. The big one was how to properly wind and compare the three ship's chronometers (finely jeweled and accurate timepieces). Chronometers, by tradition, are wound and compared each day at 1130. The chronometers were very important. At sea, in order for ships to accurately navigate using celestial navigation, knowing the exact time of when each celestial body was observed is absolutely imperative. New chronometers, or those after an overhaul, were set to the exact Greenwich Mean Time (GMT), then compared for a number of days to the Atomic Clock's Coordinated Universal Time (UTC) to determine their accuracy and error rate. Once installed on board the ship, it became the QM's job to maintain an accurate record of each chronometer's accuracy and error rate.

Each day after winding all chronometers, the QM would compare the time on each chronometer against a radio time signal (time tick) broadcasting the UTC from stations WWV Colorado Springs or WWVH Hawaii. The determined error and error rate for each chronometer was then entered by the QM into the Chronometer Record Book.

The Twelve O'clock (Noon) Report made to the captain each day by the quarterdeck watch while in port, or by the Quartermaster of the Watch when the ship was underway, included the phrases: *"Sir, the officer of the deck sends his respect;, the hour of twelve o'clock is approaching. All chronometers have been wound and compared. Request permission to strike eight bells on time, sir."*

If the chronometers were not wound every day, they ran down and stopped after about 36 hours. A QM that allowed the ship's chronometers to run down and stop due to negligence faced an Article 15 Punishment under the Uniformed Code of Military Justice (UCMJ). On Navy ships, Article 15 actions taken against an enlisted sailor were called "Captain's Mast," or Non-Judicial Punishment.

Preparations were ongoing for the next underway period for the ship to the Caribbean and Guantanamo Bay, Cuba. Janson, along with the XO, who was also the Navigator, worked on the Passage Plan for the transit to Cuba. The rest of us were kept busy with correcting the required charts and publications up to date for the passage. The date for my first time going to sea on a Navy ship was fast approaching, and I was looking forward to it.

Chip and the other QMs were briefing me and demonstrating how to take accurate gyro compass bearings. Ships at that time, when navigating or piloting in harbors and inshore waters, principally navigated by the use of gyro compass bearings corrected to true bearings taken to fixed navigation aids or other charted objects. True bearings, when drawn on a navigation chart as a Line of Position (LOP) from the navigation aid or object the bearing was taken to, were extremely accurate. Three or more true bearings are taken to multiple objects or navigation aids simultaneously. The true bearings are drawn out on the chart as LOPs. The resultant intersection point formed by the crossing of multiple LOPs represented an accurate fix position of the ship.

At home, Jan was settling in as a Navy wife. A good estimate of those who lived at Robin Hood Apartments would probably be at least 90 percent or more were military families. Everyone that lived there was friendly and helpful; it was essentially a military community. Since moving in, Jan had become fast friends with several neighboring wives. I recall very little or no crime in the area. For husbands who had to stand overnight duty or leave their families for periods of time on military obligations, the sense of community and security there was reassuring.

It's difficult to fully describe the culture and climate that came with living in Robin Hood. When husbands were away, their families had the support of his neighbors, especially the other wives who seemed to close their ranks in providing support and friendship to the families going through the experience of short-term separations or longer-term deployments. With families in a constant cycle of moving in and out of the apartment complex, the community and support culture seemed to remain unchanged and intact. As the time for the ship's departure to the Caribbean drew nearer, both Jan and I felt it would be fine for her and our son to stay there. Additionally, her brother Joe lived nearby, and she could call on him if any help was needed.

Finally, the day came for the ship to depart Norfolk and begin the trip to the Caribbean and Cuba. The process and feelings for me regarding leaving my family never changed throughout my time in the Navy. I was always torn between my desire not to leave my family, but at the same time feeling compelled and motivated to go do my job. Early on the morning of our departure, Jan and our son drove with me to the D & S Piers to drop me off at Pier 23. After saying goodbye to her and our son, I grabbed my bag and headed down the pier. On walking away, I had to fight the urge to look back, forcing myself to just keep walking down the pier until arriving at the ship's gangway and going on board.

Later that morning, the ship took in its mooring lines and got underway. After maneuvering away from the pier, the ship entered into the first outbound shipping channel and began the transit through Chesapeake Bay. After about an hour underway, the ship passed the last major aid to navigation, Cape Henry Lighthouse, located on the south side of the entrance to Chesapeake Bay. From there, the ship proceeded out into the Atlantic Ocean.

On the bridge during the sea and anchor detail when getting the ship underway, there was a lot of activity. Everything was happening with each person acting with smooth confidence doing their respective jobs. My station that morning was under instruction with Chip as the starboard bearing taker. A bearing taker's job is to identify each aid to navigation as it appears from the Passage Plan, and when ordered, to take and report the gyro compass bearings to the aid.

In taking gyro compass bearings for navigation, the device most commonly used is a telescopic alidade. The alidade uses a telescopic sight with a magnified view. In the alidade's telescopic view, the image of an object and the reflected view of the gyro compass card can be seen simultaneously. A hairline sight is lined up on the object's center and the bearing can be read directly from the gyro compass card. We wore sound-powered phones and made our reports to the bearing recorder at the Navigation plot with the navigator and senior QM. The bearing recorder would relay which navigation aids or objects to shoot for the next round of gyro compass bearings.

Rounds of bearings are taken at two or three minute intervals when a ship is engaged in the shallow water piloting navigation phase. Once the ship was in safe deeper water away from any hazards to navigation or shoal water, the sea and anchor detail was secured and the normal underway watch rotation is set. The passage was planned for a ship's speed of advance of 16 knots (18.4 mph) from Norfolk to Guantanamo Bay. The passage would take three and a half days via the Florida Straits then to the Windward Passage, a strait between the eastern tip of Cuba and the western tip of Hispaniola.

My assignment was to stand under instruction watches with Chip, in order to learn the duties and the job of the Quartermaster of the Watch (QMOW). The QMOW stood watch in a three-section rotation, four hours on watch, and eight hours off watch. I was assigned along with Chip to the 1600 to 2000 and the 0400 to 0800 watch rotations. The ship headed south off the coast of Virginia. Later in the afternoon and into evening, the winds and the sea waves were building as the ship approached the area offshore from Cape Hatteras, North Carolina. Seaward passages off Cape Hatteras are well known by mariners for the treacherous and often stormy waters off the coast of the Outer Banks. The area is also known as the Graveyard of the Atlantic, as it is estimated that over 600 ships have been wrecked there as victims of shallow shoals, storms, and war. As the sea waves mounted, the ship began rolling and pitching heavily as it pushed through the waves. Soon the ship was rolling side to side up to 25 to 30 degrees and pitching heavily fore and aft.

The Gearing class destroyers, just like the earlier Sumner and Fletcher class destroyers of World War II, were well known for how they behaved in a seaway. A vessel underway at sea will have six motions: pitch, roll, yaw, heave, sway, and surge. Pitch, roll, and yaw are rotation motions (side to side), while heave, sway, and surge are linear motions (forward and aft). For example, if the ship is rolling from one side to the other, it will also sway, which is caused by the wind, currents, or the ship's own propulsion exerting forces on the hull. 15 to 20 degrees of roll on a destroyer in a seaway was normal. At the same time, the ship will pitch, heave, and surge. Pitch is the up/down rotation of a vessel about its lateral axis (fore and aft); heave is the up-and-down motion; and surge is linear forward and aft motions caused by wind-generated sea waves. Just like rolling, the motions of heavy pitching, heaving, and surging are just part of the ride.

These six vessel motions on destroyers were almost always excessive, depending on the weight distribution and the location of the ship's centers of gravity. Most naval personnel think of destroyers in terms of their constant rolling and pitching at sea. The old joke was that Navy destroyer crews should also get submarine pay, since a lot of the ship's hull and sometimes the superstructure is underwater at least half of the time.

Destroyer crews had to get their sea legs under them quickly in order to function and do their jobs. A matter of pride for a destroyer sailor was when the ship was experiencing heavy rolls and excessive pitching, but they could walk the ship's passageways, including going up and down ladders, with a full cup of coffee and never spill a drop. Almost all destroyer veterans have stories of when they had to walk up and down on the passageway bulkheads in order to stay upright and maintain equilibrium during heavy rolling of the ship.

There was no place on these ships for anyone prone to motion sickness or seasickness. If a new sailor did get seasick, they had to learn how to overcome it one way or another. No mercy or compassion was shown to a seasick sailor by anyone. Some actually viewed seasickness as a sign or indicator of poor character and mental weakness. The belief was that one could overcome seasickness with will power and mental strength. To a degree, I think part of that belief is true. The cardinal rule was, "You *always* clean up your own puke." When a sailor was too sick to follow this cardinal rule, it wouldn't be forgotten by the person who ended up cleaning up their mess.

The real rub came when a crew member was too sick to stand their watch or do their work. Someone else would have to stand an extra watch or do extra work to make up for the seasick slacker. There were several crew members who often were prone to getting seasick, but these guys never let it interfere with standing their watch or doing their work. Even if they carried a bucket or plastic bag around for when they got sick, they didn't let the seasickness stop them, and the crew respected them for it.

About halfway through the watch on the 1600 to 2000, I learned that Chip suffered from seasickness. But Chip didn't let it slow him down. After his first round of vomiting he got a garbage bag, tucked it in his belt, and kept going. Chip was not the only one, some of the other bridge watchstanders got sick as well. For me, other than some minor queasiness, I generally felt okay. It was about focusing on getting some sea legs under me more than anything else. After a while the bridge was ripe with the stench of vomit, and that made it even more challenging for everyone.

Destroyers of this era had to be manned with substantial crew sizes. Literally nothing on these ships operated automatically, without human monitoring, or intervention. These ships existed before computer monitoring, proportional-integral-derivative controllers (PIDs), or programmable logic controllers. Every piece of equipment or machinery had to have human hands to operate every valve, switch, or controller. At the same time, a lot of the equipment or machinery had the potential to injure or kill its operator.

The ship's boiler produced superheated steam. The superheated steam generally is delivered from the boilers via piping systems while under a vacuum at a pressure of about 600 pounds per square inch (psi) at a temperature of 850 degrees Fahrenheit. In this state, superheated steam is a high-pressure gas that is then used to drive the ship's steam propulsion turbines and turbo-generators. You could say the generated steam is not only used to propel the ship, but also to generate the electricity for every electrical system on board. Compressors generated high pressure (HP) air for use in various machinery and equipment. For the ship's engineers, just about everything in the fire rooms (boiler rooms) and engine rooms had the potential to injure or to kill them.

The rest of the ship was not hazard-free, either. Steel ships, with their electrical distribution systems, do not provide for a natural electrical ground. One was always standing on a steel deck while operating, in some cases, high voltage and high amperage electrical equipment. Many systems required hydraulic pressure to operate, such as winches, guns systems, and directors. Combine all of this with the obstacles every crew member had to navigate in their daily movements around the ship, with vertical ladders and ladder wells leading from deck to deck, deck hatches, escape scuttles, and watertight doors. Slips, trips, and falls were common accidents and caused a substantial number of injuries.

What might be hard for some to keep in mind, especially if they have never experienced shipboard life, is that the ship is not only a work place, it's also home. On warships, the ship is a platform from which a trained crew will fight to defend against or attack any enemy no matter what the threat, be it from the air, another ship, land, or below the sea's surface. Crew amenities on destroyers of the Gearing class were close to nonexistent. Recreation, as the work-watch schedule permitted, might come from the movies shown on the mess decks during the evenings, playing cards, or reading books. Destroyer sailors tended to read a lot of books in what little spare time they had, because there wasn't much else to do.

The bridge on ships of that era did not have air-conditioning systems; ventilation, when weather conditions allowed, came from keeping the bridge wing doors open and raising some of the bridge windows to the open position. In heavy weather, with wind-generated sea spray and rain, bridge windows and doors stayed closed. As it was summer, the temperature and humidity on the bridge built quickly, and along with the heavy rolling and pitching motion of the ship, it became the recipe to make just about anyone seasick.

The officer of the deck commented, "For those of you who have never been here before, welcome to Cape Hatteras weather." Other than that, my first under instruction watch as the QMOW went well. However, after four hours of the ship's rolling, pitching, and people puking, I was ready to go below.

So far, my first day at sea had gone about as well as could be expected. At about 1945, the oncoming QM relieved us and took over the 2000 to 2400 QMOW watch. Before going below, we left our names and bunk numbers in the wake up/call logbook to ensure we would be woken up in time for the morning 0400 to 0800 watch, then went to the chartroom one deck below the bridge. The chartroom also served as our makeshift lounge, since there was room for several chairs and stools. One of the other QMs was there, so the three of us shot the breeze for a while before going below.

On my way below, while heading aft in the ship, I encountered at least three guys lying on the passageway deck at different locations, all suffering from seasickness. The ship's junior corpsman was checking on one of the guys I came across. I told the corpsman the location of the two other sick guys; he indicated that he was aware of them and would be checking on them. I made my way to M&B division berthing, where I was still sleeping until a rack and locker opened up in operations berthing, one compartment further aft.

The ship was rolling even heavier and with more force than before. Getting back up to the after head located on the main deck while wearing shower shoes, a towel wrapped around my waist, and carrying my douche kit was a challenge. Taking a shower was even more challenging. Once done in the aft head and shower, I went back below to the berthing compartment and hit my rack for the night. My first day at sea had come to an end.

By the next day of the passage, everyone had gotten into the underway routine. By early afternoon, the weather and seas had improved after the ship cleared the Diamond Shoals area and headed south and further out to sea away from the coastline. The ship was now rolling and pitching considerably less than the night before. For those that stood watches, the day revolved around the two four-hour watch standing periods. Time between watches was either spent working on assignments or finding something to do during your off-watch periods at night. Each QMOW stood with Chip was filled with learning more and more about the watch duties and responsibilities. Chip put my training evolution onto a fairly steep learning curve. One of the most important duties is to maintain and keep an accurate navigation plot of the ship's position on the navigation charts.

Open sea navigation requires obtaining a fix of the ship's position at least hourly. The navigation plot is updated with dead reckoned (DR) positions in between obtained fix positions. The only electronic aid to navigation other than radar for fixing the ship's position was the Loran "A" receiver. "Loran" is an acronym for Long Range Navigation. Loran was a hyperbolic radio navigation system developed in the United States during World War II. Simply put, Loran was a system by which hyperbolic (curved) lines of position were determined by measuring the difference in the times of reception of synchronized pulse signals from two or more fixed land-based transmitters. The synchronized pulse signals were converted and used as Time Difference, Lines of Position (TD LOPs).

Navigation charts had the Loran stations and the hyperbolic lines of position at set increments (TDs) overprinted on the chart. Two or more measured TDs when plotted on the chart, crossing at an adequate angle from each other, formed the Loran fix position for the ship at the time of reception. Operating the Loran "A" receiver could be a challenge and in some cases, atmospherics and poor weather conditions could interfere with the Loran radio pulse signals. In open seas away from land, the only other means of fixing the ship's position was by the use of various methods and techniques of celestial navigation, using the sun, moon, planets, and selected navigational stars to navigate by.

QM1 Janson did not stand QMOW watches; his primary job was to shoot the sun using a marine sextant to observe the sun's altitude, which then can be computed into an LOP, several times throughout the day to obtain celestial running fixes, including finding the ship's latitude by observing the sun at Local Apparent Noon. Additionally, Janson, sometimes with the XO, would observe the stars and planets on the marine sextant during morning and evening twilights to obtain a "star fix" of the ship's position. That was the extent of our abilities in open-ocean for obtaining the ship's position. It was still the era where one had to master the art and science of navigation to be proficient in ship navigation. No namby-pamby GPS for us; it didn't exist then, anyway.

The QMOW performs a myriad of tasks throughout the watch. Besides continually maintaining the navigation plot of the ship's position, some examples of his duties are the taking and recording of weather and sea state observations every hour, encoding weather observations into a synoptic code for radio transmission to the Fleet Weather Central, and making the deck logbook entries. There are a number of other tasks, such as maintaining the navigation record books, comparing the gyro compass course with the magnetic compass course every 30 minutes and at every course change, then determining the compass error. Other areas of the watch required communication of any and all ship's position information in relation to the Passage Plan to the officer of the deck, navigator, and the captain.

The normal underway bridge watch section, besides the QMOW, was made up of at least nine other crew members: two officers, the OOD, and the junior officer of the deck (JOOD). The OOD typically was one of the ship's department heads, usually a lieutenant, and the JOODs were the ship's division officers from different departments. The OOD on a naval vessel is the officer in charge of the ship. He reports directly to the captain. During the period of his watch, except for the captain, all personnel on board are subordinate to the OOD with the caveat that the XO may direct or relieve him if he sees fit.

The JOODs are junior officers training to ultimately become qualified OODs and were usually ensigns or lieutenant junior grades (Lt. j.g.). Typically, the JOOD is also the conning officer. The conning officer has the conn and is the only person authorized to verbally give helm and engine order commands to the helmsman and lee helmsman. The BMOW, the Boatswain Mate of the Watch, was a Boatswain Mate (BM) rating, with the rank of third class or second class petty officer. His function is to assist the OOD and supervise the other bridge watchstanders.

Seaman from 1st division (Deck Force) served as the helmsman, lee helmsman, forward and aft lookouts, messenger of the watch (MOOW), and the IJL circuit phone talker. The IJL circuit phone talker relays reports from the lookouts to the OOD and contact information from the surface and air radar trackers in CIC. The lee helmsman, or lee helm, manned and operated the Engine Order Telegraph (EOT), but also served as the IJV circuit phone talker for direct voice communications with the main engine room, B-2 called "Main Control." An Engine Order Telegraph (EOT) is a device on the bridge used to give orders to the engine room from the conning officer.

By tradition, naval ships also keep time by the striking of the ship's bell. The ship's bell is always located at the 1MC intercom system on the quarterdeck while in port and on the bridge while the ship is at sea. Every four hours of the watch period is equivalent to eight bells, one bell for each half hour of the watch. For example, four strokes on the bell sounded during the 0800 to 1200 watch would indicate the time is 1000. Eight bells are sounded at 0800, 1200, 1600 and 2000. The striking of eight bells at noon comes from the days of sailing ships, when time was kept by sand trickling through a half-hour glass. One bell for was rung for each passing half hour. At the striking of eight bells, it was time to relieve the watch. The striking of the ship's bell were suspended at "Taps," 2200. Starting at "Reveille" at 0600, the striking of the bell resumes. For example, immediately after Reveille is announced over the 1MC, four strokes are rung on the bell.

The other use of the ship's bell was while the ship was in port. The bells are rung for commanding officers and dignitaries coming aboard or leaving the ship. The number of strokes on the bell is equivalent to the number of side-boys to whom the officer or visitor is entitled. A ship's captain rates four side-boys or four bells. Every morning while the ship is in port, the watch on the quarterdeck, upon seeing the captain approaching the gangway, would sound over the 1MC four bell strikes followed by the voice announcement, "Rich arriving." After the captain had come on board and cleared the quarterdeck area, one stroke on the bell would be sounded over the 1MC, meaning the captain was on board.

When the ship is underway, QMs must stand all of their watches with the ship's commissioned officers, the OODs, and JOODs. I had already developed a general dislike for Navy commissioned officers, but also quickly realized that I needed to put that aside in order to be a good QM. The QMOW gets to know all of the officers. Principally, they are in a position to observe both good, and sometimes bad, character traits in their officers. In one respect, this was good because it allows the QM to learn which officers he might be able to trust, and at the same time he gained the understanding of which ones to never trust. This is a learned trait that develops over time in most quartermasters.

On the fourth afternoon since leaving Norfolk, the ship arrived at the entrance to GITMO. The sea and anchor detail was set and the ship began its inbound transit through the bay to moor alongside one of the docks at the naval base. This time, I was assigned as the port bearing taker and at least for me, the inbound transit went well. After the ship was moored at the dock, the sea and anchor detail was secured. I got a chance to take a look around at GITMO from the ship's bridge and signal bridge. The waterfront at GITMO looked pretty isolated from the rest of the base. There were several other ships docked; one in particular that caught our interest was a Turkish Navy destroyer tied up on the other side of the dock from us.

The next morning, two events occurred. First, the personnel from the Fleet Training Center (FTC) arrived on board to begin the all-day briefings on the ship's refresher training (REFTRA) evolutions that we would be involved in for the next five or six weeks. The other event caused a little excitement on the waterfront. From the bridge, someone spotted the base commanding officer's black sedan coming down the pier along with some Navy security vehicles. A Navy captain jumped out of the sedan and quickly made his way up the gangway of the Turkish destroyer, followed by several other officers and security personnel.

Someone up on our signal bridge yelled down for us to look at the forward mast on the Turkish destroyer. On looking through binoculars for several moments, we realized what we were seeing. Rigged from the masts of the Turkish destroyer we could see two big fiber lines hanging down from the masts with hangman knots made up in the lower ends. The Turkish ship was preparing to execute two of their crew members by hanging.

The base commander obviously had learned of the Turk's planned executions and was there to put a stop to it. It didn't stop the executions, as we learned later that day. Within an hour, the Turkish destroyer got underway and proceeded out of Guantanamo Bay. Later that afternoon, the Turkish ship returned and docked at the same berth. The FTC guys told us that the Turkish ship had gone out to sea, carried out the two executions by hanging, then probably buried the dead crew members at sea and returned to port. Day one in GITMO was memorable.

The next day, the ship's refresher training began in earnest. During refresher training at GITMO, every day started essentially the same way. The ship got underway from the dock at around 0700, but before going out to sea the bridge crew and navigation teams were tested with two separate training events while outbound. The first event, "blind navigation," was training for restricted visibility navigation. Bedsheets were hung over all the bridge's windows so that no one could see out, except for in front of the captain's chair. The navigation team was expected to navigate away from the dock out to a point in the bay using only radar navigation and dead reckoning (DR). Upon arrival at the point in the bay, the next evolution began.

On a modified navigation chart, three-ship channels were laid out through a simulated minefield. The FTC trainer would indicate which channel the ship should navigate in through the simulated minefield. In mine warfare countermeasures, ships navigating in minefields de-energized their electric degaussing coils, which changed the magnetic signature of the ship, and navigation lost the use of the electronic gyro compass and surface radar for navigation. As a result, the navigation team then had to switch to taking relative bearings, to navigation aids, or other objects.

Gyro compass repeaters are equipped with a relative bearing compass rose, so bearing takers could easily switch to taking relative versus gyro compass bearings. Relative bearings use the ship's head (dead ahead) as the reference of 000 degrees. Relative Bearings are then measured from dead ahead, 000 degrees through 359 degrees, in a clockwise direction around the ship. Relative bearings must be converted to true bearings from the ship's magnetic compass course in order to be plotted on the navigation chart as true bearing LOPs for fixing the ship's position. The ship is expected to navigate out to sea and stay in the designated imaginary channel with no visual markers. All navigators find this evolution challenging and it was common for them to mistakenly drive their ships out of the imaginary channels on the initial attempts.

Once the ship was out at sea offshore from GITMO, the rest of the training day commenced. Much of the day was spent at GQ, "Battle Stations" for various battle problems. Battle problems could range from the ship undergoing an NBC attack (nuclear, biological, or chemical), torpedo attacks, or air attacks. The ship always suffered from some simulated battle damage to train and test the ship's damage control, as well as its firefighting parties to see how they responded to and handled each simulated emergency. Some days included live fire exercises of the ship's 5-inch/38 caliber guns, firing at both surface and air targets. At the end of each training day at sea, the ship proceeded into port. The navigation team would be tested again each afternoon with a precision anchoring evolution of the ship before going to a berth at the dock for the night.

After docking, the FTC trainers gave the captain and all officers a debriefing on the crew and ship's performance for the day and then they would depart the ship for the night. If there were problems or discrepancies that needed to be corrected before the next day, the affected division or divisions sometimes found themselves working long into the night. The next day, the training started all over again as soon as the ship got underway. The training was progressive and as crews gained more proficiency the FTC trainers increased the complexity of problems or battle damage. By about week four or five of training, most ships' crews are peaking out in proficiency and skill and ready to pass the final battle problems, and most importantly, leave GITMO.

While in REFTRA, Janson and the XO decided that my station for GQ and underway replenishment (UNREP) would be at the lee helmsman station. The lee helmsman station was fairly easy. It was a simple matter of repeating orders back to the conning officer, then immediately ringing up the ordered engine's bell on the EOT. For example, "Engines all ahead standard; make turns for 15 knots" was the initial order, and the lee helmsman verbally repeated the order while ringing up the ordered engine's bell and then setting the required shaft revolutions for the ordered speed in knots on the shaft revolution indicator. Once Main Control answered by matching the main engine and speed/shaft revolutions command on the EOT, the lee helmsman reported, "Sir, engines are all ahead standard, with indicated turns for 15 knots." The lee helmsman waited for the reply from the conning officer of, "Very well," indicating that he had heard and understood the report.

Chip was the primary master helmsman from the QM gang. A QM, who was also the qualified master helmsman, was the assigned helmsman for GQ and UNREP evolutions. It also had been decided that Chip would train me to ultimately become the next master helmsman. During several GQ drills, with permission from the OOD and conning officer, Chip and I would switch stations. He would take over as the lee helmsman and I would take the helm under instruction.

A helmsman must concentrate on three pieces of steering equipment: the steering gyro compass repeater, the rudder angle indicator, and the rudder follow-up indicator. Additionally, the helmsman must always know the current "checking course." The checking course is the magnetic steering compass heading for the current gyro compass course being steered. In the event of failure in the steering gyro compass, the helmsman is expected to immediately switch to steering the checking course per the magnetic steering compass.

I didn't mind steering in open waters during GQ, but steering the ship for UNREP was another matter. Steering the ordered courses during any underway replenishment evolution must be accurate and precise. The helmsman must stay focused and maintain a high level of mental alertness during every second of the operation. A steering mistake or error committed by a helmsman while alongside another underway ship could end in disaster. The prospect of being the next master helmsman didn't sit too well with me. I didn't really have the self-confidence to do it, nor did I want the responsibility.

For those not familiar with UNREP operations, the following is a short description: UNREP is a method the Navy uses for transferring fuel, ammunition, and stores from one ship to another while underway. UNREP for fueling at sea (FAS) operations are completed by using a ram tension wire system called STREAM (Standard Tensioned Replenishment Alongside Method). The receiving ship comes alongside the replenishment ship at a distance of approximately 30 yards. Both ships are normally running at a speed of 12 knots (about 13.8 mph). As the command ship of the operation, the replenishment ship provides all lines and equipment needed for the transfer. A gun line, which is a pneumatic line thrower or shot line, is fired from the replenishment ship and used by the receiving ship to pull across a messenger line. This line is used by the receiving ship's crew to pull across other equipment such as a distance line, phone line, and the transfer rig lines.

Alongside connected underway replenishment is a risky operation, as two ships are running side by side at speed. Each ship must hold to precisely the same course and speed for a long period of time. The hydrodynamics set up by the two ships running close to each other cause a suction between them. A slight steering error on the part of one of the ships could cause a collision or part the transfer lines and fuel hoses. At a speed of 12 knots, just a one-degree steering error can produce a lateral (side to side) speed of about 20 feet per minute. For this reason, experienced and qualified helmsmen are required during the replenishment. The bridge crews must give their undivided attention to the ship's course and speed.

In case of an emergency, ships' crews practice emergency breakaway procedures, where the receiving ship separates the transfer rig at an accelerated pace. An emergency breakaway may save the ships from having a collision, but it is possible to lose stores or cause damage to replenishment equipment on either ship. Worst-case scenario, crew on either ship can be injured or killed. Chip, Janson, and the XO all insisted that I would be the one to replace Chip as the next master helmsman. It was apparent that they were essentially going to force me into it without regard for my reservations and my lack of confidence about being able to do the job.

Chip was a short timer, so I was seen as his ultimate replacement. A sailor would often declare his short timer status when he reached 180 days to go until his enlistment expiration date. Many short timers would buy the "short timer chain" and carry it with them at all times. A short timer chain was a small chain with 180 links. Each day, the short timer would cut off or remove one link from the chain, counting down the days.

Don't misunderstand; being a short timer had nothing to do with having a bad or poor attitude. The short timers still performed their jobs to the best of their abilities, it was just that they had no intention of staying in the Navy. Most of them had reached the level of peak qualifications and had extensive practical experience. Chip would still be around long enough to make it through the first months of the upcoming WESTPAC deployment.

Shipboard life while in GITMO was not always easy. Life below decks could be best described as barely tolerable. One must remember that GITMO is located in the tropics, and steam ships while in training steamed on their plants around the clock. Our ship generally had poor air conditioning in the berthing compartments. The heat from the steam plant and from the hot tropical sun permeated throughout the structure of the steel ship. Some nights, sleeping was nearly impossible because of the heat. Poor ventilation, body odor, dirty socks, and other odors gave the berthing compartment a distinctive aroma.

After about a week in GITMO, a rack and locker opened up in operations berthing, so I was able to move in. The QMs all had their racks located generally in the same area of the compartment. I now had my permanent home on board. An enlisted sailor's

Typical arrangement of after berthing compartment, starboard side on Gearing class destroyers.

bunk (rack) was constructed from a steel tube frame measuring about two feet wide by six feet long. A canvas backing was laced into the steel tube frame with tightened small fiber lines forming the rack (i.e., the term "rack" versus "bunk"). One long side of the tube and canvas rack was attached to two spaced steel hooks on stanchions or the bulkhead, and the other long side was hooked onto two spaced steel chains secured to the compartments overhead or stanchions. A two-inch thick mattress was then placed on the tube and canvas rack frame.

This arrangement allowed for the racks to be raised and secured out of the way if necessary. Generally, the racks were in tiers three high—an upper rack, a middle rack, and a lower rack. The senior guy got the middle rack, the next senior guy got the top rack, and the junior guy got the bottom rack. The bottom rack was a bitch, because it was suspended directly above three deck lockers, one for each rack.

The bottom rack had to be lifted up several inches to allow someone needing to get into one of the deck lockers. If a sailor was in the bottom rack, they often had to get up to allow someone access to their locker. The alternative was if the person needing to get into a locker was strong enough to just lift up the sailor, rack and all with one hand, then could use the other hand to retrieve items from their locker. A sailor's rack was important to them; it wasn't just for sleeping; it also served as a place to read or relax. It was the sailor's primary domain because it was the one space on board that could be called their own. Generally, everyone respected each person's rack. One would never take anything from someone's rack or rack storage bag without permission.

There is a society on board naval ships much like the class levels in a hierarchy. Obviously at the top of the hierarchy is the captain, followed by the executive officer, then the ship's officers serving as the different department heads and division officers. The captain and XO had their private cabin and stateroom. The rest of the officers lived in "Officer's Country" in private or semi-private staterooms. The officers dine (mess) in the Wardroom separate from the crew. Due to the privilege of their rank, the steward ratings prepare and serve the officer's meals in the Wardroom. The Wardroom, in addition to a large dining table, has a nice lounge area with couches and sitting chairs. The stewards clean the Wardroom, make each officer's bunks, do their laundry, take care of their uniform needs, and clean their heads and shower rooms. Compared to the enlisted crew, the officers live well at their upper-class level in the hierarchy.

Next in the hierarchy are senior enlisted, the chief petty officers (CPO). They too live and mess separately from the crew. They live in the CPO Mess. The CPO Mess has a dining area and a small lounge area. Mess cooks from the galley are assigned to the CPO Mess to serve meals, but also clean the mess and berthing areas. The CPOs have their own separate but small head and shower room. The CPOs live a bit better than the enlisted crew, so they are in the middle class level in the hierarchy.

Niched in between the CPOs and the rest of the enlisted crew are the first class petty officers (paygrade E-6). These guys, for the most part, we called "Lifers," meaning they were in for at least a 20-year Navy career. The first class petty officers had several extra privileges, such as having their own table on the mess decks. They were allowed to eat early at each meal served on the mess decks. As mentioned, in the berthing compartments the first class always got the middle rack. Another perk in the berthing compartments was that first class petty officers got both stand-up lockers and the normal deck locker.

Last in the hierarchy is the rest of the enlisted crew. They generally must wait in chow lines to get their meals, then eat it on the crew mess decks. They clean their own berthing areas, heads, and shower rooms. Each compartment has a communal laundry bag where crew members deposit their dirty laundry. Each berthing compartment has someone designated as having the collateral assignment of laundry petty officer, who ensured the laundry bags are delivered to the ship's laundry once per week and picked back up when the laundry is done. Most sailors learn to say goodbye to their socks and skivvies as they put them in the laundry bag, knowing they will probably never see them again. Enlisted crews have no lounge areas or recreational areas and generally use their Work Centers to gather in after hours, or spend their spare time sleeping or reading in their rack. They are in the lower class level in the hierarchy.

At least on board USS *Rich*, there were not many overweight or fat sailors, and there was a good reason for this. The food served on board wasn't very good. Hell, mostly it was just barely edible. A lot of guys ate only one meal a day just to survive, usually breakfast. Breakfast usually was a bit more edible. It's hard to screw up eggs, bacon, or sausage and toast unless a cook really tried. For most meals, about the only way to make the food edible was to cover it with salt and pepper, and often that still was not enough. In that era of the Navy, providing there was a knife sharp enough to cut it, it's the only place known to mankind where beef steak can expand in your mouth as you chew it. On one occasion while on a working party loading food stores, we handled boxes of frozen meat stamped with packing dates more than 10 years old.

It wasn't a matter of bad cooks; it had more to do with the quality of the food. Generally, food that came out of a can was probably okay to eat. Freezer burn was the major issue that affected most of the perishable food. The alternative when it was available on board was fresh bread, peanut butter, and "horse cock" (cold cuts). These kinds of foods became the survival rations until they were gone. One had to get used to trimming off the green ring (from freezer burn) around the outside edge of each slice of horse cock before eating it. To counter the food issue, many guys set up "gedunk lockers." The term "gedunk" is Navy slang generally used when referring to snacks or snack type foods. Sailors would find cabinets or install metal lockers that would become their gedunk lockers. Gedunk lockers were always locked with personal padlocks.

While the ship was in port, sailors would stock up on their gedunk. Common gedunk items were crackers, cheese spreads, canned meats, chips, candy, or other food items that could be stored unrefrigerated for long periods of time. The gedunk locker was seen as a survival locker; when there was nothing else to eat, at least a sailor could fall back on his stockpile. Gedunk was another perk in belonging to the lower class level in the hierarchy.

The weeks of REFTRA at Guantanamo Bay seemed to drag by slowly. One consolation was that RFETRA was pretty much limited to Monday through Friday, which meant the ship was in port on weekends. Crew members not in the weekend duty sections were free to go on base liberty from 0800 to midnight. The Guantanamo Bay Naval Base in its entirety is physically located in Cuba, and what's unique is that it is a completely isolated and self-sufficient installation. There are a number of Naval and Marine Corps commands located at Guantanamo Bay. The base is much like other naval bases in the United States in many respects with Navy Exchange stores, enlisted and officer clubs, and recreational services. What was unique about Guantanamo Bay was that there were not very many private motor vehicles. But it did have plenty of iguanas and mongooses.

The military did not allow service members stationed at Guantanamo Bay to have their personal vehicles shipped in. Essentially, a service member reporting in for assignment at GITMO inherited their motor vehicle from the person they were relieving. The private vehicles seen around the base were old, mainly model years from the 1950s and early 1960s. Some had been repaired and repaired again to keep them running. A lot of the car bodies had rusted away due to the high level of corrosive salt air from the surrounding bay and ocean, so there were some cars being driven around that sported homemade plywood bodies.

The Guantanamo Bay Naval Base was leased by the U.S. Government from Cuba in 1903, for the amount of $2,000 annually to be paid in gold coins until 1934, when the payment was set to match the value in gold paid in U.S. dollars. The U.S. paid to build and maintain fences marking the boundary of the leased area of about 45 square miles. Apparently, relations with Cuba went well until the 1953–1959 revolution in Cuba. In 1939, pipelines were constructed to supply the base with water from the Yateras River about 4.5 miles northeast of the base. The U.S. government paid a fee for this; in 1964, it was about $14,000 a month for about 2,500,000 U.S. gallons (9,000 m^3) per day. In 1964, the Cuban government stopped the flow of water to the base. To meet the need for water, it was imported from Jamaica by barge, then a desalination plant was relocated from San Diego and rebuilt at Guantanamo Bay.

When the Cuban government accused the U.S. of stealing water, the base commander, Rear Admiral John D. Bulkeley, ordered that the pipelines be cut and a section removed. This was the same John D. Bulkeley who, as a lieutenant and PT boat skipper in World War II, evacuated General Douglas MacArthur from Corregidor in the Philippines. The U.S. and Cuba placed some 55,000 land mines across the "no man's land" around the perimeter of the naval base, creating the second-largest minefield in the world and the largest in the Western Hemisphere.

This was the GITMO that existed during my first visit there for REFTRA. Several things the Guantanamo Bay Naval Base did offer visiting fleet sailors were swimming, snorkeling, and fishing. The waters around Guantanamo are pristine, clear, and teeming with sea life and fish. The base ran Navy buses, just old school buses painted haze gray.

The buses were the primary way to get around the base other than walking. One of the favored spots for swimming and snorkeling was at Fisherman Point near McCalla field. There was an old concrete dock there with ladders that reached down to the water. Many of us quickly learned that these waters were also favorite spots for barracudas and sharks. The swimming and snorkeling were spectacular, even with the occasional barracuda or shark encounter.

One other amenity available just about everywhere on the base was alcohol. Even the gas station sold beer, plus there were several locations around the base that were open-air bars with cabanas. Nothing beat sitting in the shade of a waterfront cabana, sipping cold beer on a hot tropical afternoon. These outdoor bars often provided a little side entertainment in the form of the iguanas. Iguanas tended to hang around the perimeter of these areas, waiting for any form of food that might come their way. Sailors would feed the iguanas potato chips, lettuce, or the vegetables from their sandwiches. The iguanas became much like any other animal when it came to getting easy food.

At night, there was the enlisted club. Many Atlantic fleet sailors remember GITMO's infamous White Hat Club. On most nights, the club offered music usually supplied by a disc jockey (DJ), a dance floor, some arcade games, and lots of cheap booze. On weekend nights, the dance floor was divided with a large ship mooring line strung between two wooden end stanchions through the center of the dance floor. One side of the dance floor was for the drunk fleet sailors who wanted to dance; the other side of the dance floor was reserved for enlisted sailors stationed at Guantanamo to dance with their wives or girlfriends. On particularly rowdy nights, shore patrolmen (SPs) were stationed around the dance floor to prevent fleet sailors from leaving their side of the dance floor. One wouldn't think it, but there was an awful lot of fun at the White Hat Club.

This club was also associated with the well-known "Bloody Mile." The enlisted club closed at 2330. Starting, about 15 minutes before closing, SPs would arrive in force and begin to herd the fleet sailors toward the main exit of the club. Waiting outside was a truck with a trailer about 40 feet in length. The trailer was actually a freight trailer modified to carry passengers. The trailer had two commercial bus-type doors installed on one side, one door in the forward section, and the other door toward the rear of the trailer. Inside the trailer there were installed steel seating benches arranged throughout. There were window openings, but with installed steel bars. Many sailors referred to this vehicle as the "cattle car."

The Navy and Marine Corps SPs would make sure everyone boarded the cattle car. Once it was loaded with drunk sailors, with doors shut and guarded by shore patrol, it began the trip from the club down to the waterfront where the fleet ships were docked. The trip was called the Bloody Mile because crew members from one ship would often decide it was a good idea to beat the shit out of crew members from other ships. So full-on brawls were common during the trip. A lot of old sailors today can look at their scars and reminisce about old injuries sustained during their trip down the Bloody Mile.

The way to avoid the Bloody Mile experience was to leave the club a bit before closing, however, this meant walking along areas of dark roads and walkways back to the ship. Some areas were a bit remote, and just off the roads or walkways were overgrown with dense vegetation. Here was the domain of the mongoose. The story of the mongoose's presence in Cuba was that they had been introduced years before to manage rodent and snake populations. Over time, with few natural predators, the Small Indian Mongoose spread out over a large range and took to eating almost anything. These mongooses were omnivores and ate many small animals and fruits. They were known for their swift, aggressive behavior. More than one sailor had a tale of a mongoose encounter while making the long and dark walk back to their ship.

After about a month in GITMO with the REFTRA routine, we got word that the ship would get a four-day port visit to Montego Bay, Jamaica. This would be my first real foreign port visit. Montego Bay lies on the northwest coast of the island of Jamaica. The ship left Guantanamo Bay late on a Thursday afternoon to make the 207 nautical mile trip to Montego Bay. The overnight passage took about 13 hours and the ship arrived at the "Alpha" Anchorage area near the beaches about 0700 the next morning.

After the ship was secure in its anchored position, liberty call was announced for all crew members, except those in the duty section. The ship's crew was equally divided into four duty sections; as it turned out my duty section in the rotation would not have duty for the three days in Montego Bay. The ship was scheduled to be in Montego Bay Friday through Sunday.

By this point, discovery of another source of financial income had come my way. There were those that had scheduled duty section assignments over the weekend and were looking for someone to stand their duty. A duty standby was allowed as long as the sailor taking the duty for another sailor was equally qualified for their duties and watch station. Now that I had had some time in the operations department, I had gained various in-port watch station qualifications. So, I became a hot commodity once I let it be known that I was willing to standby on Friday and Sunday in return for a payment of $25 per duty day. I wanted Saturday off to go ashore and see Montego Bay.

I took one guy's duty on Friday for $45, as he was the highest bidder, and another guy's duty on Sunday for $35. I made both guys pay up in advance. At that time, I only kept $20 per payday, the rest of my monthly pay going to Janice. Now, I had an extra $80 to enjoy and spend during my day off in Montego Bay.

The touristy sections of Montego Bay were nice. I went on liberty with some of my buddies from engineering. We did a lot of walking around, taking in the sights and spending some time in the afternoon relaxing on the beach and having some drinks. All of the Jamaicans we came across were very nice and friendly.

On a couple of occasions, we found ourselves away from the beach area and farther off the beaten path sections of the town. Starting several blocks away from the hotels, restaurants, and night clubs, we found areas that only could be described as ghettos. The people in these areas were living in abject poverty. More than one of us was taken aback a bit by the filthy and extremely poor living conditions. On getting back to the ship that night, I had seen all I cared to of Montego Bay. Monday was spent with the ship making the passage back to Guantanamo Bay to start REFTRA again on the next day, Tuesday.

The first week of September was when everyone received their Report of Enlisted Performance Evaluation. At six-month intervals, enlisted personnel were evaluated by their supervisors and seniors. For junior enlisted not in leadership or supervisory positions, their evaluation was limited to the categories of professional performance, military behavior, military appearance, and adaptability. This was my first performance evaluation since reporting on board in May. For those of us in the Navigation division, our performance evaluations were written by the XO, since he also served as the ship's navigator.

For whatever reason, the XO seemed to like me, because he did tolerate a certain degree of my bullshit. He gave me mid-upper level ratings, but in his written comments on my performance, he sized me up pretty well. Several of the XO's comments about my performance were right on the money: "On some jobs, however, he does not put forth his best efforts. It appears he is eager to do well only the jobs he likes. Though somewhat moody, TROWBRIDGE gets along well with his shipmates."

I do admit to being moody at times. The term moody, as used by the XO was a mild way of saying I could be an ornery little dickhead. Though I often could keep up a good front, I still was principally struggling with knowing that the machinist mate rating was out for me, and I was no longer sure about being in the Navy at all. At the same time, I recognized there were no other real choices. I knew I was stuck in this situation for three more years where everything seemed out of my control, and I didn't like it. At 19 years old, three years might as well have been forever.

In spite of my personal feelings, the ingrained farm kid work mentality in me still prevailed. If they wanted a deck cleaned and waxed, when it was done, that deck would shine like a newly minted nickel. If they needed a steel bulkhead chipped down to bare metal, sanded, preserved, and painted, it would look like a new bulkhead when finished. When on watch on the bridge, quartermasters are held to a bit of a higher standard than other sailors. While underway on the bridge, we constantly worked in close quarters with the captain, XO, and all of the officers. Therefore, we were expected to always maintain a high standard of military appearance and military bearing. However, on several occasions my general attitude of what could be called "pissed off-ness" would shine through. For example, if one of the officers standing the JOOD or OOD watch acted in a condescending or patronizing manner, I would make remarks bordering on insubordination, or instead of volunteering information, I would wait for that particular officer to realize they needed certain information from me and would have to ask for it. So, yes at times, if a certain officer pissed me off, I could be a bit of a dickhead.

On the other hand, I had realized a concept that my experiences had validated. This concept actually became my mantra: "Hard work and production talks, while bullshit walks," meaning I learned that by being a consistent hard worker, when my temper or general pissed off-ness sometimes got the best of me, a bit of latitude and leeway were often exercised by my seniors. Obviously, there were other sailors on board who had the same general attitude as me, but I found that some of them got hammered if they exhibited unmilitary behavior or were insubordinate with seniors. What was the difference? Usually those that got hammered also were slobs, lazy, poor workers, and usually displayed a shit-head attitude. For me, this was a very valuable life lesson.

The next two weeks in GITMO went well, with the ship finally passing all of the required battle problems. It was time to start the trip back to Norfolk. However, we had received notification directing the ship to first go to San Juan, Puerto Rico, for another port call before returning back to Norfolk. The visit to San Juan would be another three-day visit. After the visit in San Juan, the ship would then make the four-day passage to Norfolk.

By this time, I had completed the qualifications as Quartermaster of the Watch and was now standing QMOW bridge watches on my own. Our QM2 had come off the watch bill rotation to spend more time learning the elements of passage planning and had allowed for Janson to spend more time training him on the duties of the assistant navigator. The ship departed Guantanamo Bay and began the two-day passage to San Juan; the crew's morale was high now that REFTRA was over and behind us.

I didn't go ashore in San Juan. I just wanted to go home to Norfolk. The ship was able to moor at a dock near the downtown section of San Juan. I stood duty all three days while the ship was there; one day was my duty day, the other two days I stood duty for other guys, making another $60. The guys that did go on liberty mainly talked about going to a night club in San Juan called the Black Angus. The rest of their time was spent on the beaches or the hotel bars and night clubs. The one visual that always stood out for me was the El Morro Fort, officially Castillo de San Felipe del Morro, located at the entrance to San Juan Harbor. The El Morro Fort is a huge, six-level fort, named in honor of Spain's King Philip II, built between the years 1539 and 1540.

The day we left San Juan as the ship passed below El Morro Fort, the XO came out onto the starboard bridge wing where I was the bearing taker. He began waving at some people up on the fort. I could see it was a woman with a couple of kids he was waving to. I asked him if those people on the fort were his family. He replied that his wife and kids had been able to fly down to spend the weekend with him in San Juan. I believe my reply was, "That's great," but I still remember the feeling of envy.

The XO was a lieutenant commander. One thing different about him from other officers was that he was a "Mustang." Mustang is a slang term which refers to a commissioned officer who began his career as an enlisted service member. Commissioned officers who are Mustangs often more highly respected by the average enlisted sailor. Mustang officers are often seen as being more empathetic, even handed, and fair leaders than their counterparts who gained their Commissions through other officer accession avenues. I would say the XO fit into that category of naval officer; he was fair and had a no-nonsense professional approach to everything, but at the same time could display a sense of humor when it mattered.

Four days later, the ship entered into Chesapeake Bay and made the hour and half long transit through the southern sections of Chesapeake Bay to the Norfolk Naval Station. Our berthing assignment was the D & S Piers at Pier 23. The crew was going to be granted a four-day liberty weekend. I was excited about having three days off at home with Jan and our son until my next duty day. After tying up at the dock and securing the ship, the word for liberty call was passed throughout the ship on the 1MC intercom.

I made my way to the quarterdeck and headed down the gangway. Jan was on the pier across from the gangway. Our son, now almost 10 months old, saw me and recognized me right away. He broke free from Jan's hand, running toward me. I caught him at the bottom of the gangway as I swept him up into my arms. I was surprised at his ability to run; seven weeks before, he still hadn't been walking all that well. With him in my arms, I covered the distance across the pier to hug and kiss Jan. Once again, I was back where I wanted to be.

As I was in one of the last groups departing the ship, Jan had been waiting since the ship tied up about an hour before. While waiting, she had overheard some people talking on the dock about cases where destroyer sailors didn't always make it back. She became worried after watching groups of sailors leaving the ship and she couldn't find me among them. I didn't realize this until she told me about it later while driving home. I couldn't understand why someone would be talking about negative stuff like that within earshot of young wives and families.

This was a day of firsts for both of us. It was my first time returning from the sea, and it was Jan's very first time waiting for and meeting my returning ship. The only shadow on this day was that it was now mid-September and the ship would be departing on its WESTPAC deployment the following month.

6. THE PASSAGE AND LONG TRANSITION

The week after the ship's return to Norfolk from the Caribbean, preparations began for the deployment departure date of October 17.

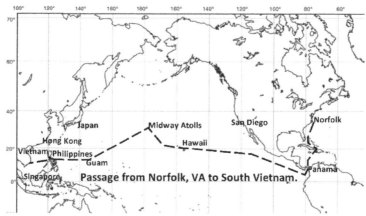

Approximation of USS Rich's passage from Norfolk to South Vietnam.

The initial passage plan was laid to take the ship from Norfolk to the Panama Canal with a planned one-day transit of the canal from Cristobal on the Atlantic side to Balboa on the Pacific side, with the ship docking at the Rodman Naval Station overnight. The next morning the ship would depart from the Panama Canal Zone bound to Pearl Harbor,

Hawaii, then to Midway Atoll, and after that to Guam in the Mariana Islands. From Guam the ship would proceed to the Subic Bay Naval Base in the Philippines. During the passage from Midway Atoll to Guam the ship would be crossing the International Date Line. From Subic Bay, it would be on to Vietnam. The transit from Norfolk to Subic Bay in the Philippines represented a total passage distance of 11,200 nautical miles.

We had decided that after the ship departed, it would be best for Jan and our son to fly home to her parents in Stacyville. The deployment posed some unknowns. The biggest unknown was the unknowns. Sounds a bit dramatic, right? What might help illustrate our concerns are some examples of naval actions in Vietnam during the spring and summer months of 1972. These naval actions in Vietnam were not well covered by the news media for the months of April through August:

- During the earlier mentioned Battle of Dong Hoi Gulf, on April 19, North Vietnamese MIG aircraft attacked U.S. Navy destroyers. In that battle, one destroyer, USS *Higbee* (DD 806), suffered damage from a bomb hit and USS *Sterrett* (CG 31) shot down two attacking MIG aircraft with her Terrier missiles. Later that same day, *Sterrett* and *Higbee* were attacked by high speed patrol craft launching Styx anti-ship missiles. *Sterrett* successfully repelled the Styx attack with Terrier missiles, and then, with the 5-inch/54 caliber gun, fired 11 rounds of air fragmentation at the radar position of the two-patrol craft, which resulted in enemy losses and the sinking of both patrol craft. This battle resulted in special armaments and sensors being provided to destroyers for combating low flying aircraft and anti-ship missiles.

- May 8, the Navy's 7th Fleet laid extensive minefields in the channels and approaches to North Vietnam's port of Haiphong.

- July 17, USS *Warrington* (DD 843) struck two mines that detonated under her port side and suffered severe damage in her after fireroom, after engine room, and the main control room.

- August 27, Operation Lion's Den, or the Battle of Haiphong Harbor, occurred, which involved one of the few ship-to-ship naval battles of the Vietnam War. The operation was carried out by four ships designated as Task Unit 77.1.2., which included USS *Newport News* (CA 148), an 8-inch gun cruiser; USS *Providence* (CLG 6), a 6-inch gun missile cruiser; USS *Robison* (DDG 12), a guided-missile destroyer; and USS *Rowan* (DD 782). The two cruisers and two destroyers conducted a brief night raid against the North Vietnamese forces protecting the port of Haiphong. After the bombardment, the ships were threatened by four Russian-built torpedo boats. Two Navy A-7 Corsairs from USS *Coral Sea* (CV 43) assisted. The Task Unit's ships and aircraft were able to sink three of the four torpedo boats. Vietnamese coastal defense gunfire were heavy during the attack. *Newport News* reported 75 rounds of very accurate hostile fire; *Rowan* reported 50 rounds of accurate fire as close as 20 yards and straddling the ship. *Robison* reported 140 rounds of very accurate fire, the closest being 15 yards off the port beam. *Providence* counted 60 incoming rounds.

I kept discussions with my wife to a minimum of the recent actions by Navy ships off the coast of Vietnam. I'm sure others on board probably minimized these types of discussions with their wives as well. Some of the old salts onboard who had been to war before gave some good advice to young married sailors. Sailors rarely speak in terms of straight and plain language; they tend to use a lot of made-up axioms and analogies instead. I heard one old salt put it this way: "Silence, along with your discretion, is the better part of valor," meaning, be careful about saying what you know to your wives.

Some years later, while serving as the senior enlisted advisor on board one of the Navy's modern guided missile frigates, I discovered once again the importance of following that advice. In early August 1990, Saddam Hussein's Iraqi army invaded Kuwait and our ship was notified to be ready to deploy in seven to ten days for an unspecified period of time. The crew obviously knew about the Iraqi invasion into Kuwait. The unofficial assumption was that our ship was going to war, but what our actual mission would be was open to wide and varied speculation.

Several days into our deployment preparations, I received a phone call on board the ship from the wife of one of our crew members. During the phone call, the young wife pleaded with me to persuade the captain to let her husband off the ship and not make him go to war. The wife was highly distraught; she told me her husband had said the ship was going on a dangerous top secret mission and that he could likely be killed. I finally begged out of the phone call with a "Let me look into this."

Within the hour, I sat down with the sailor in private about my phone call with his wife; my news caught him by surprise, and it was easy to see he was highly embarrassed. I asked him what on earth he had said to his wife. His reply astounded me when he said, "Well, Master Chief, I wanted my wife to go to bed with me and she didn't want to, so I told her about how dangerous our mission was going to be to make her feel sorry for me." I had to stop myself from telling the kid he was a little f**king moron.

I told him to go home now and get things squared away his wife, and to tell her he had lied. To ensure that he would be honest with her, I explained that I would be calling his wife to let her know that he had lied to her and that he was on his way home to tell her the truth. The truth at that point was that no one knew what our mission would be, not even the captain. I didn't hear any more on the matter. For months afterward, anytime I happened to pass by the involved sailor, he would not look me directly in the eye. I do know his marriage did not survive the deployment.

About two weeks before USS *Rich*'s imminent deployment to WESTPAC, a number of steps were taken to prepare the crew, legally and otherwise. A group of Navy lawyers were brought on board for the mandatory drawing up of our wills and the process of naming a power of attorney who would have control of our legal and financial affairs in our absence. Everyone was issued their Geneva Conventions Card.

At that time, the Geneva Conventions Card was issued in addition to your Military Identification (ID) Card, which also had the Geneva Conventions statements on it. Article 17 of the Conventions required that active duty military members have duplicate identification to facilitate their identification as prisoners of war. The idea was that in the event that you were captured by the enemy, you were supposed to show the card to your captors, informing them that you were protected by the terms of the Geneva Conventions and should be treated humanely, in accordance with Conventions. Not that I had any plans of becoming a prisoner of war. It was a moot point anyway, because so far in the war, North Vietnam's position had been that captured U.S. military personnel were war criminals, not prisoners of war (POWs).

We were also given a new set of identification dog tags. Dog tags were corrosion-resistant metal plates worn on a neck chain and were primarily used for identification of dead and wounded sailors; they had personal information and conveyed your blood type and religious preference.

Next, a Navy photographer took official pictures of everyone in their dress uniforms. In my photograph, my uniform still had the fireman's red stripes with the MM insignia sewn on, though officially I was now a seaman, striking for the QM rating. The entire process of the wills, power of attorney, and the pictures was a bit sobering.

The year's events leading up to our deployment had been busy both on the national and international scenes. The political situation by mid-1972 was being driven by the events in the news. In February 1972, the last draft lottery was held. Starting the end of military conscription in the U.S. during the Vietnam era, no one from the last lottery was called to duty. Some of the other key events that had occurred so far in 1972 were:

- At the end of March, the Easter Offensive began after North

Vietnamese forces crossed into the DMZ of South Vietnam.

- In April, the Nguyen Hue Offensive began, prompted by the North Vietnamese Offensive; the U.S. resumed bombing of Hanoi and Haiphong Harbor.

- In May, Operation Linebacker and Operation Custom Tailor began large-scale bombing operations against North Vietnam by tactical fighter aircraft.

- In June, the Associated Press published a photograph of naked nine-year-old Plan Thi Kim Phuc running down a road after being burned by napalm, and President Richard Nixon announced that no new draftees would be sent to Vietnam.

- In July, actress Jane Fonda toured North Vietnam, where she was famously photographed sitting on a North Vietnamese anti-aircraft gun.

- In August at the Republican National Convention, President Richard Nixon and Vice President Spiro Agnew were re-nominated for a second term.

- In September, the North Vietnamese released three American POWs, the first since 1969—Navy Lieutenants Norris Charles and Markham Gartley, and Air Force Major Edward Elias. Still, 539 American POWs remained in captivity and more than 1,000 Americans were listed as missing in action and/or were unaccounted for. Eleven Israeli athletes at the Summer Olympics in Munich were murdered after eight members of the Arab terrorist group Black September invaded the Olympic Village.

- On October 8, a major breakthrough happened at the Paris Peace Talks between Henry Kissinger and the North Vietnamese, where the U.S. declared it would withdraw its forces from South Vietnam without North Vietnam doing the same.

For people of my age, it was a pivotal year. We could now vote in the federal and state elections. The Twenty-Sixth Amendment to the U.S. Constitution now prohibited the states and the federal government from using age as a reason for denying the right to vote to citizens of the United States who were at least 18 years old. My home state of Iowa ratified the Twenty-Sixth Amendment on March 30, 1971. As a result, I was able to obtain an Iowa Voter Registration Card and in early October, received my absentee ballot in the mail. I voted the top of the ticket for Richard Nixon and Spiro Agnew of the Republican Party. Most of us knew and understood that it was the Democrats, starting with President John Kennedy, who had gotten us into the Vietnam War; hopefully, the Republicans would finally get us all the way out.

Bringing the war in Vietnam to an end with a peaceful and honorable resolution was part of Nixon's platform and it appeared he had made significant progress to that end during his first term. Nixon's opponent, Senator George McGovern, appeared to be just another left-wing extremist or another bullshit Democrat full of hot air. I mailed my absentee ballot the day before the ship departed on deployment. It was going to take the ship at least a month to make the passage to Vietnam. With a young man's optimism, I mused that maybe Nixon would have a cease fire in effect before we arrived.

Meanwhile at home, as much of my time as possible was spent with Jan and our son. Our boy was growing and would be 11 months old by the time the deployment began. I was having difficulty imagining what he would be like after nine more months. My time was somewhat limited as work on the ship was brisk Monday through Friday, with a duty day every fourth night where I had to stay on board overnight.

Over the summer, Jan had made more friends with some of our neighbors. We began to chum around with one married couple in particular who lived in our apartment building. This couple had two young boys. The wife, Constance, was very nice, and her husband Jerry was a Navy cook stationed on board the aircraft carrier USS *America* (CV-66). We had been saving money for Jan and our son's flight back to

Iowa. Our plan was to keep the apartment, with several of our neighbors agreeing to keep an eye on things for us while we were gone. The days raced by, and before we knew it, there was only one more day left before it was time for me to leave.

The night before departure, I took more uniforms and clothes to the ship, and our friend Jerry came with me. After we got my bags to the ship and got on board, we headed down to the operations berthing compartment. The berthing compartment was dark, smelly, and hot; the air conditioning was not working again. While stowing my clothes and gear in my deck locker, Jerry suddenly said, "Holy shit, you're going to live here for nine months?" I asked him what he meant. His reply didn't surprise me much as he said, "I just can't believe that people have to live this way."

My reply to him was something like, "Well, I guess living conditions on aircraft carriers are better?"

He nodded and said, "Absolutely. This is unbelievable."

After finishing putting my gear away, I took Jerry on a short tour of the ship. Before we headed up to the bridge, I first took him down to the B-4 engine room. The ship was steaming on its boilers and the plant was in a hot status. With the engineering plant lit-off, there was a lot of ambient noise in an engine room from blowers, pumps, compressors, and other equipment.

One of my snipe buddies was on watch at the main throttle board. I went over to him to let him know I was showing a friend from an aircraft carrier what a real ship looked like. He grinned and pointed at the thermometer on the control board, which read 110 degrees, and he shouted to me over the blower noise, "Just be careful." Jerry didn't want to stay in the engine room very long.

Since he was a cook, I was sure he would want to see the galley and mess decks area. His reaction was not much better than what he had expressed about the berthing compartment, just another, "Holy shit." I think Jerry kind of freaked while we were still on the mess decks when a crew member came up through the deck hatch wearing only a towel around his waist and flip-flops. Seeing the look on Jerry's face, I explained that the only route from the weapons berthing compartment to the forward head and showers was through the mess decks. He asked, "Do guys do that during meal hours, too?"

I told him, "Yes, I'm sure they do."

After a tour of the bridge and CIC areas, we headed back home. More than once during the drive home, Jerry expressed his surprise about the low level of living standards on board my ship. I found his reaction to my ship a bit amusing, so just to jerk his chain a little, I told him, "That's why destroyer sailors have to be superior to and tougher than other sailors." After saying that, I silently realized, *Shit, I'm starting to talk like a damn "tin can" sailor.*

The next morning, wives and families were allowed on the pier to see the ship and their loved ones off. There was a large group of people and sailors gathered near the ship's gangway. Jan and our son came down the pier with me, and we stayed together for as long as possible until it was time to say our final goodbyes. Leaving Jan and our son this time was much harder for me to do since this time we would be measuring our period of separation not in weeks, but for nine long months instead. As before, walking away from them and going on board wasn't easy.

Shortly afterward, all crew members were mustered as being on board, and at 1125, the ship got underway from Pier 23. The ship navigated through Chesapeake Bay then on out to sea, bound for the Panama Canal Zone. The passage of 1,860 nautical miles to the canal-zone would take the ship about four days. That afternoon and evening, the weather off Cape Hatteras gave us a break. The weather was clear; the seas were good, with waves only about 4 to 6 feet in height. We were now bound for the Western Pacific and ultimately the Gulf of Tonkin and the near coastal waters of Vietnam.

After the ship cleared the Diamond Shoals waters off the coast of North Carolina, the ship's course was set to proceed southward to the

Straits of Florida. After several days the ship progressed from the southern end of the Straits of Florida, then courses were steered to follow a southeastern route direction along the northern coast of Cuba to the Windward Passage. Once again, the ship transited the Windward Passage between the eastern tip of Cuba and western tip of Hispaniola. This time, instead of turning west to Guantanamo Bay, Cuba, the ship was brought to a southwesterly course to proceed south between Jamaica and Haiti. Then, the course was set to the breakwater at Cristobal and Limon Bay where ships enter the Panama Canal waters.

The *Rich* arrived at the Panama Canal Zone early morning on October 21. As our ship approached the Cristobal breakwater and entered into Limon Bay, the Panama Canal Pilot boarded the ship from the pilot boat. Within a short period of time, the pilot ordered the ship to begin maneuvering to the first lock, the Gatun Lock. Seeing Gatun Lock for the first time makes for an impressive picture. The three successive lock chambers look like a huge staircase. The lock area itself is a lot of concrete and buildings located on either side of the lock. Beyond the grass areas on either side of the lock began the tropical jungle of dark trees and dense foliage.

For many on board, this would be their first trip through the Panama Canal. The canal should be considered one of the man-made wonders of the world. Its length is about 44 nautical miles (about 50 statute miles) from the Atlantic coast to the Pacific coast. While going through the Panama Canal, a ship will be raised and lowered 85 feet. After going through Gatun Lake and Gaillard Cut, the ship enters Pedro Miguel Locks and is lowered 31 feet. After Pedro Miguel Locks, one mile downstream the ship next enters the Miraflores Locks to be lowered about another 54 feet to the level of the Pacific Ocean.

As the ship proceeded to and along the lock wall of the Gatun Lock, small boats came out to the ship to deliver the canal line handlers. Then wire ropes were sent over to the ship from small electronic locomotives called Mules. The Mules ran on steel rail tracks laid along the top of the lock walls and were located on both sides of the locks. After the Mules passed wire ropes to both sides of the ship, they were made fast to the ship's deck bitts.

Once the wire ropes were secured, the Mules began to winch-in, taking the slack out of the wire ropes. The Mules were then used to tow the ship on the wire ropes alongside the lock walls, and ultimately towed the ship into each lock chamber and assisted the pilot in positioning the ship within each lock chamber. This process would be repeated at each of the lock chambers throughout the ship's canal passage.

The Gatun Locks consisted of three successive lock chambers. When a ship left the Gatun Locks and entered Gatun Lake, it had been raised 85 feet to the level of the lake. Gatun Lake was a man-made lake and covered an area of about 164 square miles. The shipping channel through the lake was about 15 nautical miles in length. Upon leaving Gatun Lake, you arrived at the more historical section of the canal, the Gaillard Cut, also known as the Culebra Cut, which traversed about eight miles through the Continental Divide of Panama, the highest point on the isthmus.

Construction of the Culebra Cut was considered to be one of the great engineering feats for its time. The French began digging the cut in 1881. Up to 6,000 men worked in the cut using explosives, steam shovels, and dirt trains to remove the earth and rock out of the cut. The United States took over the work on the canal in 1904, but the digging and blasting through the Culebra mountain ridge that created the cut was not finished until 1913.

After the ship passed through the Gaillard Cut, the first of two more locks were reached. The first lock, Pedro Miguel, had one chamber, and lowered the ship 31 feet. From Pedro Miguel, the ship moved into Lake Miraflores and proceeded about one mile to the Miraflores Locks. The Miraflores Locks had two chambers, which lowered the ship the remaining distance, depending upon the height of the Pacific Ocean tides, back to sea level. Being a military vessel, the ship proceeded from the Miraflores Locks about eight more miles to the docks at the Rodman

Naval Station across from Balboa. The canal transit had taken over eight hours, so the ship moored at the Rodman Naval Station docks at about 1600 that afternoon.

Except for the duty section, the crew was granted overnight liberty. My section had the duty that night, so no liberty in Panama City for us. The ship was scheduled to get underway the next morning at 1000 to begin our passage to Pearl Harbor. QM1 Janson asked that Jeff, one of the other quartermasters, and I double-check the time, speed, and distance calculations in the passage plan from Panama to Hawaii. We initially got a bit distracted from the task when something caught our eye on the first navigation chart leaving the Canal Zone out to the Gulf of Panama.

On the chart was a location just down the coast labeled "Leper Colony." The Leper Colony was located just west on the coast from the Pan-American bridge. We looked in the *Sailing Directions* publication and sure enough, it discussed the community of Palo Seco. Palo Seco was a leprosarium, or hospital, operated in the canal-zone since the disease-ridden days of canal construction, and was actually funded by the U.S. Congress. Both of us were surprised about the existence of the colony. I associated leprosy with biblical stories, not modern times. The rest of our night in Panama was spent checking latitude and longitude coordinates, re-measuring distances, and calculating time, speed, and distance to double-check the estimated time of arrivals (ETAs) at each route leg waypoint.

The next morning, down in the berthing compartment, returning crew were talking about their night in Panama City. One place mentioned by many was a spot called the Blue Goose. The Blue Goose in Panama City was a brothel that was supposedly sponsored by the Panamanian government. One guy aptly described the place as probably being much like a Prohibition era roadhouse, where anything went. Those of us who had duty quickly grew tired of hearing how we had missed out on all the fine women and what a great place the Blue Goose was.

The other thing the crew was happy about was that it was Sunday. Once the ship was out to sea and secured from the sea and anchor detail, for those not going on watch, "holiday routine" would be set. The holiday routine meant that those nursing their hangovers and/or suffering from exhaustion because they had been up all night while on liberty would be able to hit their racks and get some sleep.

At 1000, the ship got underway from the Rodman Naval Station dock. Once the ship was fair in the outbound channel, it proceeded to pass under the Pan-American bridge (The Bridge of the Americas) and headed outbound to the Gulf of Panama, and then on to the Eastern Pacific Ocean. The passage distance of close to 4,700 nautical miles lay ahead of us from the Panama Canal to Pearl Harbor. This distance was approaching the upper limit of the ship's fuel/cruising range capability. It was going to take a little over 12 days of steaming for the ship to travel that distance at an overall speed of advance (SOA) of 16 knots.

That afternoon and evening the ship made the passage through the Gulf of Panama, making its way into the Eastern Pacific Ocean. By the next day, it became apparent to many of us that the waters in the Eastern Pacific Ocean were much different from those found in the Atlantic. Here the ocean seemed smooth, with small sea waves and long ocean swells. It became common to sight marine life such as whales, dolphins, sea turtles, and different species of sharks. For a number of days, the weather was great, with plenty of sunlight, azure blue skies, light winds, and calm seas.

Each morning, the deck crew would work at clearing the decks of the dead flying fish that had landed on the weather decks and died during the night. The first three or four days of the passage, the ship steamed near the coast along the Central American countries. During daylight hours, particularly along the coasts of Costa Rica, Nicaragua, El Salvador, and Guatemala, the various volcanic mountains could be clearly viewed in the distance. This area along Central American isthmus was sometimes called the "Ring of Fire" for the 29 volcanoes found ranging from Guatemala to Panama.

For me, each day standing my watches on the bridge as the QMOW helped me learn more about ship navigation, ship control, weather, and meteorology. My proficiency in accurately fixing the ship's position by visual compass bearings, surface radar, and Loran continued to improve. A lot of my spare time was spent studying the practical use of celestial navigation and astronomy. I had perfected tasks such as finding the true wind speed and direction from the apparent wind speed and direction. Apparent wind speed and direction were created by the ship's forward movement and had to be converted to true wind speed and direction using vectoring solutions.

The ship regularly conducted various emergency drills each week. During man overboard (MOB) drills, I began to learn how to plot out the ship's MOB maneuvers using Maneuvering Boards, and advised the conning officer of estimated bearing and range to the point of the MOB. Other emergency drills, which required the ship to go to GQ, provided opportunities to gain more time and proficiency in steering the ship as the GQ helmsman.

When the ship was at Watch Condition III, with watch rotations being four hours on, off eight hours, once per week, every watch station on board would "dog the watch." Dogging the watch allowed the crew to rotate through all the watches. In order to do that, it was necessary to split one of the watch periods in half to create an odd number of watches on that day. This allowed the watchstanding crew to shift to a different watch rotation instead of one watch team being forced to stand the mid-watch every night.

Some others and I really didn't care for the practice of dogging the watch. After about a week in a particular watch rotation, my body acclimated to when it could sleep, then we would dog the watch and the adjustment period would have to start all over again. The concept of circadian rhythm or internal body clock disruptions were unheard of at that time. So, every week, we purposely disrupted our internal body clocks, which for many caused several days of fatigue until our bodies once again adjusted to the schedule change.

Many aspects of shipboard life could be difficult. Adding to the difficulty was the existence of what I call the "dark underbelly" of the old destroyer life. The draft was winding down, but a fair number of our crew members were of a bit of a different cut. The only reason some were in the Navy was because a judge somewhere had given them the choice of either joining the military or going to jail. Others had simply joined the Navy after losing their draft deferment. Not to say all of them were bad guys, because most weren't.

A lot of these sailors were a bit older, and some were streetwise. There are distinct maturity differences between young men over the age of 21, as compared to many 18- or 19-year-olds. With the smaller crew sizes of surface combatant ships, a social pecking order was always present and sustained. Cliques made up of the older sailors were common and controlled the on-board gambling, loan scams, and drug dealing.

Some of these groups saw any new 18-year-old sailor reporting onboard as their next victim or score. One common tactic was one of the group members making a very friendly approach to the new crew member and inviting the younger guy to meet the rest of the group. It wouldn't be long before they would draw their newest score into a "friendly" card game. Normally, after several games, the friendly card game would turn into gambling and betting. Usually, by the time the card game was over, the new sailor would have lost a lot of money. If he didn't have the cash to pay up, now he had a gambling debt, sometimes amounting to hundreds of dollars. From that day on, his new so-called friends would be waiting at the end of the pay line each payday to collect their debt payments.

Another common scheme were the payday loans. When a sailor was short on cash between paydays, there were always guys that would loan them money to be repaid the next payday. Deals like a loan for $10 with a repayment of $15 were common. The loan repayment scales were normally $20 for $15, $27 for $20, $40 for $30, and so on. Great interest rates for the loaner. Sailors were decades ahead of today's popular payday loan industry.

So, what happened when someone failed to pay their gambling or loan debt as agreed? Ah, that was part of the underbelly. For failing to pay on time, the consequences ranged from just stern verbal warnings to the debtor and/or direct threats of violent action. On occasion, if the debtor failed to pay, there was physical retribution. However, if the group also dealt drugs, they would make the offer of allowing the debtor to work off part of the debt, usually requiring him to make the drug deal deliveries and drop-offs for them. This minimized the risk of any of the core group members getting caught.

The third clique was the guys that just sold drugs. To my knowledge, there were just a handful of crew members actually involved in the low-level selling of mainly marijuana. I think most had smuggled a lot of weed on board, more than needed for their own personal use, and decided to sell their excess. At that time, the punishment if caught using or dealing any type of drug was severe. If the charges went beyond Captain's Mast (Article 15, Non-Judicial Punishment) to a Court Martial, upon conviction it could end up involving a lengthy sentence to military or federal prison. Because of the severe penalties if caught, both dealers and their customers were very careful about what crew members could be trusted and which ones were a risk of being potential informants (narcs).

Personally, during my time onboard, I made it clear that I was a non-gambler, didn't borrow money, and didn't use drugs. I learned there was fine line between being a non-user and not being suspected of being a narc. I had been approached early on by the different groups after coming on board. I was always polite but stern in a friendly way with them. Once they understood that I couldn't care less about their activities, they tended to leave me alone.

Every week the junior QM made the rounds on the ship, winding and setting all of the ship's clocks. One day, while the ship was on its passage from Panama to Hawaii, I inadvertently gave myself a problem. When entering a compartment to wind a clock, I walked into the middle of a drug exchange between four or five guys. They quickly hid what they were doing and I pretended not to notice what had been going on. Later that day, a buddy of mine let me know I needed to watch my back, and the word was out that I might be a narc. Being labeled as a narc could be hazardous to your health. In some cases, those involved with drugs would try to intimidate the narc into keeping his mouth shut.

That night I had the 2000 to 2400 watch, and after getting off at midnight, I first went below to the berthing compartment. There, I stripped off my uniform shirt and T-shirt and made my way to the after head to wash up. Sure enough, while washing up at one of the lavatory sinks, the overhead red lights went out. Fortunately, I was at one of the end sinks next to a battle lantern mounted on the bulkhead. I quickly switched on the battle lantern's light in time to clearly see at least three people coming at me.

Keeping the bulkhead to my back, I punched the first guy in the throat. Thankfully, he went down fast. I could see the next guy was big, and I kicked him hard in the knees; as he went down, I hit him in the face hard with my right fist. What helped me a bit with the second guy was that the force from my blow to his face also caused his head to hit one of the sinks with a loud thud. He faded away into the dim light and darkness.

The third guy stopped in his tracks about four feet away. I recognized him and said his name. I think I told him he could either leave or come on and finish it. In the poor light he just seemed to vanish and was gone, leaving his two buddies. As I picked up my gear to leave, I could clearly see the other two guys still lying on the deck. I walked over and told both of them, "Never come after me again."

I wasn't sure of the purpose of the three guys rushing me. Was it just to intimidate or to actually do a beat down? Had I just put a stop to it all, or would it escalate further? Only time would tell. I have never considered myself to be a tough guy, and in this case, I'd just gotten lucky. I had learned to be a somewhat decent fighter as a teenager, but I tended to avoid fights. Back in the berthing compartment, my breathing was rapid, plus my hands were shaking. Guessing symptoms of a post-adrenaline rush, I shook it off.

Now, I was too keyed up to sleep, plus maybe the bastards might try again, so I got dressed, went up to the chart room, and spent the rest of the night sleeping in a chair. Later upon waking up, my right hand was stiff and painful. I turned on the white lights in the chart room to see the knuckles on my right hand were scraped and the top of the hand was swollen, so I hadn't escaped the fight injury free.

Later, going down to the chow line for breakfast, the second guy from the fight was in the chow line ahead of me. I was pleased to see dark nasty bruising and swelling around his left eye and cheek, with a goose egg on his right temple. Smiling, I said good morning to him, and asked him what had happened to his face. He looked away as he said something about falling down a ladder. All I said to him was, "Too bad."

Some of the other guys in line grinned at me with knowing smiles. That also told me that my problem was over. Slips, trips, and falls were common accidents on board destroyers. So, when anyone in a leadership position inquired after someone's injuries and they were told it was from a fall or a trip, that answer was easily accepted. From that day on, I never had any further issues with any of the on-board cliques.

Another aspect of a destroyer sailor's life was all about freshwater, or the lack thereof. All ships generally had to make their own freshwater. Ships with steam propulsion and auxiliary plants typically had at least two distilling units or evaporators that made all of the freshwater for the ship. Basically, seawater was pumped to a distilling unit from a sea chest located in the ship's underwater hull. Low pressure steam was circulated through tubes in the distilling plant, flashing the seawater surrounding the tubes into vapor. The vapor was cleaned by moisture separators then passed on and condensed from a vapor back into a liquid form called distillate or freshwater.

On the Gearing class destroyers, as with most naval ships, water conservation was practiced at all times while the ship was underway. Shower heads on ships had valves where shower water could be easily turned on and off. The crew could only take Navy showers, where the person ran just enough shower water to get wet, shut off the shower, soaped up, ran enough shower water to rinse off, and done. Crews only took "Hollywood" showers where they could use all the water they wanted when the ship was in-port and receiving freshwater from the pier. USS *Rich* often was plagued with evaporator operation or mechanical problems, which meant the ship's freshwater making capacity was sometimes severely reduced. When these evaporator issues occurred, the ship would be put on strict "water hours."

The priorities for freshwater usage were as follows: (1) Boiler feed water; (2) Cooking and galley; (3) Ship's laundry; (4) Drinking water; and (5) Head sinks and showers. If there was enough water, shower hours might be practiced where the showers were turned on for only several hours each day, or they might be secured all together. All shower piping valves would be shut and padlocked. Usually, only one of the ship's officers had the keys to the shower valve padlocks.

It was common for our crew to go days, sometimes several weeks, without showers. On occasion, some crew members would get possession of the shower valve padlock keys and attempt to sneak in a shower, but they almost always got caught. When everyone hadn't showered for days, body odor in the air became normal. If someone clean walked up, it was immediately noticeable that the person didn't stink and they were easily caught.

The usual punishment for those who violated water hours or no showers rules was the standing of extra watch hours at the evaporators in the engineering spaces. In Main Control (B-2, forward engine room) and in B-4 after engine room, the evaporators were located close to the main steam condenser and the deaerating feed tank, the hottest places in the space. Air temperatures of 125 degrees Fahrenheit and higher were common. The captain decided how many punishment evaporator watches a violator or violators might have to stand.

It wasn't just the lack of showering; when the ship's laundry was also shut down, after a number of days, no one had clean uniforms. We wore our cleanest dirty clothes. Most of us wore our socks and skivvies for as long as we could stand them, then just threw them away. Fortunately, the ship's store always seemed to carry a good supply of socks and skivvies that were cheaply priced, so at payday, we could replenish fairly inexpensively.

For our uniform dungarees and shirts, the only option was to tie them securely onto a small fiber line, then stream the line over the stern of the ship for about 15 minutes, giving our uniforms a thorough washing in seawater. It was common to find makeshift clotheslines in various spaces around the ship for drying uniforms. Before putting on a dry saltwater-washed uniform, it was a good idea to first shake as much salt as possible out of the cloth.

To help relieve the laundry and uniform issue, uniform standards were relaxed a bit. Since the air temperature was generally warm or hot, it was acceptable for the enlisted crew to do away with the wearing of their dungaree shirts and just wear T-shirts, dungaree pants, boondockers, and a ball cap. Except for when the ship was in port, this became the standard working uniform for most of the deployment.

One practice that sometimes would help alleviate the lack of freshwater for showers was finding rain squalls. In the warm Pacific Ocean waters, many afternoons the warm tropical air rising aloft would form cumulonimbus vertical development clouds. In tropical waters, cumulonimbus clouds would sometimes drop tremendous amounts of rainfall, but without the lightning and thunder associated with thunderstorms (i.e., the squall). If the squall line wasn't too far off of the ship's intended track, the OOD would call the captain, requesting permission to maneuver into the squall. If the captain granted permission, the OOD would have the word passed over the 1MC announcing throughout the ship, "Now rain squalls are off the starboard bow."

This was a cue for anyone not on watch to grab their soap, towel, and shower shoes, strip off their uniforms, and then race to the weather decks. It was an opportunity to take a free rain shower but out on the deck. It was a sight to see, the different open weather deck areas filled with buck-ass naked guys rushing to get wet in the downpour and soap up. One risk of taking a rain squall shower was that it might quit raining before getting all of the soap rinsed off, which did happen on some occasions. The only solution was to use a towel to wipe off the soap, which was not good.

Sometimes the OOD would maneuver the ship, trying to keep it in the area of heaviest rainfall to allow everyone time to complete showering. If the rain was heavy enough, the side benefit to the ship itself was that the rain provided an easy freshwater washdown, helping to get a lot of the accumulated salt off the superstructure and deck surfaces.

The ship's crew fell into the underway routine on the long passage to Hawaii. The weather and seas stayed calm as the ship cleared the west coast of Mexico well south of the Baja peninsula. According to the passage plan, the ship's courses were steered to direct the ship toward the Hawaiian Islands. About a week out from Panama, people began to take note that they were feeling really good, no longer suffering from colds, flu, or other short-term illnesses. The lack of these nuisance illnesses was explained pretty simply; the bacteria and viruses had run their course and were now gone. The members of the crew had been isolated long enough, without contact with people from off the ship, to get and stay healthy.

Some people commented that they felt better than they had in a long time. This experience of living in a cold- and illness-free environment was short-lived. It came to an end as soon as the ship entered into a port and the crew came into contact with people. In port, people coming on board or crew members having contact with people while off the ship introduced a new crop of bacteria and viruses on board. Then the cycle started all over again.

After more than another week of steaming, during the early morning hours of November 3, the ship began its approach from east of the island of Molokai. The intent was for the ship to pass north of Molokai and south of Oahu on the route to the entrance of Pearl Harbor. My watch was the 0800 to 1200 that morning and as Diamond Head on Oahu came into view, everyone on the bridge got a bit excited. The sea and anchor detail was set at noon, and as the ship continued along the south coast of Oahu, the city of Honolulu and the hotels along Waikiki Beach could be clearly seen.

The ship docked in the inner harbor at Pearl Harbor at 1300 that afternoon. Shortly after docking, we learned from the newspapers that President Richard Nixon had been reelected to a second term. What Nixon's reelection signified to some of us was that maybe, just maybe, we might be making a wasted trip.

The ship's stay in Pearl Harbor was for less than two days. We docked on Friday afternoon and there was liberty for the crew starting late Friday afternoon and all day on Saturday. Liberty expired for everyone at 0800 on Sunday. The ship was scheduled to depart Sunday morning at 1130. Many snipes didn't get liberty on Friday, since the ship needed to take on fuel oil, lube oil, fresh water, repair, and spare parts. The other crew members assigned to the Friday or Saturday duty sections spent most of their duty day loading stores, food, and other ship supplies on board.

On Friday night, Chip and I went on liberty together in Honolulu. Like most sailors, we ultimately made our way to the famous Hotel Street area in the Chinatown district. Hotel Street was populated with hundreds of bars, night clubs, nude shows, tattoo parlors, and brothels; a sailor's paradise on earth, if you will. Chip and I hit a good number of different bars and night spots. In one club, both of us were highly impressed with all of the gorgeous women at the bar. We ordered and got our drinks, sat at the bar, and surveyed the room.

After both of us spent some time ogling around the room, Chip turned to me and said, "I think some of these babes are probably hung better than we are."

I asked him, "You mean they're men, not women?"

Chip grinned and said, "Look, they have Adam's apples; only men have those."

Even with our awareness of what type of bar we were in, we stayed and had several more drinks before moving on; the view was just too good. Knowing this would be our last night of liberty until the ship got to the Philippines, we decided to hit as many bars as we could and drink as much as we could. After a night of substantial drinking, we made our way back to the ship sometime during the early hours of Saturday. I was in the Saturday duty section, which made for a long hard day of battling my hangover well into the afternoon.

Sunday, at 1130 in the morning, the ship took in her mooring lines as we got underway, leaving Pearl Harbor. The passage plan distance from Pearl Harbor to the Midway Islands was 1,150 nautical miles. About 70 hours later, on the morning of November 8, the ship began its approach to the Midway Islands. The ship steered a northerly course, heading directly between Sand and Eastern Islands until we could make out the channel, then we steered onto the navigational range markers, which were visually used to steer the ship in the center or axis of the channel.

The two main islands in the Midway Atolls are Eastern Island at the southeast end of the atoll, which is triangular in shape, about 1.2 miles long, and 6 to 12 feet in elevation. The largest island, Sand Island, is on the south side of the atoll, about 2 miles long in a southwest direction, composed mainly of white coral and sand.

Just west of Eastern Island, close to the shipping channel, is Spit Island which really looks like a large sand bar, about 15 acres in size. As we made the approach, my sea and anchor detail assignment was as the starboard bearing taker. On Spit Island, there were several rusting ship and boat hulks we assumed had been there since World War II. The waters around the islands were a brilliant turquoise color. In the shipping channel waters I was able to spot green sea turtles in the water along with large patrolling sharks. There were big monk seals nesting on the shore of Eastern Island. We were bound for the Naval Air Station docks on Sand Island. The ship arrived and docked for refueling at the dock on Sand Island at 0930. It was going to be a short stay in Midway, just long enough to refuel the ship, which would take about four hours.

If you're a nature fanatic, Sand and Eastern Islands should be on your bucket list of places to see. The islands are teeming with hundreds of species of birds and other wildlife. The seabird the area is principally known for is the Laysan albatross, more commonly called the "gooney bird" because of their awkward, somewhat un-acrobatic landings, and their strange mating rituals. However, once the gooney bird is airborne with a wingspan up to six feet, their grace in flight is impressive.

Once the ship was docked and fueling was in progress, the crew was free to leave the ship and explore the area.

The area immediately outside of the dock area was more like a park setting, with shelters, picnic tables, and benches. There were literally hundreds, if not thousands, of gooney birds sitting everywhere on the ground; it was definitely a place to watch your step, as the birds also pooped everywhere. At that time, the Navy still operated the air station on Sand Island and it was the normal refueling location for Navy and Military Sea Lift ships bound to or coming from Vietnam.

Since the crew was off the ship, ice cold beer was broken out and anyone who wanted could have their limit of two beers. The beer tasted great since it was free of the formaldehyde preservative found in most beers meant for prolonged storage before drinking.

The ship departed from the dock on Sand Island at 1330 bound for Arpa Harbor, Guam. The passage plan distance was 2,635 nautical miles from Midway to Guam. The passage would take a little less than seven days of steaming through the mid-Pacific Ocean waters. The next day, November 9, was a major event when the ship crossed over the International Date Line, from west longitude to east longitude. The weather for the next week at sea was generally good, with fairly gentle winds and mostly clear skies. There was a distinctive and significant sea swell coming in from a general direction south of west, which caused the ship to take on a rhythmical fore-and-aft up and down pitching while meeting and slicing through each swell.

With the passing days and weeks at sea, I continued learning more about ship navigation, weather, and maintenance of navigation charts and publications. Chip and the QMs were always willing to lend assistance, so coupled with studying on my own, reading, and practice helped me to continuously improve. Now after nearly four months of working as a quartermaster, I was feeling better about my life as a "fresh air sailor" and doing less mourning about the loss of what I thought was my destiny of being an engineer.

As the ship got to less than 1,000 nautical miles from Guam, there was a change in direction of the sea swells. They had increased in size and were more frequent. This change in the seas was explained that night when we received a weather message with tropical storm warnings with the storm center located northeast of Guam. The ship arrived at the entrance to Arpa, Guam, early in the morning on November 15.

After picking up the harbor and docking pilot in the entrance channel, the ship was maneuvered to its assigned dock in the inner harbor. The purpose for the stop was the same as it had been at Midway, to refuel the ship. One big difference for this stop was the bags of mail waiting on the dock. The ship had not received mail since leaving Pearl Harbor 10 days before. In those days, getting mail was a big deal, as the primary means of communication with wives and families was via letters sent and received by mail. The ship's postal clerk would always hurry to get the mail sorted and everyone on board waited to hear the announcement over the ship's 1MC intercom system, "Now, mail call."

It turned out that this mail call was disappointing for some. The ship, an Atlantic Fleet ship, had been away from home port just under one month. The assigned Fleet Post Office (FPO) was New York. Now that the ship was in the Pacific theater, mail to the ship had to be rerouted from FPO New York to FPO San Francisco, then flown to Hawaii and from there to Guam. In other words, there hadn't been enough elapsed time yet for all the mail to catch up to the ship. The average time to get a letter sent from home in the U.S. was about four weeks. We would find out later in Vietnam that the amount of time to receive a letter from home would increase to about six weeks; for packages it was about seven to eight weeks. It would take about the same amount of time for mail sent from the ship to get home, about six weeks.

There were two cardinal rules married sailors needed to learn and follow: (1) Never write and send a letter to your wife chewing her out for not writing you, because as soon as you sent that bitching letter, you would get a letter from her the next day; (2) both of you should sequentially number all of your letters, so you each knew when a received letter was out of sequence. Other military couples we had met who had been through family separations and deployments had explained to Jan and me how important it was for each person to sequentially number their letters. Following these rules really helped avoid misunderstandings and prevented either party from needlessly getting pissed off. I have no statistics to back this up, but by simply following the mail cardinal rules, it's possible that many married military couples avoided further martial separation stress and/or committed revenge screw-ups.

After refueling the ship in Arpa, we got underway at 1400 that afternoon and steamed back out to sea. Once the ship was in open water, a westerly course was set to the San Bernardino Strait in the Philippine Islands. The passage plan distance was 1,655 nautical miles from Guam to Subic Bay on Luzon via the San Bernardino Strait. The passage would take a little less than three days of steaming through the Western Pacific Ocean waters. The planned overall SOA was 23 knots versus the normal transit speed of 16 knots. The next day, November 16, we had caught up to Typhoon #29, Typhoon Ruby. By today's standards, Ruby would be a Category 3 Typhoon on the Saffir-Simpson Scale. The Saffir-Simpson Scale provides some indication of the potential damage and flooding a hurricane will cause at landfall, so it's meaningless to a mariner at sea. The winds in this typhoon were forecast to reach up to 110 knots (126 mph).

The danger for any ship at sea in the vicinity of an Atlantic hurricane or Pacific typhoon has to do with the size of the body of water (the fetch area) and the fetch. Fetch is the area in which ocean waves are generated by the wind. It also refers to the length of the fetch area measured in the direction of the wind. With sustained and mounting winds in a large fetch area, like an ocean, the winds can generate big sea waves. As the surface pressure lowers in and around the storm's center, the wind circling in a counter-clockwise direction (in the northern hemisphere) about the storm's center will increase both in velocity and intensity nearly in step with lowering surface pressure. The longer the period of time the wind is in place, the higher the potential is for the sea waves to build to their maximum height. Sea wave height is measured vertically from the wave trough to the crest at the top of the wave. So, when one states the seas are 20 to 25 feet, they mean the distance from the wave trough to the top of the wave crest is 20 to 25 feet.

The ship began to experience ever-increasing waves, and the wind had veered around to the west and southwest. Each hour, both the wave size and wind speed continued to incrementally increase. By the afternoon, the ship was in the midst of a powerful Pacific typhoon. The good news was that we were fairly certain the ship's position was on the left side of the typhoon's track, also called the navigable semicircle. We also knew we were in a position ahead of the storm's track and possibly could just outrun the storm.

Destroyers were fast ships, but because of their propensity to excessively pitch, roll, and yaw, big waves could cause the ship's stern and propellers to come clear of the water's surface. When that happened, the propeller might experience over-cavitation, possibly causing damage to the propeller or propeller shafting. Generally, when maneuvering destroyers in big sea states, propeller shaft revolutions are set to not exceed 12 knots, which is considered prudent in avoiding damage to the propulsion system.

The other issue was with speed. When the ship's hull was pounding into the seas, it could put too much stress and strain on the ship's hull structure and strength members. Many ships have experienced hull failure in big sea conditions where the result was a quick foundering and sinking of the ship.

Generally, the convention for tropical storm avoidance maneuvers was for a ship in the northern hemisphere and on the left side of the storm's projected path or the navigable semicircle to bring the wind on the starboard quarter, hold course, and make all possible headway.

On November 16, my first watch for the day was the mid-watch. The pass down from the prior 2000 to 2400 watch included information that the captain and XO had decided to keep the ship's true course of 285 degrees (15 degrees north of west) and had ordered speed of 23 knots throughout the night to see if we could get ahead of the typhoon. The idea was that carrying out a storm avoidance maneuver would take us too far south away from our intended passage. Since we believed our ship was ahead of the storm track, the decision was made to make best speed possible and proceed with our intended route in accordance with the passage plan.

The "Night Orders" from the captain included instructions to closely monitor the barometric pressure, wind, and sea state and inform him if there were significant changes, particularly a steep drop in barometric pressure. Throughout the watch, the wind and the size of the sea waves continued to build.

By the time the 0400 to 0800 watch came on, the ship was rolling 25 to 30 degrees to either side and heaving and pitching fore-and-aft. I went below to the berthing compartment with the intent of getting a couple hours of sleep. The berthing compartment was hot, humid, with loose water sloshing around on the deck, plus someone had gotten seasick and not cleaned it up. After about an hour of trying to sleep while hanging onto my rack to keep from getting thrown out of it from the violent rolling of the ship, I decided to get up.

I spent the next hour or so dozing in a chair up in the chart room. After reveille, I made my way down to the galley to see if anything was going to be served for breakfast. There were only a couple guys in line at the galley, so it didn't take long for one of the cooks to make me a couple of fried eggs and bologna, because that's about all they could make in the rough sea conditions. With my eggs and bologna on my tray, I made the trip one deck below to the mess decks to make toast and hopefully get some juice or coffee. It was too much of a challenge to keep the food tray from flying off the mess deck's table and eat at the same time, so I slapped the eggs and bologna into two slices of toast. After a long night, that fried egg and bologna sandwich tasted great. From that day on, fried egg and bologna sandwiches became my favorite breakfast.

After breakfast, I went back up to the chart room and talked with the QM on watch for a while as he attempted to get some usable TD lines of position from Loran. Having nothing else to do, I went back up to the bridge to see what was going on. Now that the sun was up, I could see the huge waves coming at our ship one after another. I watched the anemometer, which at one point indicated the apparent wind speed at 95 knots, which I quickly converted to the equivalent true wind speed of about 70 knots. The QM on watch showed me that with 23 knots of speed rung up, based on two successive Loran fix positions, the ship was really only making about 14 knots good over the ground. With the present weather conditions, it was going to be a long day at sea.

By the afternoon watch (1200 to 1600), the fetch had done its job. This was my first tropical storm experience on a ship underway in open ocean. The winds and seas had become dangerous. We began to record true wind gusts in excess of 90 knots (104 mph), but the waves were approaching 40 feet in height, slamming in one after the other just off the port bow. Except for wind gusts, the sustained true wind speed consistently ranged between about 65 to 75 knots (74 to 86 mph). On what was known as the Beaufort wind force scale, we were in maximum force 12 conditions where the air was filled with foam and spray; the sea was completely white with driving spray; sea wave height was 45 feet; plus, visibility was very seriously affected. For mariner purposes, we stopped trying to estimate the height of the waves at 50 feet, and from that point on it was just called 50 feet plus.

The ship was experiencing heavy rolling and pitching, and we could see as the waves broke over the bow that the forward gun, mount 51, was submerging with each breaking wave. Above the helm station, mounted from the overhead, was a clinometer used for measuring the angle of roll. During some of the more severe rolls, the helmsman would call out the angle of roll from the clinometer. On many rolls, the helmsman would wait until the ship was at the end of a roll and call out the angle of the roll. He began to report roll angles of 40 or more degrees. At the same time, to reduce pounding, the ship's ordered speed was slowed from 23 knots down to 15 knots.

Everyone on the watch kept doing their respective jobs in spite of the ship's extreme motions. Each person did their best in trying to hang onto anything that could prevent them from being thrown around the bridge. Suddenly, the OOD and I saw something coming at the same time through the bridge windows. The OOD yelled to everyone, "Hang on."

For our ship, the height from the waterline to the bridge level was about 40 feet. What the OOD and I had seen was a huge mountainous wave towering above the ship coming in fast, just off the port bow. From my position on the starboard side of the bridge near the chart table, I had to bend over and look up to see the crest of this wave. As the wave slammed into the ship, we rolled heavily and fast to starboard, and the helmsman yelled out the angles from the clinometer: 55 degrees, 60 degrees, and finally, 67 degrees. I was watching out the window of the starboard bridge door, and it looked as if the starboard bridge wing was about to dip into the water. The ship seemed to hang at that angle forever, then finally the ship began to shudder. Groaning noises sounded as it slowly began to roll back upright.

Just as the ship came upright and began to roll to port into the wave trough, another monster wave, just as huge as the last one, slammed into the ship. The ship was heeled over about 25 degrees to port when this wave hit the ship. This time the ship acted differently from before. The ship went into "green water." The green water in this case meant that both the entire ship's hull and superstructure submerged into the breaking wave. As the ship went underwater, the helmsman yelled out the clinometer reading of 50 degrees to port.

Looking out the bridge windows kind of reminded me of being in an aquarium; the entire bridge was submerged. For several moments, it seemed the ship would just stay underwater, but once again the shuddering and groaning noises began as the ship recovered from the roll. Within several seconds we once again could see the seas and sky through the bridge windows. What we had just experienced was not just one, but two successive rogue waves.

At that time, the term was not used. Many scientists considered rogue waves to be just a myth and were not real. Well, I can tell you, the damn science was wrong. Back then we just described those waves for what they really were: big ass waves.

That afternoon the ship took green water several more times; all of the waves were just big ass waves, period. Several hours after being relieved of the watch at 1600, the severity and forcefulness of the ship's rolling and pitching seemed somewhat reduced as compared to what it had been earlier in the day. I hadn't eaten since breakfast; many in the crew had also not eaten that day, as it had just been too rough. Those who had them got by eating saltine crackers. I put in a wake-up call on the bridge for 2300 and hit my rack to try to get some sleep before the mid-watch.

When the messenger of the watch woke me at 2300, I hopped up and out of my rack. As I was dressing, I realized that the ship's rolling and pitching had lessened even more. I made my way to the galley to see what was being served for mid-rats (midnight rations). Damn, another score of a fried egg and bologna sandwich with coffee and bug juice (a type of Kool-Aid) for my mid-rats meal. Now, I would be going on watch with something in my stomach.

On arriving on the bridge, it appeared that the weather conditions had improved considerably from seven hours earlier. The QM and the OOD seemed sure that Typhoon Ruby was well astern of us now and we were continuing to open the distance. It appeared the immediate danger from the typhoon was over. I chalked it up as my first experience with a tropical storm at sea. Over the next 12 hours of steaming through the Philippine Sea, the weather conditions continued to improve; by morning, the western skies were fairly clear and the sea waves had reduced to a more than manageable height of 16 feet or less.

The next afternoon, the ship was approaching the San Bernardino Strait. The San Bernardino Strait is a strait in the Philippines connecting the Philippine Sea with the Samar Sea. The strait separates the Bicol Peninsula of Luzon Island to the north from the island of Samar to the south. As the ship approached the northern entrance of the strait, we sighted Mount Bulusan to our north. Mount Bulusan is one of the active volcanoes in the Philippines.

The passage plan distance from the entrance of the San Bernardino Strait to Subic Bay on the southwest coast of Luzon was about 240 nautical miles. Most of the transit would take place at night through the northern islands' passages to Subic Bay. After getting off watch, the Navigation Detail was set for the rest of the passage. As we came closer to northern point of Samar Island and the San Bernardino Islands, the topography of the islands ranged from high bluffs and cliffs to areas of dense vegetation and jungle.

One of the junior officers made the comment that many of the islands are so remote and isolated that it was possible there still could be Japanese soldiers from World War II in the Philippine Island jungles. It turned out his comment was not that far off the mark. Less than two years later, during the spring of 1974, Second Lieutenant Hiroo Onoda of the Japanese army made world headlines when he emerged from the jungle on Lubang Island after 30 years. Lieutenant Onoda was convinced that World War II was still being fought. In 1999, his book was published titled *No Surrender: My Thirty-Year War*.

The QM gang stayed on the navigation detail throughout the night as the ship navigated its way through the Ticao Passage, then between Ticao and Burias Islands into the Sibuyan Sea. The navigation detail is different from the sea and anchor detail. When the navigation detail was set, the QMs assisted the navigator in more frequently fixing the vessel's position. Here the method of navigation is all piloting navigation, where the vessel's movement is directed by frequently determining the ship's position using visual compass bearing and/or radar bearings and ranges to fixed and charted aids or objects. Soundings (actual depths of the water under the ship's keel compared to the charted depths) to help confirmed the actual position are also used. The westward passage took the ship through the Sibuyan Sea, then through the Verde Island Passage. From the Verde Island Passage, the ship steamed northwest along the coast of Luzon to Subic Bay.

The ship docked the next morning, November 18, at the Subic Bay Naval Station in Subic Bay Harbor at 0710. The transit from Norfolk to Subic Bay had taken one month and one day, 32 days total. Of the 32-day transit, almost 29 of those days had been at sea. The ship would remain in Subic Bay for six days while making the necessary preparations and alterations to enter the combat zone of Vietnam. Our ship was docked at Pier 16-17, Rivera Point Ship Repair Facility.

The ship was moored with our starboard side to outboard of USS *Hepburn* (DE 1055), and USS *Parks* (DD 884) was moored outboard on our port side. We were scheduled to depart Subic Bay early in the morning on Friday, November 24. The passage plan distance from Subic Bay to Military Region I located in northern South Vietnam was about 805 nautical miles. The passage to Vietnam would take close to 37 hours at the planned passage speed of 22 knots.

From our berth, USS *Warrington* (DD 842) was clearly visible where she was moored at another berth in the ship repair facility. The ship was abandoned now and had a mystic look about her similar to that of an empty and deserted old house. On July 16, Warrington had come under the rapid and heavy fire of North Vietnamese shore batteries. The destroyer had been able to take prompt evasive action and avoided damage. Later that same afternoon, though, the ship was rocked by two underwater explosions close aboard on her port side. It turned out that the ship had not received warning messages and entered an area where U.S. aircraft jettisoned bombs and mines, so the mines the ship had stuck were ours. She had suffered serious damage in her after fire room, engine room, and in the main engine room or main control.

Warrington's crew had been able to control the damage and flooding from the mine explosions, which enabled the ship to retire from the area under her own power. Ultimately, it was determined that the ship was so badly damaged that she had to be towed to Subic Bay. Once the ship was back at Subic Bay, the Navy's initial intent was to repair the ship and return her to service, but in August, an inspection and survey found her to be unfit for further naval service. *Warrington* was decommissioned on September 30 in Subic Bay. The now deserted and dark USS *Warrington* stood as a stark reminder to me and many in our crew of what could happen to any ship operating in the waters along Vietnam's coast.

While the ship was in Subic Bay, the crew and the ship repair facility personnel were carrying out many different preparations. All types of equipment and supplies were loaded. About 200 flak jackets were loaded on board, a type of body armor, but they wouldn't stop a bullet. They were effective at stopping flak or shrapnel from high explosive weapons. Flak jackets were bulky and hot to wear, weighed about eight pounds, and were made from layers of ballistic nylon.

Starlight Scopes, which were night vision devices, were added to the bridge equipment. We found later that these devices were bulky, awkward to handle, and required moonlight to actually function well at night, so their use was limited.

For close in-ship protection, ship repair weapons personnel installed Browning .30 caliber medium machine guns at various locations on the ship, including just aft of the port and starboard bring wings. Several M2 Browning .50 caliber heavy machine guns were installed as deck guns on the ship's main deck. The gunners mates and fire controlmen were busy with maintenance tasks on the 5-inch/38 caliber main guns and the Fire Control radar and director systems.

Over the course of several days, we moved the ship around the Subic Bay docks multiple times using tug boats. We made each movement with tug boats as "dead stick" moves since the ship's engineering plant was in cold iron status. One move was to the ammunition depot docks to do a complete ammunition on-load of 5-inch artillery rounds and powder cases, small arms ammunition, chaff, and flare rounds. The next stop was over to the fuel docks to refuel the ship, then back to our original berth at Pier 16-17 Rivera Point Ship Repair Facilities.

The day after our arrival in Subic Bay was my first opportunity to get off the ship to call home. The Subic Bay Naval Base had a huge International Telephone Exchange office. In the world of today's cellular and smart phones and international dialing, the procedure for making an international call in 1972 probably will seem really archaic. To make a telephone phone call from Subic Bay to the United States was a process. One had to remember that the local zone time in the Philippines was 13 hours ahead of the time in the U.S. Central Standard Time zone. If you wanted your phone call to be received early to mid-evening back home, you needed to make the phone call at local times of 0730 to 0830.

At the telephone exchange office, the first step is to fill out your call request form. On the call request form you had to say what would be the phone call duration. Once you submitted your completed call request form to a clerk, they would collect the payment for the phone call and hand you a slip of paper with the telephone assignment and your waiting number. Depending upon the time of day and how busy they were, your wait could range from minutes to several hours. Once they called your waiting number, you made your way to the assigned telephone. On picking up the telephone, an overseas operator would be on the line to verify the telephone number of the party you are calling. The overseas operator would make the connection to the long distance operator in the U.S. The U.S. long distance operator would dial the phone number you were calling. Once you could hear ringing on the line, you prayed that somebody on the other end would pick up the telephone.

Luckily, Jan answered the telephone after a couple of rings. I had paid for 20 minutes of phone time, which might seem like an ample amount of time. Yet while on the phone with Jan, time went by like a flash. As always, it was great to hear that all was going well at home with her and our son. We had last spoken when I had called her from Pearl Harbor about two weeks before. We filled the last minute of the phone call with each of us telling the other how much we missed one another and multiple exchanges of "I love you." Then, the operator terminated the call and the phone line went dead.

After hanging up the phone, a sense of loneliness and sadness suddenly came over me. In my mind, a voice was telling me, "This was the last time you will ever talk her." I didn't know exactly why these depressed feeling were happening. As I had learned to do early in life, I shook the bad vibes off and made the walk back to the ship.

Something had been happening with me since departing Guam and had been weighing on me, which I had kept strictly to myself. I had begun to have two different recurring dreams. Both dreams were unsettling, disturbing, and always ended in the same way. In the first dream, the ship was out at sea. I would be on the ship's bridge wing, looking out over the water to the visible horizon. I would spot a small dark dot near the horizon some distance out. The dot appeared to be moving through the air coming closer and directly at me fast, traveling at a high rate of speed. Just as the dot would get to me, I could see it was going to hit me right between my eyes, then, *Bam*, sudden total black darkness and silence. At that point, I would startle myself awake.

The second dream was in certain respects similar to the first. I would once again be on the bridge wing, except this time the ship was very close to a shoreline. The shore area looked to have low sandy beaches backed by high sand dunes and a dense tree line further inland. On the water between the shore and the ship, two small impact geysers of water from shore gun fire appeared. One after another, the successive small impact geysers would appear each time getting closer in range as if the rounds were being walked out purposefully with each firing to eventually get to and then hit the ship. The last set of impact geysers appeared very close to the ship and just a little to my left, then "Bam," the same sudden total black darkness and silence. It would end the same way, with my startling myself awake.

The only way I could interpret the two dreams was that my subconscious mind was telling me that I was going to die. Sounds a bit melodramatic, doesn't it? My rational side told me to just ignore the dreams and forget them. Obviously, neither of them came true. However, there was a later event when that sense of déjà vu hit me right afterward, where I realized what had just happened was very similar to the second of these two dreams.

7. FIRST ARRIVAL

While in Subic Bay, the crew was granted all-night liberty each day. The only place to go was right outside the main gate of the base, Olongapo City. I reckon that any sailor who has ever been to Subic Bay has memories from their time in Olongapo City. It was an easy walk from the docks to Magsaysay Drive and then to the main gate. Right outside the main gate was a combination vehicle and foot bridge leading into town, spanning a drainage canal from the Santa Rita River.

The drainage canal was famously known as "Shit River." Crossing the Shit River bridge was everyone's first experience as they make their way into Olongapo City. Down on the water in small boats beneath the bridge there were always a bunch of beggar Filipino kids from the barrio. The kids would beg sailors to throw coins in the water so they could dive and retrieve them. The name Shit River was accurate because the canal was ripe with sewage and dirty water from the town. We heard that many of these kids didn't live to be very old, because most died of diseases from their constant exposure to the water.

Ahead of the bridge huge billboard-type signs advertising Sansui and Pioneer stereos; a huge Marmont Restaurant sign was on the right. After the bridge, Magsaysay Drive continued as the main drag.

175

Magsaysay Drive was always busy and bustling with sailors, pedestrians, Jeepneys, motor scooters, and bicycles everywhere. Jeepneys are still used today, and are the most popular means of public transportation in the Philippines. They got their start as Willys Jeeps, left behind when America departed the Philippines at the end of World War II. Jeepneys are Jeeps modified to carry more passengers, and they're painted with all kinds of brilliant colors with lots of chrome and highly decorative cloth awnings. Some people consider Jeepneys to be works of art.

What also lined Magsaysay Drive were countless street vendors, bars, restaurants, shops, and night spots; another paradise for sailors on earth. Street vendors constantly came up to us trying to sell us "monkey meat" cooked on wooden skewers. I think most of the monkey meat was really dog meat, or only God knows, some other small animal. Along Magsaysay Drive, the sidewalks were concrete, but the road was mostly an unpaved dirt road with a narrow concrete slab running right down the middle. Fortunately, it didn't rain much while we were there. They told us that when they got heavy rains the streets turned to mud.

Live music could be heard coming from each bar out in the street. You would hear Chicago coming from one bar, Deep Purple from the next, then Janis Joplin and the Rolling Stones. We weren't hearing records or recordings; these were live Filipino bands and singers in each bar. It was a marvel to listen to them; if you closed your eyes, you would swear the real band or artist was playing on each stage as they were that good. Just imagine thinking you were hearing Johnny Cash, so you walked into the place. There on the stage was a Filipino less than five feet tall, wearing black jeans and a western style shirt, with cowboy boots, singing "Ring of Fire."

Olongapo City was under martial law and had been for many years, so the town had mandatory curfew starting at midnight until 5:00 a.m. each morning. The words of warning were, "Do not get caught violating curfew; the Olongapo City police have the authority to shoot anyone on sight they find on the streets after curfew." So our crew had overnight liberty in a town with a mandatory curfew starting at midnight. Now there was the formula for the making of some damn good sea stories.

The U.S. Marines, the Armed Forces Police with their notorious white helmets, Navy shore patrols, and the local Olongapo City Police all rigidly enforced the curfew laws. For the sailors on liberty, the curfew dictated that the daily partying had to start early. While aboard the ship, they routinely reminded us that while on liberty, we were still responsible for acting in a civilized manner, and that we represented the United States Navy to the Filipino people. Uh-huh. Yeah, right!

I recall one club on the right side of Magsaysay Drive that had a small pond out in front with a wrought-iron type fence around the water. The pond held live crocodiles about five feet in length. A woman with a large basket would sell live baby chickens to customers. Once you had bought your baby chicken, you were supposed to toss it in the pond for the crocodiles. Usually the one of the crocodiles would at first just push the baby chick around, as if playing with it, then suddenly it would open its jaws wide and chomp down. Just another oddity one could see in Olongapo City.

Most bars on request would serve the Filipino delicacy "balut." A balut is a developing bird embryo (usually a duck or chicken) boiled and eaten from the shell. Baluts were sold as street food or in bars, usually served with beer. Some guys felt that it was some type of rite of passage to eat a whole balut and wash it down with beer. I had no desire to try one, which was justified when most people who did eat one hurled it up anyway. No thanks!

One thing about Olongapo City: everything was cheap. One Philippine dollar, or peso, was equivalent to about 15 U.S cents. For example, the standard price for one San Miguel beer was about two pesos. A good meal at one of the restaurants might cost twelve pesos, about two U.S. dollars, including the tip. A big day/night on the town, which included a meal, all the alcoholic beverages you could drink, drinks for the bar girls, and for some, taking a bar girl home, cost between $8 and $10, or around 53 to 67 pesos for the whole day.

Anyone who ever entered any bar in Olongapo City experienced the immediate visit from the bar girl. The Filipino bar girl experience could be a nuisance, especially if one just wanted to have a drink or two alone or with a buddy. It was a bit like trying to walk onto a used car lot just to look at the cars and not wanting to be bothered by a salesperson. That just wasn't going to happen. However, the Filipino bar girls were something to behold, always well dressed, young, attractive, and very friendly. Usually the first full sentence you heard from any Filipino bar girl after the word "hello" was the question, "Buy me a drink, Joe?"

Most guys would just order a San Miguel beer. All had to quickly learn another guideline: never buy a bar girl her requested drink unless you didn't mind being stuck with that particular girl for the entire night. The drinks bought for bar girls were served in small glasses not much bigger than shot glasses. Their drinks contained no alcohol and usually it was just iced tea or cola, but it cost about twice as much as your beer.

Often, once guys found a bar they liked, they would selectively buy the bar girl of their choice the "drink." Once one had bought their bar girl several drinks and was starting on their way to getting a bit drunk, the girl would often whisper in their ear, "I be your girlfriend? Okay." Many sailors on their first visit to the Philippines would answer that question with "Okay," not realizing it was a bit like agreeing to "go steady," at least for the week. If the sailor went home with that girl for the night, in the bar girl's mind, the girlfriend deal had been consummated. Her expectation was now that for the duration of the sailor's stay, he would come to her bar and be with her every night. Now, how many sailors do you suppose would actually do that? Not many. They would "butterfly."

Sailors butterflied when the next night they would go to a different bar and go home with a different bar girl for the night. A butterfly cheated on bar girl number one with bar girl number two. Amazingly, girl number one would know about the butterfly act with bar girl number two the next day. If the man was stupid enough to go back to the bar where girl number one worked, within moments after entering he would hear the immediate accusation, "You butterfly with other girl."

The bar girl despised butterflies because a sailor discarded them so quickly after he had them, like a butterfly. A butterfly was someone who moved from one bar to another, a little like bar hopping, only here it was girl hopping. A guy that was a butterfly was the lowest of the low on a Filipino bar girl's shit list. It was best to back out slowly and go to another place. I'm sure there are some sailors who bear scars caused by expertly wielded "butterfly knives" at the hands of highly pissed-off Filipino bar girls.

There was an interesting phenomenon associated with Filipino bar girls and certain sailors. I witnessed this phenomenon personally more than once and it seemed to only affect young and really naïve (you can read that as stupid) sailors. It occurred when a young sailor returned from a big night or two in town and made an announcement to his shipmates. The sailor would profess his absolutely amazing luck in finding the only Filipino bar girl in the world that was different from the rest; she was the love of his life, and therefore, the ideal marriage partner.

Luckily, back then, enlisted personnel in pay grades E-5 and below needed to get the permission of their commanding officer to get married. This often did not deter the sailor from submitting his "request chit" immediately up his respective Chain-of-Command: *Request permission to get married before the ship departs from port.*

This is where leadership and some counseling had to happen to make the sailor understand that his request was not a good idea. Surprisingly, many senior petty officers and division officers would exercise good patience and some degree of tolerance in dealing with their sailors. Often, they would calmly explain to the individual concerned that if this girl was really the one, he should take his time, complete the deployment first, then see if the feelings were still the same. Below decks, fellow sailors were more pointed. They would just tell the guy to wake up and not be a dumbass. To my knowledge, no one from the *Rich* crew actually married an Olongapo City bar girl. However, some guys did end up carrying reminders of their recreational activities from their time in Olongapo City.

Navy ships published and distributed their plan of the day (POD) every day, seven days a week. The daily POD covered the routine and ship's schedule of activities for the day and was an effective communication tool between the command and the crew. The POD also included notes pertaining to various topics ranging from world event news to more specific information regarding evolutions or tasks the ship would be carrying out that day. As an example of POD notes, the following was published in the ship's POD as Note 3, nine days after the ship departed from Subic Bay:

3. *PERSONAL CLEANLINESS*

It has become obvious since our departure that the lovely girls of Olongapo City are not the most hygienic in the world. Their unsanitary habits, coupled with a lack of soap and water on the part of some RICHMEN, have resulted in what is called balanitis. This is not venereal disease, but it does result in severe pain and inflammation of the penis and surrounding area. It is commonly associated with poor local genital hygiene habits. All hands are reminded, that even though you must take a Navy shower to conserve water, don't forget to wash, rinse, and dry your genital area thoroughly.

On the other hand, however, there have been a dozen cases of bona fide VD reported on board since Subic Bay and the number is increasing every day. VD can be easily cured if reported early. So if in doubt, contact the friendly chief corpsman in Sickbay. All consultations are kept in the strictest privacy, of course.

The day before the ship was to depart from Subic Bay was also Thanksgiving Day. The ship's cooks served the traditional Thanksgiving dinner on board. Of course, turkey, mashed potatoes, gravy, and all the traditional side dishes were on the menu. The cooks tried to do well, but Navy food was still just Navy food; it couldn't hold a candle to Thanksgiving Day meals back home. Most of us found that the turkey, cranberry sauce, and biscuits were the best parts of the meal. Later, they probably carried the rest of the prepared meal to the dumpsters on the pier, where it belonged.

Our six days in Subic Bay raced by and the next day it was time to once again get the ship underway and leave. At 0652 local time, Friday, November 24, USS Rich got underway and departed from Subic Bay bound for Military Region I (MR1) in northern South Vietnam. The passage plan distance from Subic Bay to MR1 was 806 nautical miles. It would take the ship about 35 hours at the planned speed of advance of 22 knots to arrive near MR1. Material condition "YOKE" was set throughout the ship, all ship fittings marked with black *Xs* and *Ys*, Circle *X* and Circle *Y* are closed. A modified condition YOKE was sometimes used at sea when cruising independently in good weather, calm seas, and in port in peacetime. Material conditions established the fighting and watertight integrity of the ship to maintain its survivability. The determination of the material condition set at any time was the responsibility of the commanding officer, who might authorize modifications to any material condition.

That afternoon during the 1200 to 1600 watch, the ship exercised the crew at GQ. Material condition "ZEBRA" was set throughout the ship. When condition ZEBRA was set on a ship, it provided the greatest degree of subdivision and watertight integrity to the ship. ZEBRA was the maximum state of readiness for the ship's survivability system. It was set immediately and automatically when general quarters was sounded and whenever the ship entered or left port in wartime. Condition YOKE provided a greater degree of watertight integrity than condition "X-RAY," but to a lesser degree than the maximum condition. YOKE was normally set at sea and in port during wartime.

During this GQ, the 5-inch/38 caliber twin mount guns were fired as an exercise to refresh the gun and fire control crews. The ship fired a total of 36 high explosive rounds using 36 rounds of full service powder cartridges. Eighteen rounds were fired from mount 51 forward, nine rounds from each gun, and eighteen rounds were fired from mount 52 aft, nine rounds from each gun.

On Gearing class destroyers all 5-inch/38 caliber twin gun mounts sat on a base ring stand. Each gun mount's ammunition handling room, called the "upper handling room," was found directly below the mount. For example, the upper handling room for the after gun mount 52 was right smack in the middle of the operations berthing compartment (where I lived), which was located on the first deck, one deck below the main deck of the ship. Though the 5-inch/38 caliber twin gun development dated from the 1930s, the weapon technology was still valid for use in naval gunfire applications like Vietnam. The 5-inch/38 caliber gun mount was equipped with horizontal periscopic sights with movable-prism sight setting, two powered fuze setting projectile hoists, two powered powder case hoists, powered training drive, and elevating drive.

The 5-inch projectile has three major parts: body, fuze, and the explosive charge. The projectile body is a machined steel tube with a conical head at one end. At the conical head and rear ends are threaded openings for installing the shell's filler and to hold the fuze. Around the tube near the base is a copper alloy ring called the "rotating band." This band has a diameter larger than the gun's bore, and when the projectile and powder case are rammed into the chamber, the band is jammed into the grooves of the bore's rifling. It forms a gas seal between the projectile and the gun's bore. Also, as the projectile travels down the gun's barrel, the rotating band grips the rifling to impart spin to the projectile.

Shortly after the gun firing exercise, the ship was secured from GQ stations and material condition YOKE was set throughout the ship. The ship was maneuvered to bring her back to the passage plan's intended route track and the normal underway watches were set. Apparently, all had gone well during the GQ and live gun fire exercises. We assumed the captain and the XO were satisfied and believed the ship and the crew were ready to go into combat operations.

During the early afternoon on November 25, as the ship navigated through the Paracel Islands and reefs in the South China Sea, we sighted the lighthouse on Triton Island four miles off the ship's port bow. That night, at 2048, we sighted the light on Cu Lao Re Island, an island off the mainland of Vietnam, at a range of 18 miles. By the end of the 2000 to 2400 watch, the ship was closing in on area MR1.

The long title for the acronym MR1 is the Republic of Vietnam Government in I Corps Tactical Zone/Military Region 1 (ICTZ/MR1). Military Region I was located in northern South Vietnam and contained the following northern provinces: Quang Tri, Thua Thien, Quang Nam, Quang Tin, and Quang Ngai. MR1's area was essentially from Quang Ngai northward along the South Vietnam coastline to the DMZ. Most referred to the area of MR1 simply as the "gun line."

Just off the coast of Quang Tri Province in the area of MR1, but very close to the DMZ, was a gun line position designated as, "Point Allison." Naval gunfire in South Vietnam was under the control of the U.S. Marine Corps 1st Air and Naval Gunfire Liaison Company (ANGLICO).

ANGLICO was a Fleet Marine Force detachment consisting mainly of forward artillery observers, close air-support specialists, and radio operators.

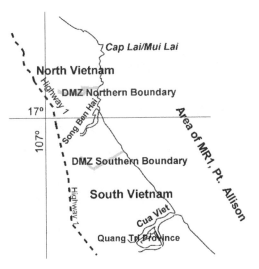

Quang Tri Province and DMZ. Offshore MR1, Point Allison.

From the 7th Fleet, the naval gunfire liaison officer (NGLO) at a corps headquarters received the name of the ship allocated to naval gunfire support (NGFS) in the corps area. When a ship arrived, the NGLO would then direct the ship to report to a given position and instruct the ship's commanding officer to contact the divisional or brigade NGLO.

The divisional NGLO would sometimes visit the ship, giving a briefing on conditions in the NGFS area. The briefing included information on concentrations of enemy troops, possible mined waters, the types of ammunition required, the extent of the ground force area of operations, and the location of "specific fire zones." Specific fire zones were the areas declared by the South Vietnamese government as having no friendly civilians living in them. Any movement detected within the specific fire zones could be considered either Viet Cong or NVA.

To be most effective, naval gunfire requires observed or "spotted fire." Spotted fire allows for quick corrections if projectiles are not falling on or hitting the target. Spotted fire was the usual form of NGFS. When a ship arrived at its NGFS station, it would establish radio contact with the Marine Corps "spot team" assigned to the ground force. Forward observers acted as the spotters and were usually airborne in a light aircraft or helicopters, but sometimes they were on foot with forward elements of the ground forces. The ground commander requested clearance of the general target area from the Vietnamese province chief and informed the spot team of his requirement for NGFS. The ground commander was either the U.S. Army or Army of the Republic of Vietnam (ARVN) or the South Vietnamese Army (SVA).

The forward observer spot team notified the ship of the target description and grid coordinates, the type of ammunition required, and the number of guns required to be ready to fire. The ship then fired on the target with the spotter correcting the fall of the projectiles and directing fire onto any new targets, for example, new enemy troop movement.

Navigation and exact positioning were essential for accurate gunfire support. Along most areas of the Vietnam coastline, navigating the ship accurately was difficult. Many areas had long stretches of straight, sandy beach line, backed up by low marsh or rice paddies inland, which provided very few suitable navigation reference points. Some ships made "positioning buoys" with radar reflectors that could easily be identifiable on radar. Ships often designed and built the buoys and anchored them in position. After positioning the buoy and knowing the precise location of the buoy, visual compass bearings or radar bearings and ranges to the single buoy could be used for accurate navigation.

Dropped positioning buoys were supposed to be recovered or sunk before a ship departed from the area. On occasion we would discover anchored positioning buoys made by other ships that they had not removed. These buoys were of no use for navigation until we knew the positioning buoy's precise position. Our ship made several of our own positioning buoys out of old 55-gallon drums and scrape steel, which gave the buoy good radar reflection qualities. The positioning buoy would be put over the side of the ship and we would let go of its anchor and chain, allowing it to sink to bottom, hopefully setting the anchor.

One method of determining a positioning buoy's exact location was the use of sextant angles, which could be performed very quickly and accurately. Once the buoy was secure in its anchored position, someone, (a QM), had to get on top of the buoy with a marine sextant in hand. Three different visible features or objects were necessary that were also printed on the navigation or grid chart. Combat grid charts often had structures, ruins, trees, steeples, water tanks, and building positions accurately overprinted on them. Of the three features or objects, the center object was the most important. With the marine sextant turned on its side, the horizontal angle was measured to an object left of the center object, and a second angle was measured to other objects to the right of the center object.

Marine sextants have index and horizon mirrors that allow for viewing two objects through its scope simultaneously, normally the visible horizon and a celestial body. But here, the angles are horizontal angles measured on the sextant from the center object to the left and right objects and the two angles are recorded. The major hazard for the person taking the sextant angles was that an NVA or Viet Cong soldier on shore could decide to shoot their ass off the buoy. Back on the ship, using a device called a three-arm protractor, the observed angles to the left and right objects are set on two moveable protractor arms, and the center arm is fixed. With the three-arm protractor, the positioning buoy's precise position can be plotted and marked on the grid chart. Once completed, the ship now had an effective aid to navigation.

The quartermasters had to quickly learn new ways to plot positions on the chart. We were now using combat grid coordinate charts for ship navigation and for plotting target positions relayed to us by the forward observer spotting teams. We were accustomed to plotting the terrestrial coordinates for latitude and longitude. Now we had to learn how to plot target positions relayed by spotters using just the grid coordinate position quickly and accurately.

During gunfire support missions, two quartermasters would be on the watch team. When the spotter passed a target's grid position, one QM would record and plot the target's grid position on the chart. The other QM would work at fixing the ship's position on the chart using radar ranges and bearings or compass bearings to geographic features, or to our positioning buoy. After the ship's position was plotted, the QM on the navigation plot used a machine called the parallel motion protractor (PMP). The PMP arm is aligned to the chart's true north/south axis to find the true bearing from the ship to the target. This true bearing was the "gun target line" to the target.

The Marine spotter would initiate a fire mission by first giving the "warning order" over the radio. The next radio calls from the spotter would pass the target grid location and the target description. They would give the target grid coordinates in six digits; for example, "Target coordinates are 6, 9, 4, 1, 8, 3. Break. I say again, target coordinates are 6, 9, 4, 1, 8, 3. How copy? Over."

Typically we could expect the accuracy of the target grid coordinates to be within 100 meters (328 feet) of the actual target. Combat grid charts were laid out in square grids. For example, on a grid chart of the 1:50,000 scale (1-inch on the chart, equals 50,000 inches of the earth's surface), the lengths of the horizontal and vertical sides of each grid square are 1,000 meters. Both sides of the grid are broken down into units of tenths, which allowed plotting the target's position to an accuracy of at least 100 meters.

Sometimes, the spotter would add to his radio message, "Danger close," meaning our gunfire will fall within 750 meters of friendlies or friendly troops. To prevent firing on friendly troops and civilians, we strictly adhered to the following procedures:

1. Upon receipt of target coordinates, we recorded and plotted them at two different stations, CIC and on the bridge, by different persons on separate charts. We read the coordinates back to the spotter for possible error.

2. CIC and bridge compared navigational and target positions and agreed to them before reporting, "Ready."

3. Any information we repeated to the spotter over the radio was closely monitored and checked.

4. We monitored and double-checked the plotting of target coordinates.

5. We carefully plotted and cross checked the gun target lines between CIC and the bridge.

6. CIC checked target locations and descriptions against the chart for possible dangerous or doubtful situations.

7. We questioned spotters on any missing or questionable elements of the standard mission format.

Many of us on the bridge crew became well-versed about the types of 5-inch projectiles we were firing and how they performed over or on the target. Our 5-inch projectiles had a high initial velocity, which resulted in a high striking velocity and a flat trajectory at short ranges. This made our fired 5-inch projectiles particularly effective against targets presenting a nearly perpendicular face to our line of fire. In the support of say, ground forces with gunfire, where plunging or enfiladed fire (raking gunfire) is better, the high initial velocity was a disadvantage. Either opening the range to the target or using reduced charges could overcome this disadvantage. Typically, instead of taking the time to maneuver the ship to open the range, we would often reduce the charge. However, reducing the charges also reduced the maximum effective range of the gun by 20 to 50 percent.

The Marines from the ANGLICO spotting teams were highly proficient in selecting the appropriate projectile and fuze for the ship to fire on their selected shore targets. For the most part they asked for high explosive or HE projectiles. However, their directions for types of projectile fuze varied depending on the type of target. The various fuze types are the mechanical time fuze, base detonating fuze, point detonating fuze, and the Variable Time (VT) fuze. The VT fuze is really a proximity fuze, it is an electronic fuze in the nose of the projectile and does not require impact to trigger. The VT fuze is designed to detonate close to the target and performed very efficiently in shore bombardment. It's good for bursting the shell at the correct distance above the target for maximum damage over a large area to light vehicle-types and personnel.

When a 5-inch projectile explodes, the projectile's body yields under the pressure until it fails and breaks into sharp-edged fragments. Most

USS Orleck (DD 886) firing all four 5-inch/38 caliber guns on targets in Vietnam. Photo courtesy of the USS Orleck Association.

of the sharp-edged and dangerous fragments come from the side walls of the projectile. The exploding fragments are primarily concentrated in a narrow zone called the "side spray." The angle of the side spray depends on what the fuze delay is and the projectile's angle of fall. A quick fuze and low angle of fall will produce a side spray almost perpendicular to the line of fire. A slower fuse delay and a high angle of fall will concentrate the fragments almost parallel to the line of fire.

By the time of the mid-watch on November 26, the ship was on its station in MR1. The ship had checked in with the NGLO and the Marine spotter. We started the wait for our first gunfire support mission assignment. The ship essentially steamed at various courses and speeds in a box-shaped area for the remainder of the mid-watch and through the 0400 to 0800. We received no fire mission tasking during those two watches. During the 0800 to 1200 morning watch, we received orders to go out to the sea area of Yankee Station to complete an underway replenishment for refueling operations.

That afternoon, our ship found and approached United States Naval Ship (USNS) *Taluga* (AO 62). *Taluga* was a World War II era Cimarron-class fleet oiler. During underway replenishment for FAS operations using the STREAM rig, a span-wire is passed to the receiving ship. The span-wire is then suspended under tension between the two ships, and trolleys attach a series of hose saddles to the span-wire. The actual fuel transfer hoses are suspended between the saddles. The receiving end of the hose rig is tipped with a coupling, the probe fueling coupling.

Once the probe fueling coupling is latched into the fuel receiver on the receiving ship, the delivery ship will commence the pumping of fuel. The FAS operation was completed after about an hour alongside. After refueling, the ship broke the FAS rig, maneuvered away from the *Taluga* and headed back to MR1. The ship arrived on station and reported in over the radio to the NGLO and Marine spotter shortly after 1900.

The 2000 to 2400 watch undertook the ship's first gunfire support missions. The mission load was light. There were only three fire missions called for. A total of only 12 high explosive (HE) rounds were fired at assigned targets during the entire watch. For fire missions at night, the flashes of the gun's muzzle needed to be suppressed, so only flashless powder cartridges are used to propel the 5-inch HE projectiles. Muzzle flashes at night could quickly give away the ship's position to the Vietnamese enemy on shore.

Starting on the mid-watch, November 27, the ship went to Watch Condition II. For watchstanders that shifted the crew into the six and six-hour watch rotations. The mid-watch would now be from midnight to 0600. During the mid-watch, the ship received and completed seven gunfire support missions, but only expended a total of 24 rounds for the watch. For the morning watch (0600-1200), things picked up a bit, where the ship received and completed only one gunfire support mission. This fire mission would last more than an hour and a half; it started with the "commence fire" order at 1005, and they ordered "cease fire" at 1145. The fire mission was completed with only 39 rounds fired. By the afternoon watch, the fire mission tempo picked up considerably.

The afternoon watch (1200-1800) was a long one. We received and completed ten gunfire support missions throughout the afternoon. A total of 234 rounds of high explosive (HE) with full service powder cartridges were fired during the watch. During the afternoon, the ship had moved to within less than three nautical miles off the mouth of the Cua Viet River, about four miles south of the DMZ. They ordered the afternoon's fire missions to help suppress or stop the NVA troop movements that had been detected both north and south of the river. After several fire missions, the spotter would give us feedback on our shooting. During several of these calls, we heard comments such as, "Good shooting." On one call, the spotter yelled into the radio, "Fire for effect, fire for effect; you're blowing the hell out of them!"

The afternoon watch was mine. Luckily, the destroyer we had relieved had already put down a positioning buoy off the entrance to the Cua Viet River. They passed their buoy's grid coordinates to our ship by flashing light message, signalman to signalman. The coastal area north and south of the Cua Vet River was mostly sand dunes and low-lying beaches, which made for extremely poor radar return. Having the positioning buoy to use for navigation made it much simpler to accurately determine the ship's position by radar. Our afternoon was busy plotting each new

Picture taken from Bridge of mount 51 firing both guns. Just imagine being this close for 300 or more rounds fired per day.

target's grid coordinates, then fixing the ship's position, followed by determining the new gun target line to each new target.

We maneuvered the ship to keep it broadside to the beach, so both gun mounts 51 and 52 could be brought to bear on the targets. This maneuver also increased the number of rounds fired within each salvo. After a while, the almost constant shaking, harmonic vibrations, and ringing throughout the ship caused by each round as we fired came to feel almost normal. However, most in the bridge crew were starting to experience high-pitched ringing in our ears from the almost constant firing from mount 51, the forward gun mount. Hearing protection was not considered and wasn't available, anyway. Some stuck cotton balls or pieces of balled or wadded-up toilet paper in their ears, trying to lessen the effects from the 5-inch guns.

The evening watch (1800-2400) became even more intense. There were only five gunfire support missions completed during the watch, but they were big ones. On the beach under the cover of darkness, the NVA activity had intensified. From the Marine spotter we learned that friendly ground forces near the DMZ were in a bad position and were being attacked by the NVA. Almost every one of the five fire mission messages included the "Danger Close" warning in the spotter's radio call.

During the next six hours, the ship would fire a total of 374 HE rounds with full service powder cartridges. Several times during the watch, the spotter requested the ship fire illumination (star-shell) rounds, affording the Marine spotter a better view of the situation over the target area. After the illumination rounds extinguished, the spotter would call to resume the fire mission attacking the NVA at adjusted target coordinates.

In our first 24 hours at MR1 in Vietnam, USS *Rich* expended about 72 percent of its 5-inch/38 caliber magazine capacity. The ship had fired 632 HE 5-inch rounds and 16 illumination rounds for a total of 648 rounds.

During the next mid-watch on November 28, the gunfire mission continued with our ship staying in its position offshore from the Cua Vet River entrance. During the first 30 to 40 minutes of the watch, there was only one gunfire mission, shooting about six illumination rounds over target positions provided by the spotter. Then the action slowed until about 0300. The ship commenced fire at 0305 and did not cease fire until 0625. The gunfire mission became much as it had the previous watch, with the spotter calling for gunfire and more illumination rounds over detected NVA positions.

The cease-fire order came shortly after sunrise. The ship had fired 77 HE rounds and 14 illumination rounds for a total of 91 rounds fired over the course of the six-hour watch. After daylight, the Marine spotter reported that all was quiet in the target area and requested that the ship stay at stand-by and on station. At this point, the weapons officer reported to the OOD on the bridge and to CIC that there were less than 75 rounds of unfired 5-inch ammunition remaining on board.

The ship stayed on station that morning until about 1100. The ship checked out of its station with the NGLO and the ANGLICO spotter to go out to sea to rendezvous with USS *Flint* (AE 32) to transfer some new crew members reporting on board and rearm the ship with a full on-load of ammunition. USS Flint was a Kilauea-class ammunition ship, which was capable of underway replenishment at a sustained speed of 20 knots. The transfer-at-sea method for an ammunition on-load was normally completed with the CH-46 Sea Knight helicopter for vertical replenishment (VERTREP). Our ship met up with USS *Flint* at 1230 and at 1240, the VERTREP operation began.

Once a VERTREP operation begins, it's really fast-paced. Two CH-46 helicopters rotate flying pallets of projectiles and powder cartridge cases from the ammunition ship to the deck of the receiving ship. They sling the pallets on a wire rope strap from the underside of the helicopter's fuselage on a hook. As they land each pallet on deck, an air crewman releases the wire rope strap. On deck, before anyone touches the pallet, they must electrically ground it to the ship removing any potential static-electric charge that may have built up during the flight. After electrical grounding, the pallet's steel securing straps are broken and the projectiles or cartridge cases are removed one by one from the pallet. Each projectile or cartridge case is passed from sailor to sailor in formed lines leading down to the main deck and ultimately to the below deck magazine handling rooms.

An ammunition on-load is an "All Hands" evolution. Everyone not on watch, including all officers and chiefs, had to work in the lines passing each projectile or cartridge case from person to person until the on-load is complete. The loading started at 1345 in the afternoon and wasn't complete until about 1830 that evening. We loaded 863 HE projectiles, 48 White Phosphorus projectiles, 48 illumination projectiles, and 819 full service powder cartridges. The white phosphorus (called WP or Willy Peter) projectiles are for smoke screen or incendiary use and are fitted with a time fuze.

Each projectile or powder cartridge was muscled by hand from the flight deck to the magazines. Each 5-inch projectile weighs about 55 pounds and a powder cartridges in its case weigh about 20 pounds. An hour and a half after the VERTREP operation was completed with the USS Flint our ship was back on station at MR1, awaiting the assignment of our next gunfire support mission.

One thing many of us noted when our ship would head out to Yankee Station for FAS or other replenishment operations was how many Vietnamese sampans we would find 40 to 50 nautical miles out in the Gulf of Tonkin. These sampans were fishing boats, but so many were tiny, with only one or two people on board. Very few were motor-propelled and instead used sails and oars. The issue with the sampans on some days was that they were everywhere. When deep draft replenishment ships had ships alongside at a speed of 12 knots, receiving fuel or stores with the STREAM method, making significant course changes is not a viable option.

On several occasions where our ship was alongside replenishment ships, we would see Vietnamese sampans dead ahead. There was no other option but to keep going and hope the sampans got out of the way in time. More than once we watched sampans come right between the alongside ships, with the sampans nearly capsizing in the waves and suction vortexes between the two ship hulls. At night, the sampans were still there but we couldn't see them. There is no doubt that a number of them were hit and sunk by naval vessels during the war. This seemed to me to be just another common occurrence in Vietnam, where we probably killed the same people we were supposed to be helping.

In less than two days, our shipboard life had changed completely. It no longer bore any resemblance to the old normal underway routine. The major changes were not much sleep for anyone and very little time for food. Showers and clean laundry would now be a thing of the past. For the next several weeks, there would be no sleeping in our berthing compartments. For example, the operations berthing compartment where I lived also contained the upper handling room for mount 52, the after gun mount. With ongoing gunfire support missions essentially around the clock, there was constant activity in and around the mount 52 upper handling room. They had commandeered many racks to hold empty powder cartridge cases. Ever try sleeping directly under a shooting 5-inch gun? Probably not going to happen. When not on watch, at GQ stations, or in the middle of underway replenishment evolutions, sleep was in the form of short cat naps. We napped anywhere we found enough deck room that was out of the way. Many found that their flak jackets also served as quite decent pillows.

Another issue that had developed was stowage of the empty powder cartridges cases. Empty powder cartridge cases were being stowed in berthing compartments and anywhere there was available space. In some areas, it was a matter of finding ways to navigate around or through the stacks of empty cartridge cases in order to get around the ship. Empty cartridge cases were saved with the intent to transfer them back to the ammunition ships during the next underway replenishment. Normally, the empty cartridge cases were sent back to the ammunition supply ship (then called retro-grade) near the end of each replenishment evolution.

Meals now mainly came from C-rations, since most of the cooks and mess cooks were assigned to the gun crews, working either in the magazines, handling rooms, or in one of the gun mounts. C-rations, or the Meal Combat Individual (MCI), were distributed around on the ship to the crew at least once, sometimes twice per day. Each C-ration or MCI was packed in a small, rectangular cardboard box. Each box contained individual cans with a meat-based entree item, crackers/candy, a flat spread, and a dessert item.

The C-ration boxes also came with the P-38 can opener and a mini cigarette pack, containing five cigarettes (Marlboro, Winston, and Kools). The P-38s and the cigarettes were the two more popular items. There were some nonsmokers on board who would trade their cigarette packs with smokers for their C-ration canned items. At first, some felt the C-rations were an improvement over the food served in the ship's galley.

The evening watch (1800 to 2400) back on station at MR1 was uneventful. Starting on the mid-watch, November 29, the first gunfire support mission call came in from the Marine spotter just before 0100. That fire mission lasted until the cease-fire order at 0525, with 174 HE rounds fired. Thus began the routine from watch to watch for the next two days. The ship stayed in its assigned sector ranging offshore from Quang Ngai to the south and to Vinh Son in the northern part of the sector. During the prior 48-hour period, the ship had fired 375 illumination and HE rounds in gunfire support missions.

On the afternoon of November 30, the rumor around the ship was that we were going to attack Tiger Island that night. The rumor had some truth to it. The actual name for Tiger Island is Hon Co Island, and it was considered part of the Quang Tri Province. The rumors about Tiger Island were that the NVA had many 8-inch/203 mm artillery gun batteries, surface-to-air missile installations, and more sophisticated Soviet (Russian) fire control and coastal radar installations on the island. Many naval ships had previously carried out attacks on Tiger Island and came under heavy counter-battery fire from the island.

Some intelligence must have been valid, as the Navy required the carrier battle group to stay further than 50 nautical miles from Tiger Island. On one of my trips through CIC, one of the radarmen showed me the "movement order" (MOVORD) message from Commander Task Force 75 directing our ship to rendezvous with USS *Waccamaw* (AO 109) for a night refueling, then rendezvous with the guided missile destroyer USS *Henry B. Wilson* (DDG 7) and the destroyer USS *Rowan* (DD 782) for "special operations." Our ship would be attached to the Commander Task Unit (CTU) 71.1.1, embarked on board USS *Wilson*.

That night during the mid-watch, after firing 75 HE rounds as part of a gunfire support mission, we checked out of station with the NGLO and the ANGLICO Marine spotter. Then we headed out to sea to rendezvous with USS *Waccamaw* for the FAS operation. The ship got alongside *Waccamaw* at 0300 and began taking on fuel. The FAS operation took less than two hours alongside. They assigned me as the underway replenishment helmsman for this FAS operation.

It was my first time as helmsman during night underway replenishment. Chip, who had been the primary helmsman, was due to leave the ship in less than two weeks; his enlistment was done. That was putting more pressure on me to become fully proficient as the GQ and underway replenishment helmsman. After breaking the fuel rig and maneuvering away from the *Waccamaw*, the course was set taking us to the area for our rendezvous with USS *Wilson* and USS *Rowan*.

Shortly after our ship made the rendezvous with USS *Wilson* and USS *Rowan*, CTU 71.1.1 embarked on USS *Wilson* and gave the tactical order for the ships to form up in a loose column formation. Our task unit was to proceed to an attack position offshore from Tiger Island, as described in chapter one of this story.

After the afternoon action at Tiger Island, our task unit regained its formation and began the run to the next destination further north off the coast of North Vietnam. The passage to the next position would take about 10 hours, enough time to give the crew a little time to rest up. En-route, the ship received a helicopter from the aircraft carrier that delivered 32 bags of mail. A chance to rest a few hours and maybe some mail from home would raise everyone's spirits.

At 1900 our ship went to GQ stations. At 1935, our ship met up with USS *Wilson* and USS *Rowan*. USS *Wilson* was the guide ship for the formation and we took a station off *Wilson*'s port quarter at 1,000 yards. The course and speed set by *Wilson* for our small formation of ships was a base course of 000 degrees, speed 24 knots. We were going north in a hurry. The actual special operation wasn't necessarily just a single attack on Tiger Island. The assignment was for our ships to conduct a series of night raids against targets near Vinh Son, Dong Hoi, and possibly all the way north in Brandon Bay. The targets of interest for the raids were bridges, NVA bases of operation, NVA storage areas, and coastal defense sites.

The first raid was to attack the island of Hon La less than one mile off the coast of Vinh Son. There are two small islands just off the coast of Vinh Son, Hon Co and Hon La. The island of Hon La, which is less than one mile off the coast and was known to have coastal defense sites with large artillery and radar sites. The first night raid was to be carried out by the three ships in conjunction with the air raids launched from the carrier fighter/bomber air wings and U.S. Air Force bombing operations. I really think the purpose of our raid was just to tie up NVA coastal defenses so their guns wouldn't be available to use as anti-aircraft weapons.

After sunset, darken ship was set including the securing of the ship's navigation lights. For the night raid operations, ships went totally dark, and we depended upon radar for collision avoidance with the other ships in our formation. Our three-ship formation began its approach to Hon La from the southeast on a base course of 050 degrees, speed 21 knots. USS *Wilson* (DDG 7) was the lead ship 30 degrees off our port bow at 6,000 yards (three nautical miles). USS *Rowan* was astern of our ship off our port quarter at 6,000 yards. My GQ station for this raid was as the lee helmsman.

At 0034, our speed was slowed to 17 knots, and at 0046, we changed course to 325 degrees (northwest) for nine nautical miles to close the distance to Hon La. At 0119, our ship commenced the three nautical milen leg of our firing run on a course of 248 degrees, speed 23 knots. Mount 51 began firing on the assigned targets on Hon La. At 0127, we changed course to 290 degrees and slowed to 16 knots; we could see the rounds from our ships exploding and impacting almost dead ahead on Hon La and targets farther inland near Vinh Son. We could hear and see USS *Wilson* firing her 5-inch/54 caliber guns off our starboard bow as she headed off in a northerly course direction. USS *Rowan* positioned off our port quarter was firing her mount 51 5-inch/38 caliber guns. At 0134, the XO who had the conn ordered "right full rudder," and as the ship came about to starboard, the XO ordered, "Steady as you go, on course, 027 degrees."

The ship was now nearly broadside to Hon La, and both gun mounts 51 and 52 let loose with long barrages of 5-inch fire. We stayed on our course at 16 knots for about 2 nautical miles. The IJL phone talker with CIC began to relay EW reports of a J-band fire control radar lock-on and tracking, bearing 265 degrees (south of west) from the ship. Within moments, the EW reported a second J-band fire control radar lock-on and tracking, bearing 295 degrees (west-northwest) from the ship. The XO ordered the helm and lee helm, "right full rudder, engines all ahead flank, make turns for 27 knots."

Within moments, the next helm command came, "Steady as you go, on course, 095 degrees." Just as the ship steadied up on the new ordered course, four airbursts detonated with the loud *"KEERAACK"* sounds of their high explosives above the ship.

From the bridge we could hear hissing noises and a sound like someone was throwing steel bolts at the ship; it was shrapnel coming down like rain. To evade getting hit by the counterbattery gun fire, the XO ordered the steering of a short weaving pattern about the base course of 095 degrees, 15 degrees to port for 30 seconds, then shift the rudder to come back 15 degrees to starboard for 30 seconds, and so on.

We turned our stern toward Hon La, which only left mount 52 unmasked and clear to return counterbattery fire as we moved away. The BMOW was taking gyro compass bearings from the bridge wing

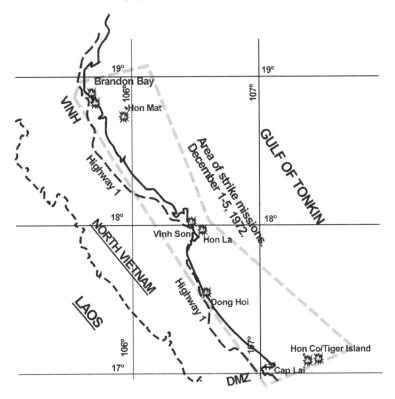

Area for CTU 71.1.1 strike missions and attacks, December 1-5, 1972.

gyro repeaters to the muzzle flashes on Hon La. The IJL circuit phone talker was passing the BMOW's gyro compass bearings to the weapons officer in CIC. The *"KERUMPF"* noises began from chaff launching systems. The *"KEERAACKs"* came repeatedly, one after the other, as the rounds in each incoming salvo detonated.

The lookouts and sonar reported splashes close aboard on the starboard side. We could hear the shrapnel whining and hissing noises from all around us. Mount 52 was now consistently firing, *"KABOOM, KABOOM … KABOOM, KABOOM"* four-round salvos, fired as quickly as the gun crews could reload and fire the next salvo. After about three or four minutes, the North Vietnamese counterbattery began to wither and then the counterbattery stopped; we were now probably now out of range of their guns or the chaff had been effective in confusing their J-band radar.

The cease-fire command came at 0150. We could hear USS *Rowan* now off our ship's starboard quarter still firing on Hon La. The entire raid had lasted about 20 minutes from commence fire to cease fire, but it seemed like it had lasted for hours. Our ship had fired 196 HE rounds on the Hon La targets and in returning counterbattery fire.

The after-action report showed that the three ships combined had fired more than 600 HE rounds during the raid. They estimated that the North Vietnamese on Hon La had fired more than 250 rounds of counterbattery at the three ships with no direct hits. Other than minor shrapnel hits, all ships were undamaged. Now, all of us understood that we had gotten ourselves into an actual shooting war.

USS *Wilson* signaled that the ships form up into a diamond formation. We left Hon La astern of us as our ships moved away to the southeast. The formation course was 125 degrees, speed 18 knots. The night's work was over, and at 0224 the ship secured from GQ stations and set Watch Condition III, three watch rotations, four hours on, eight hours off. The formation was now headed farther south along the North Vietnam coast to the next target.

Chip and I had been rotating between the helm and lee helm

stations throughout the night. By the time we were relieved, we had been at our GQ stations for almost eight hours. All of us were tired and hungry, and in about one more hour, I was to take over the 0400 to 0800 QMOW.

We made our way to the mess decks to see if they had put anything out. We were pleased to see that some homemade bread, peanut butter, and horse cock had been put out at the serving line. Nothing better than a peanut butter and bologna sandwich with bug juice at 0300 in the morning. The first class commissaryman (cook) had been taking the time when he could to make homemade bread. The bread was great; the question often became, what to have with it? Canned peanut butter never seemed to be in short supply, but peanut butter sandwiches were not enough to live on. Nonetheless, when available, the fresh-baked bread was appreciated by all.

Some of the snipes were on the mess decks partaking in the homemade bread with us. One of the machinist mates from B-4 engine room asked us, "What in the hell happened up there during GQ?" He added, "Man, it was like someone had a huge sledge hammer and they were banging away at the starboard hull. It was freaky as shit and it was loud. I thought the damn hull was going to blow in on us. We lost count after about thirty-five booms and bangs on the starboard side."

Our three-ship formation steamed south until around 1300 that afternoon. USS *Wilson* detached our ship to proceed independently to an area designated as "Surveillance Station Alpha and Bravo." We were there to watch for NVA traffic on Highway 1, south of Dong Hoi. We spent the afternoon maneuvering at various courses and speeds to close the coastal area. Late in the afternoon we established radio communications with a Marine spotter flying in a Cessna Bird Dog observation plane. At 1800, GQ stations were set throughout the ship. The spotter had a convoy of trucks thought to be carrying NVA troops south on Highway 1 and passed the initial grid target coordinates over the radio.

The ship ran up the coast to be in a position north of the targets on

Highway 1, and at 1820, it came around to course 150 degrees to position us parallel to the coastline. We commenced fire at 1854 on the targets, sending five consecutive salvos of four rounds per salvo. We put 20 HE rounds on the targets in less than four minutes. The spotter notified us to cease fire, all targets were destroyed. Our ship stayed at GQ stations, but maneuvered away from the coast headed back to Surveillance Station Alpha and Bravo.

Later, just after 2000, the maneuver completed earlier was repeated again to hit more targets on Highway 1. At 2023, about two hours after sunset, we commenced fire on the spotter's designated targets, sending five more consecutive salvos of four rounds per salvo. At 2027, the spotter notified us to cease fire, all targets were destroyed. The IJL phone talker relayed the EW report from CIC: J-band radar lock-on bearing 225 degrees (southwest). Within moments, the EW reported the second J-band radar locked-on bearing 255 degrees (south of west) and then reported an third J-band radar locked-on bearing 310 degrees (northwest).

Three J-band radars locked-on allowed the NVA to achieve deadly accurate counterbattery. Suddenly, the forward lookout and sonar reported counterbattery shell splashes off the starboard bow at 300 to 400 yards, followed by more shell splashes off the port bow at 200 to 300 yards. From the helm station, I could see some of the shell splashes, as well. Everyone stayed silent and calm waiting for the next order from the conn.

The NVA gunners were using bracketing fire in trying to find the range (distance) to us. Bracketing fire is where the first salvo is shot beyond the target, then the gun's range is reduced a set amount for the second salvo's rounds to land under the target's range. The difference in the gun's range settings between the first and second salvos is then cut in half and that range is set in the gun for the third salvo. Theoretically, the third salvo should be on the target's actual range from the gun. Bracketing gunfire works better for stationary targets, but could be accurate for slower-moving ships. However, our ship was not slow.

At 2042 we quickly came around to course 060 degrees, speed 23 knots to put more distance between us and the coastal guns and their J-band radars. Shore counterbattery fire was still coming in. Above the ship, at least three airbursts detonated with what was now becoming the familiar loud *"KEERAACK"* sound of high explosives. Moments later, three more airbursts detonated above the ship just aft of the bridge. These NVA gunners could shoot a lot better than those at Hon La last night. The detonating airburst and shell splashes just kept coming, getting closer with each salvo.

Many of us, including me, stopped paying any attention to the shrapnel noises and the loud *"KEERAACKs"*; it was better to just focus on your job. Finally, the counterbattery salvos stopped. Again, the ship had avoided any direct hits. The ship continued heading away from the coastal batteries at a speed of 19 knots until meeting up with USS *Wilson* at 2100. Our ship took our assigned station off USS *Wilson* for the night back at Surveillance Station Alpha and Bravo. The ship stayed at GQ stations four more hours, finally securing from GQ at 0152 the next morning. The three-ship formation headed out into the Gulf of Tonkin to rendezvous with the replenishment ships for refueling and rearming.

The following notes are from the ship's POD, December 3, 1972:

1.   *UNREP DAY*

Our activity this morning after securing from General Quarters will be devoted primarily to replenishment. Once again, let me remind you that this takes the cooperation of all hands to get the job done as quickly and painlessly as possible. We are going to re-arm, refuel, and take on stores this morning from three different service force ships; so let's pitch in and get it completed.

2.   *COMBAT ACTION RIBBON*

Last night, the ship was taken under fire by coastal defense batteries on the coast of North Vietnam. This will undoubtedly qualify everyone on board for the Combat Action Ribbon. YN1 name redacted, our friendly yeoman is presently researching the eligibility requirements and procedures for obtaining this award.

As the POD Note 1 on December 3, promised, the underway replenishment detail was set at 0720. We called it "the special rearming detail" and it turned out to be a marathon type day. At 0750, VERTREP started with receiving CH-46 helicopters from USS *San Jose* (AFS 7). *San Jose* was a Mars-class combat stores ship. This VERTREP was a short one and only involved several personnel transfers to and from *San Jose* and receiving repair parts and some supplies. By 0855 our ship had maneuvered alongside USS *Mauna Kea* (AE 22). *Mauna Kea* was a Suribachi-class ammunition ship. This ammunition transfer with *Mauna Kea* would be alongside using the STREAM rig method versus VERTREP with helicopters. It's still an "All Hands" effort for any ammunition on-load, regardless if it is a STREAM or VERTREP method.

That morning, the sea state conditions were not the best. It was windy and the sea wave heights ranged between 8 and 12 feet. The main deck on destroyers is close to the water, especially near the after section of the ship where the freeboard distance from above the waterline to the main deck is less than ten feet. Chip was on as the helmsman, so more junior guys like me would be available to hump projectiles, powder cartridge cases, and stores. They stationed me on the after main deck near the watertight door on the starboard side.

A line of us passed 5-inch projectiles from person to person. Every other projectile went to the after-handling room and we passed the other projectiles to the formed line of sailors all along the starboard side, leading forward to the handling room for mount 51. All of us were getting soaking wet from sea spray coming off the waves as they rolled along down the ship's side from forward to aft. The waves rolling down the side were getting bigger and taller. I had just taken a 5-inch projectile in my arms and had turned to pass it to the next person when I saw it.

Rolling down the starboard side main deck was a wave breaking about 10 feet above the deck. I could see 5-inch projectiles being thrown over the side and sailors were going down like bowling pins as they disappeared into the wave. Several of us yelled, "Watch out!" simultaneously. I threw my projectile over the side, grabbed a lifeline stanchion, and wrapped my arms around the upper wire rope lifeline. In an instant, the wave was on me. While underwater, I felt a tremendous pressure and pain in my thighs and lower legs. As the wave quickly broke and went by, the source of my pain became apparent. There were three guys who had grabbed onto my belt, thighs, and legs and were hanging onto me for dear life. Everyone quickly got up from the deck or let go of whatever they had been hanging on to. One of the chiefs yelled, "Check your buddy, make sure everyone is here!" Many were exchanging looks or letting out sighs of relief; all of us knew we had just avoided injury or even getting killed. We immediately reformed our line as more projectiles were already waiting to be passed to us. It was a close call. More than that, it was a miracle that nobody fell or went overboard.

If any of us would have actually fallen overboard, with the ship setup in the STREAM rig while alongside *Mauna Kea* the odds of anyone being recovered would have been very small. It would have taken far too long for an emergency breakaway to be carried out, where our ship could be free to maneuver and return to the area of the man overboard. The only chance of survival one might have had in that situation was if life ring buoys or smoke floats had been thrown from the ship by someone who had seen the man overboard. In this type of situation, though, it would have been pure luck for the ship to search and actually locate someone in the water. To me, that near-miss served as a reminder of how fast it could all be over.

The ammunition on-load from *Mauna Kea* was completed at 1205. After the breakaway from *Mauna Kea*, our ship maneuvered to take up a position astern of USS *Manatee* (AO 58), another Cimarron-class fleet replenishment oiler for FAS operations. Our ship set the "Special Sea and Refueling Detail" at 1215. At 1220, *Manatee* signaled our ship to begin our approach to come alongside, and by 1235 the first line was over. The FAS with *Manatee* took a little more than two hours to complete. While alongside *Manatee*, a VERTREP with a CH-46 from the *San Jose* took place as well.

Our ship completed the FAS with *Manatee* at 1405. After breaking away from *Manatee*, our ship maneuvered to take up a position astern of USS *San Jose* for another VERTREP, receiving more 5-inch ammunition delivered by CH-46 helicopters. The VERTREP with *San Jose* was completed at 1545. As I said earlier, it was a marathon type day. All from a crew most of who had not had any meaningful sleep for over a week. Many of them, if asked, couldn't say when they had last eaten an actual meal.

Now, it was time for our ship to rejoin USS *Wilson* and USS *Rowan* for another night of special operations in the hot area at Vinh Son. That night, the ship went to GQ stations at 2045, while still inbound to the next target area. Darken ship was set, including no navigation lights. It wasn't until the next morning, December 4, after 0200 that all three ships were in position north of the targets around Vinh Son. We were steering a base course of 180 degrees, speed 16 knots. The three ships in a loose column began steering zigzagging courses. USS *Wilson* was the lead ship. Our ship followed *Wilson*, and USS *Rowan* was at her station astern of our ship. At 0209, all three ships were broadside to the coastline and commenced fire with all their guns on the assigned targets.

At 0215, all ships began to encounter heavy counterbattery fire from a bearing of 180 degrees (from ahead of our ships) from the NVA shore batteries on Vinh Son and Hon La Island located to our south. At 0217 USS *Wilson* ordered cease fire. The three-ship column turned to port to steer away from the coastline, then increased speed, heading out to our designated independent holding surveillance stations beyond the range of the NVA shore batteries. After the ship arrived at our designated holding surveillance station, it secured from GQ. All three ships basically loitered at their designated surveillance stations for most of the day. Toward mid-afternoon, the ships began to move in closer to the North Vietnam coast again.

At 1600, the ship went to GQ stations. Just as before, the USS *Wilson* was the lead ship, our ship followed *Wilson*, and USS *Rowan* was at her station astern of our ship. As the column approached the coastal targets, each ship independently began to steer broad weave courses between 270 degrees and 300 degrees. Each ship had an assigned NVA coastal defense target. At 1654, our ship commenced firing 40 HE projectiles on our assigned target in less than three minutes. At 1657, we changed course to 157 degrees, speed 15 knots, moving away from the coast.

Some of us on the bridge exchanged questioning looks. The question was, "What, no NVA counterbattery?" USS *Wilson* signaled our ship to take station off her port bow at 6,000 yards. Our three-ship formation was on course 000 degrees, speed 10 knots, heading back to our offshore surveillance stations.

Early into the mid-watch on December 5, USS *Wilson* signaled for the ships to form up into a diamond formation. The formation's initial course was 158 degrees, speed 17 knots. At 0230 our ship went to GQ stations. The purpose of this attack, amazingly, was to intentionally draw NVA counterbattery fire. The idea was that with USS *Wilson*'s electronic counter measures and radar capabilities, if the NVA gun batteries fired on us, *Wilson* could track their shell trajectories and determine the gun battery positions. They increased the formation speed to 20 knots, closing the distance to the coastline. Our ship began steering various courses to begin the firing run. Now the ships were in a loose column.

The USS *Wilson* was the lead ship in the column, our ship was second, followed by the USS *Rowan*. At 0338 we commenced fire on our targets. Again, we fired 40 HE projectiles on our assigned target in less than three minutes. At 0342, the first counterbattery salvos from NVA coastal gun batteries began splashing in the water on our port and starboard bow. Within moments, a salvo of six airbursts detonated with loud *"KEERAACKs."* The airbursts seemed to be directly overhead and close on our port side. Brilliant and almost blinding white and orange-red light flashes came from each exploding shell. Once again, it sounded like someone was throwing steel bolts as hard as they could against the ship in between the hissing noises as the hot shrapnel hit the water.

Our ship made a left full rudder maneuver, increasing speed to 25 knots to clear the area. As we gathered speed on our outbound course, another salvo of four airbursts detonated directly ahead and above the ship at close range. The blinding white and orange-red light flashed through the bridge as even louder "KEERAACKs" resounded from the really close high explosives.

USS *Wilson* signaled our ship to take station on her stern. Once again, the ships were formed into a loose column, speed 25 knots, to close the coastline for the next firing run and attack. By radio, *Wilson* passed our ship the grid coordinates of our assigned target. The plan for this attack was to take out the now identified NVA coastal gun batteries.

At 0433, all three ships commenced fire on the gun batteries; our ship rapidly fired 40 HE projectiles on the target. Less than a minute after the order to commence fire, our ship began to receive heavy counter-battery fire. The lookouts and sonar were reporting splashes landing all around the ship. We could see the bright muzzle flashes off our port bow from the NVA coastal gun batteries. We kept firing on the target with mount 51. Apparently, this NVA counterbattery fire was not radar directed, as their shooting accuracy seemed poor.

A bright flash suddenly lit up the western horizon and sky from an onshore explosion very near to where we thought the gun batteries were. Then it was over; no more incoming counterbattery. USS *Wilson* signaled our ship to proceed independently to a near-shore surveillance station designated "Whisky" to maintain a visual and radar watch on the coastal area we had just attacked.

Surveillance station Whisky was close to shore, less than two miles out. It was easily vulnerable to attacks from shore. USS *Wilson* called us on the bridge-to-bridge VHF radio telephone to advise us that they could see numerous spots of white and red lights on our ship, making us visible. Light emitting from a darkened ship increases the risk of being attacked by the shore batteries. USS *Wilson* advised that our ship should move farther out to sea until the cause of our light emissions could be found and repaired.

From the bridge, the XO called the damage control officer to get the damage control teams out and investigate. Within minutes, the damage control officer called the bridge to let the XO know that they had found the sources of our light leaks. The forward port side of the superstructure on the main deck and above had been peppered by shrapnel. In many areas, the shrapnel had penetrated through the steel, leaving open holes and tears. In some areas of the ship, interior white and red lights were on in some outboard

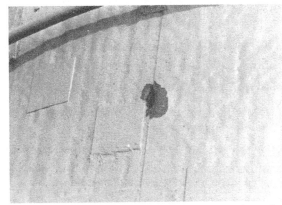

Typical shrapnel damage. This piece penetrated into the ship's forward stack.

spaces in the superstructure and the passageways, which were the sources of the light emitting from our ship.

The damage control teams were sent out with bundles of rags and screwdrivers to plug any shrapnel holes they found. Once it was thought that all the shrapnel holes had been found and plugged, the ship maneuvered to return back to station Whisky.

Through the rest of the night and the next morning, we steamed in the area on various courses, but we kept the ship's speed at around 10 knots. The next morning a number of us went to inspect the superstructure. We had been hit in dozens of places from the main deck and up. One of the seaman sweeping up loose shrapnel pieces off the deck pointed out spots of shrapnel holes and tears on the sides and near the top of both the forward and after boiler stacks.

At 1200, the ship was notified of an inbound helicopter from the carrier USS *Saratoga* delivering our mail. We maneuvered the ship to close the helicopter, and also to get the ship a bit further away from the coast. Saratoga's helicopter arrived over our deck and dropped our mail bags on deck. After receiving the helicopter our ship maneuvered to return closer to the coast. As always, mail call was a welcome break for everyone. It seemed that anytime we were lucky enough to receive mail, there was always a short lull in on-board activities for about an hour. It was a short-lived holiday of sorts.

Early that afternoon, we received a call for gunfire support from an aloft ANGLICO Marine spotter flying in a Cessna Bird Dog plane. The spotter passed us the grid coordinates for a newly located coast radar station on Tiger Island. Once our ship received permission from CTU 71.1.1, we immediately brought the ship to the required course and speed to close the island. At 1458, the ship went to GQ stations and we maneuvered the ship in close to Tiger Island. At 1530, the ship commenced fire on the target with an eight-round salvo from both mounts 51 and 52.

Within moments after firing, we got heavy NVA counterbattery in return, with multiple counterbattery splashes all around the ship. The XO maneuvered the ship farther away from the shore and then brought the ship broadside to the beach. We had good gun target lines and ranges to the gun batteries that had fired on us. Our ship opened up on the NVA gun batteries, and we fired 340 HE projectiles with reduced charges onto the targets. According to the Marine spotter's report, now acting as our forward observer, "You've blown the hell out every living thing in the target area."

After the order to cease fire, the ship stayed in the area for a short while before proceeding to take station off USS *Wilson*. After taking station off USS *Wilson*, all three ships in our task unit came to a northerly heading, now proceeding further north along the North Vietnam coastline to our next strike mission position. Shortly after 1600, the lookouts began reporting seeing many brown cloth sacks floating in the water on both sides of the ship. The ship slowed and then came to "engines all stop" to investigate the floating sacks. They could have been just bags of rice, but it all seemed a bit suspicious. The captain ordered the .50 caliber machine guns manned and to fire on the sacks. The .50 caliber gun crews had a hay day firing .50 caliber rounds into every sack they could see on the port and starboard sides of the ship. After we had fired about 400 .50 caliber rounds, none of the sacks had exploded or appeared to be booby trapped. The captain ordered the .50 caliber guns to cease fire. So far it had been a busy day, but it wasn't over. After finding the floating sacks were harmless and reporting the findings to USS *Wilson*, our ship was ordered to return back to our station in the formation.

At 2013, the ship went to GQ stations. Once again, we were on the attack. There had been NVA activity reported near Vinh on Highway 1. This province and the assigned targets in it were located around the southern parts of Brandon Bay. This attack would mean our ships would have to close the coastline from north of Hon Me and Hon Mat islands with their large coastal defense guns. The XO maneuvered the ship around and we began to close the coastline, steering a course of 250 degrees, speed 25 knots. Before we could start our attack, the ship began to receive NVA counterbattery fire from Hon Mat Island. The muzzle flashes on the island could be clearly seen from ahead of our ship. The XO ordered, "Right full rudder." Turning the ship hard to starboard, he continued to swing the ship until he commanded, "Steady as you go; steer course 125 degrees." The after lookout was reporting counterbattery splashes and detonations off the stern as the ship was turning at 25 knots.

The XO had swung the ship around almost 235 degrees from the original heading. Now the ship lay with its starboard side broadside to the coast. When the ship steadied up on 125 degrees, we launched chaff from both the port and starboard launchers. The QMs and CIC had both determined a good gun target line and range to the designated targets along Highway 1. The captain in CIC ordered, "Commence fire," and 37 HE rounds were fired on the targets. The lookouts and sonar continuously reported counterbattery splashes and shell detonations from all around the ship.

Our intent was to destroy the targets along the highway, not to get into a gun battle with the NVA, so our ship did not return any gunfire on Hon Mat. After several more minutes, the counterbattery reports stopped. The XO brought the ship left to course 090 degrees as we headed back out to the Gulf of Tonkin, opening the distance from the coast and the islands.

Ultimately, December 5 was comprised of 24 straight hours of high-speed runs, a lot of 5-inch gunfire, constant maneuvering of the ship, repeatedly taking NVA counterbattery fire, and in between we got to shoot up a bunch of rice sacks with the .50 caliber machine guns. So far in our limited time in Vietnam, our experience seemed to show that our war was going to be an unending cycle of each exhausting day piled on top of the last exhausting day.

On arriving back in the vicinity of USS *Wilson*, we discovered USS Rowan had been replaced in our unit with USS *Shelton* (DD 790). Apparently, USS *Rowan* was having engineering plant mechanical issues and could no longer perform the mission. Our three-ship task unit formed up into a diamond formation, with USS *Shelton* as the guide ship, and our unit headed south. We would spend all of the next morning completing an ammunition on-load from USS *Mauna Kea* with the STREAM method of transfer and then a FAS replenishment with USS *Cacapon* (AO 52).

Our ship was released from CTU 71.1.1, and we had orders to report to CTG 75.9. It would be back to the gun line in MR1 for us. The assigned Naval Gunfire Support Station for our ship was back to Point Allison, near the DMZ. The ship went to Watch Condition II. For watch standing, that shifted everyone back into the six-hours on and six-hours off watch rotations. Over the radio, we reported in with the NGLO and Marine spotter shortly after noon. By 1330 we received the spotter's radio call for our first gunfire support mission. It was right back in the NGFS saddle for us. By the end of the watch, our ship had fired 363 HE rounds on various targets designated by the Marine spotter. Ho hum. What had seemed exciting less than two weeks before now was, well, routine.

Many of us had not had more than two or three consecutive hours of sleep in the past five days. Now that we were back in the six and six hour watch rotations, if you could find a place to sleep, getting four or five hours of sleep at a time was possible. Doesn't sound like much sleep, does it? But it was just enough sleep to break the grip on our state of chronic fatigue. Looking back, it seems amazing how well young 20-somethings could withstand the rigors of not having much to eat, no or very few showers, no racks for some, and little to no sleep. Our physiological state probably also aided us in feeling little to no stress from repeatedly tempting the gunners on the NVA coastal defense batteries to kill us. I know many of us by this point had grown more accustomed to the experiences of our ship being fired on by the NVA. I found at least for me, the stress caused by combat action was mitigated or offset by the need for sleep or trying to meet my other basic human needs. The bad news was, we knew we would probably have to go back and do it again, but not today.

From one six-hour watch to the next, the ship was called upon for gunfire support missions mainly around the Cua Viet River. During the last ammunition on-load we had taken on extra ammunition, which had been stowed at areas outside of the gun magazines. On December 6, from 1333 to 2312 we fired 453 HE rounds onto an array of targets north of the Cua Viet River as designated by the ANGLICO Marine spotter. During the mid-watch from 0040 to 0300 on December 7, the ship fired 145 more HE rounds on targets as called in by the Marine spotter. By 0300, we had fired 598 HE rounds into the area north of the Cua Viet River area in the past 14 hours.

I distinctly remember the night of December 6, for one simple reason: I was able to get a little over five straight hours of sleep. After getting off watch at 1800, I was physically and mentally spent. The prior five days of getting little to no sleep had caught up with me. I went to the operations berthing compartment and found an empty rack away from the mount 52 upper handling room. I removed the "fart sack" (a type of fitted bed sheet with an opening at one end for sliding over the length of a mattress) from my mattress. After lying down on the empty rack's mattress, I got inside of my fart sack, much the same as one would get into a sleeping bag. The fart sack was long enough to cover me from head to toe and protected me from all the dirt, paint chips, and insulation that rained down from the overhead every time mount 52 fired. I went out like a light.

I woke up and got up a little after 2300 to get ready for the mid-watch. I felt good; the sleep had helped me considerably with my fatigue issues. As I appeared from the dark, one of the guys working outside the upper handling room looked at me in disbelief. He asked, "Were you sleeping in here?" I told him yes, and pointed toward the rack where I had been sleeping. He said, "Man, that's unbelievable; we've shot over 200 rounds in the past five hours."

I remember telling him that I hadn't heard them. To me, this experience proved that if a human being was tired enough, they could sleep through just about anything, including soundly sleeping for five hours while one deck below a firing 5-inch gun.

Early morning on December 7, we once again checked out of our station at Point Allison, heading out into the Gulf of Tonkin for FAS and rearming replenishment at sea operations. The morning into the early afternoon was spent alongside USS *Mount Katmai* (AE 16) for the ammunition on-load, then onto USS *Cacapon* (AO 52) for FAS replenishment. While the ship was en route back to Point Allison, we received a helicopter, which picked up and delivered our mail. It was always a better day when there was mail call. I was lucky, at almost every mail call, I would get one or two letters from Jan. Anytime I got letters from home, especially from Jan, it made for a better day. At some mail calls, there was time to read Jan's letters, but most of the time there was too much activity to stop and read mail, so I would just stuff them into my back pocket to read later.

The ship arrived back at Point Allison at 1648 that afternoon. Surprisingly, the gunfire mission tempo had slowed in our absence. That evening there was only one gunfire support mission, firing 45 HE rounds. That mission only lasted about 25 minutes, and it was quiet for the remainder of the evening until the next mid-watch.

One thing that was different now was that at night, after sunset, when we darkened the ship, the navigation lights stayed off. Even lighting a cigarette on the bridge at night was no longer allowed. Point Allison was offshore and adjacent to the Province of Quang Tri, which bordered the DMZ. Recently, NGFS ships had been receiving counterbattery fire coming out of Quang Tri. As far as it was known, the counterbattery fire was not radar directed, however, at night it was believed the NVA gunners in Quang Tri were using navigation lights or any other light they could see from offshore ships for targeting. For night gunfire missions, using only flashless powder cartridges was the rule.

Friday, December 8, Marine spotters called in fewer gunfire support missions than normal. Our ship still fired 298 HE rounds on different targets in Quang Tri throughout the day. However, one event was beginning to increase in frequency. We starting experience casualties in our 5-inch/38 caliber guns. At 1642, we had a "foul bore" report in the right gun on mount 51. In this foul bore casualty, the gun crew was unable to close the breech after reloading. The gun crew could remove the powder cartridge, which leaves the projectile jammed in the rifling. Part of the extracted powder cartridge's cork plug can still be wedged in the chamber behind the projectile. This "fouls" the chamber because it decreases the chamber's volume. Since the gun had been firing a good number of rounds just prior to the misfire, time is critical because the barrel could be hot enough to cook off the high explosive in the projectile, destroying the gun.

The standard procedure in clearing the fouled bore was completed in two steps. First, a fire hose was run out with a low velocity fog applicator inserted in the firefighting nozzle. With the fire hose charged with seawater from the ship's fire main system, the fog applicator was put into the end of the gun barrel, using the seawater to start cooling the gun barrel. Second, a special powder cartridge called a "clearing charge" was used, a shorter cartridge case with the wad and plug left out, its powder charge less than a full-service charge.

The clearing charge was removed from its special container and hand-rammed into the chamber. Once ready, the fog applicator spraying seawater in the barrel was removed. With the clearing charge sealed in the chamber, the projectile was fired out the muzzle. It was always safer to clear the projectile through the muzzle. The alternative, but much less safer method, was to push a bore rod down the gun's barrel to force a fuze projectile back through the chamber.

Saturday, December 9, on the mid-watch, during a gunfire support mission, an early cease fire was called at 0035 for hydraulic system repairs in the left gun on mount 51. By 0140, the left gun on mount 51 was back in action. That morning the ship checked out of station with the ANGLICO Marine Spotter to go out once again in the Gulf of Tonkin for FAS replenishment with USS *Cacapon* (AO 52). By now, I was the underway replenishment helmsman every time.

At 1420 that afternoon, our ship was back on station at Point Allison. Again that afternoon another early cease fire was called during a gunfire support mission to repair more hydraulic leaks in mount 51. After the hydraulic system repairs were complete to mount 51, the ship resumed gunfire support missions for the rest of the evening. Meanwhile, the weather along the Vietnam coast was deteriorating badly. Strong northeast winds, torrential rainfall, and building sea waves were affecting operations. There was a late season tropical storm, actually a typhoon, headed our way.

On November 30, Typhoon Theresa developed east of the Philippines. Theresa struck the Philippines on December 3. After crossing the Philippine islands, Theresa reached peak winds of 120 mph winds while in the South China Sea, which was very rare for the month of December, late in the tropical storm season. The typhoon's intensity fluctuated, but it continued westward and arrived off the coast of South Vietnam on December 9, as a typhoon with wind gusts of up to 115 mph.

On December 10, in addition to the bad weather courtesy of Typhoon Theresa, the ship's evaporator equipment was struggling. The ship had two evaporator plants for making freshwater and boiler feed water. One plant was located in B-2, the main engine room/main control, and the other plant was in the B-4 after engine room. The B-2 plant had been down for over a day with engineers unable to repair it due to not having the required parts on board.

That left the single evaporator plant in B-4 to make all of the necessary freshwater and boiler feed water for the ship. To conserve freshwater, the ship went to even stricter water hours; even the "scuttlebutts" (drinking fountains) were secured. Nearly all of the freshwater made by the single evaporator plant was diverted as boiler feed water for use in the propulsion boilers.

About this time was when I became a fully committed coffee drinker. One thing I had noticed was that even during times of severe water hour restrictions, there always seemed to be water available to make coffee. The scuttlebutts were secured and there was no bug juice available on the mess decks, but damn, there would be coffee. I had never cared much for coffee, but it was getting to the point where the only liquid for drinking that could be found was coffee. Since many of us now functioned in a state of chronic fatigue almost all of the time, coffee was the mainstay beverage.

One night during a bridge watch, I was dead tired and also wanted something to drink. The boatswain mate on watch offered me a freshly brewed cup of bridge coffee. After drinking one cup, I experienced my first caffeine jolt. It was almost like a buzz, with an added benefit of suddenly feeling more alert and as if I had some energy. Man, I was hooked, and am still a dedicated caffeine addict to this day.

The next night, on December 11, the gunfire support missions undertaken by the ship during the mid-watch would turn out to be our last, at least for a while. The single operating evaporator plant in B-4 engine room could not keep up with the demands of making enough boiler feed water. At 0400 that morning, our ship was detached from CTG 75.9 and ordered to proceed out to Yankee Station and report to CTG 77.6 embarked on USS *America* (CVA 66).

After our rendezvous with USS *America*, our ship was directed to stay within visual signaling distance of the aircraft carrier. Several helicopters arrived over our deck to drop off different repair parts for our evaporators. That night, the aircraft carrier put our ship to work, assigning us to take the "life guard" station astern of the carrier, while she was alongside USS *Wabash* (AOR 5) conducting underway replenishment for FAS.

At 0239 on December 12, our ship went alongside USS *Wabash* for our FAS replenishment. Precise steering by both ships is vital during alongside underway replenishment. Before beginning our approach to *Wabash*, she changed the replenishment course to 300 degrees (northwest-by-west). Our ship would come alongside *Wabash's* starboard side and we would be port-side-to *Wabash* for the replenishment. The idea was to put the weather on our starboard quarters, which could make for a better ride and steering. It was a tough refueling operation all around for those on the bridge and on deck because of the typhoon force winds and high sea wave conditions. Both our ship and Wabash were experiencing rolling and pitching while alongside. Obviously, being a destroyer, our ship's rolling and pitching was much more severe than *Wabash's*.

In heavy sea state conditions, steering exact gyro compass courses and not being more than one degree off the ordered course at any time can be extremely challenging for any helmsman. For me, it was a big test. This was another new experience of fighting the weather helm to stay on a precise course for over three consecutive hours. A momentary loss of mental alertness or awareness could cause you to allow the ship to get well off the intended course. The last thing any helmsman ever wants to hear from the conning officer is the command "Mind your helm," which means "Wake the hell up; your steering sucks."

Finally, at 0437, the refueling was complete and all lines were clear.

Ten minutes later, after breakaway, our ship was clear of *Wabash* and secured from the underway replenishment detail.

December 12 was also another milestone day. My mentor and friend Chip was leaving to go home. In my mind, every bit of knowledge and skill I had gained so far as a quartermaster was because of Chip. From the very first day, Chip taught, coached, and guided me in my efforts to learn and improve. Chip also had been a good friend to me, one I have never forgotten. At 0741, a helicopter from USS *America* arrived over our deck for personnel transfers. Chip and five other departing USS *Rich* crew members would be flown to USS *America* and then from there, ultimately fly back to the States for transfer or discharge. In Chip's case, his enlistment was up and he would be discharged. His days of being the short timer were over; he no longer had to count down the days until he could go home.

On December 13, shortly after midnight, our ship went back alongside USS *Wabash* on her starboard side. This underway replenishment was not for fuel, but for *Wabash* to pump badly needed boiler feed water over to our ship via transfer hose lines. The wind and sea state conditions had deteriorated even further from the morning before.

The replenishment course was 070 degrees (east-north-east), speed 10 knots. Once alongside, I was finding it extremely difficult to keep our ship on the replenishment course. Apparently, the helmsman on *Wabash* was having similar difficulties. The two ships were about 80 to 90 feet apart and both were rolling, pitching, and yawing so severely that it was considered unsafe to continue. About 25 minutes into the transfer, the captain on *Wabash* made the decision to terminate the transfer and ordered an emergency breakaway of the transfer rig. Once the rig was broken and the transfer hose was clear of our ship, we began to maneuver away from *Wabash*. With no other immediate orders from the task group commander, our ship started the trip back to MR1.

Sometime later that night, it was decided by the task group

commander that our ship should go to Da Nang, South Vietnam, in order to repair our evaporators while at the dock. At 0635, our ship began the approach to Vinh Da Nang. To reach the actual port of Da Nang, the large open bay of Vinh Da Nang had to be transited. On the approach, one first saw Hon Son Cha Island, which had cliffs that rose to elevations of 750 feet and were separated by three-tenths of a mile from the northwest entrance point of Vinh Da Nang. The effects of Typhoon Theresa were still present, with high winds and significant waves in the bay.

The port lay on the southeast side of Vinh Da Nang on the west bank of Song Han River, close within the river mouth. Initially we tried to dock the ship in the port, but the high winds made it impossible without tug assistance. Da Nang Harbor Control directed our ship to go instead to an emergency anchorage just inside the entrance to Vinh Da Nang. We backed the ship clear of the pier area, turned around, and proceeded out to the Vinh Da Nang anchorage area.

Once we arrived at the anchorage area, we let go of the port anchor. At 0756, we set the anchor in about nine fathoms (54 feet) of water. The bottom composition at the anchorage was mud, which does not provide the best holding ground. Within moments after setting the anchor, the ship began to roll severely. The winds were still gusting to 70 knots or more. The XO and I were both on the starboard bridge wing, and as the ship rolled heavily to starboard we both had to hang onto anything we could find to stay on our feet. Looking over the bridge wing as the ship rolled, I thought the bridge wing was going to actually enter the water.

The helmsman reported from the clinometer that the roll angle had reached 73 degrees. QM1 Janson on the navigation plot quickly determined that the ship was dragging anchor. We let out more anchor chain, increasing the scope to increase the holding power of the anchor. Next, we took a measure rarely exercised by a ship at anchorage: we put turns on both port and starboard engines, slowly turning the propellers thrusting ahead, and kept the helmsman on the helm using the rudders to keep the bow of the ship headed into the winds and the seas while at anchorage.

By the afternoon, the weather conditions at our anchorage area had not improved. The bridge team had fought all morning, constantly maneuvering the ship while anchored to keep the ship in safe water. At 1355 we weighed anchor and moved the ship further into Vinh Da Nang to an anchorage area closer to the port of Da Nang and in better protected waters. Twenty minutes later, we anchored the ship again at Anchorage #4 in about five fathoms (30 feet) of water; the bottom composition at this anchorage was also mud.

Finally, the Da Nang Harbor Pilot boarded our ship at 1508. The pilot felt the winds had decreased enough to allow our ship to safely dock. Once again, we weighed anchor and got underway. The harbor pilot gave the maneuvering orders as we entered Da Nang harbor and docked at pier Delta, Delta Two at 1536. As a precaution, all mooring lines were doubled up and extra mooring wire ropes were put over to the dock at the bow and the stern.

The intent and purpose for our ship docking in Da Nang was to bring on board several Navy technical experts to help our engineers in repairing the evaporators. Being at the dock also gave the ship an opportunity to take on more freshwater. The scheduled time in Da Nang was initially indefinite, until the evaporators were fixed. That indefinite schedule got blown away when the local commander warned that the threat level was very high for our ship to be attacked by mortar fire while at the dock. They believed the mortar attacks would begin shortly after sunset. This information was relayed to the task group commander by the captain.

Within a short period of time, we received orders for the ship to leave the dock before sunset and to proceed back to Subic Bay. The Navy technical experts were to stay on board and continue efforts to fix the ship's evaporators while en route to Subic Bay. The ship got underway at 1832 from Da Nang harbor and transited through Vinh Da Nang back out into the waters of the Gulf of Tonkin bound for Subic

Bay. Goodbye, Vietnam, at least for now.

Some in the crew were happy about going back to Subic Bay. That night on the mess decks, some guys were fantasizing about how great it was going to be to take Hollywood showers and get some clean laundry. Others were looking forward to maybe a night or two of liberty in Olongapo City. All were happy about not being in Vietnam. However, it would turn out to be a short-lived celebration.

At 0900 the next day, our ship went alongside USS *Wabash* for over two hours, taking on boiler feed water. After our breakaway from *Wabash*, our ship assumed the lifeguard station 1,000 yards astern of *Wabash* while she took USS *Brooke* (DEG 1) and USS *McCaffery* (DD 860) alongside for FAS on her port and starboard sides. *McCaffery* was also experiencing problems with her evaporator distilling plants. USS Brooke had actually departed the Gulf of Tonkin on December 13, bound for Subic Bay, to complete an upkeep period. She had been diverted back to Da Nang to escort our ship and USS *McCaffery* to Subic Bay. Once the two ships were completed with their replenishment with USS *Wabash*, USS *Brooke* ordered our three ships into formation for the passage to Subic Bay.

Then came good news for some and bad news for others. During the early morning hours, both of our evaporator distilling plants were fixed and operating normally. By 0830 on the morning of December 15, our ship was ordered by CTG 75.9 to turn around and proceed back to MR1, Point Allison on the gun line. By the next morning at 1030 on December 16, our ship checked in with the NGLO and the ANGLICO Marine spotter at Point Allison. Our first gunfire support mission started within 20 minutes after check in, firing 37 HE rounds on two different targets.

What's the old saying? Oh, it's "back in the saddle again." Our version was the acronym BOHICA—"bend over; here it comes again."

The afternoon watch fired 188 HE rounds on various assigned targets by the spotter. At about 1700, our ship checked out of our station with the NGLO and the Marine spotter for another nighttime underway replenishment to on-load more ammunition and to conduct a FAS. At

1820 we began with an ammunition on-load from USS *Santa Barbara* (AE 28), with the STREAM method of transfer and then FAS replenishment with USNS *Taluga* (AO 62).

By 0210 the next day, our ship had returned to Point Allison and the first gunfire support mission began 30 minutes later at 0240. This fire mission was a long one, firing 170 HE rounds on two targets for about an hour and a half. At 0500 that morning a message arrived from CTG 75.9 detaching us from gunfire support duties and directing us to rendezvous with aircraft carrier USS *Midway* (CVA 41). Our ship was being assigned carrier escort duties out at Yankee Station. The other news was that *Midway* would be going to Singapore for Christmas and our ship would be one of her escort ships. Now, there was some damn fine good news.

8. RESPITE AND SECOND ARRIVAL

It's probably worthwhile to discuss a few more details of shipboard life while our ship was involved in combat operations. I would say that sailors, if their mothers hadn't already taught them, quickly learned the value of maintaining good personal hygiene. Everyone's biggest challenge besides battling constant fatigue issues was in maintaining some level of personal hygiene while under severe freshwater use restrictions.

Except for when the most severe water conservation measures were being practiced, at least for a period of time each day the sinks in the crew heads would have just the hot water turned on. Since auxiliary steam was used in heat exchangers to heat the water supply, generally very hot water came out immediately from a faucet. Every destroyer or frigate sailor knows and understands the term "bird bath," where you bathe using just one sink basin filled with hot water. There is a method to taking a hot water bird bath: using bar soap and a wash cloth, you clean your body from head to toe. First the hair, face, neck, chest, back, and armpits are washed and rinsed. Next, it's your groin area, ass, and then feet.

When no clean laundry was available, which was most of the time, hopefully there was time to complete seawater washing of some of your clothing. Skivvies and socks were worn for as long as they could be tolerated, then were thrown away. As mentioned earlier, even when the ship's laundry was operating, generally after putting your skivvies and socks in the laundry bag, you probably would never see them again. Everyone stocked up, buying skivvies and socks from the ship's store as often as possible. I always wondered where all those damn skivvies and socks went to, but for certain they rarely came back to their original owners.

Baby powder was the mainstay for armpits, groin, ass, and feet. No deodorant, because after several days of no washing and a lot of sweat, deodorant-soaked armpits and clothing were absolutely disgusting and intolerable for anyone to be around. I recall some crew members who didn't keep up with even the minimum hygienic practices, and for some of them the result was severe crotch rot, heat rashes, athlete's foot, or toe rot. They paid the price, and so did anyone else who had to be around them.

Another challenge to our continued existence was food. At MR1 and during special operations, the crew's daytime hours were filled with GQ battle stations, standing watches, and working on the gun crews. When not at GQ stations or on watch, most nights were spent with everyone humping 5-inch projectiles, powder cartridge cases, or boxes of stores all night, or standing-by on the in-haul/out-haul lines on the FAS or STREAM rigs.

Almost all of the cooks had assignments on the gun crews and underway replenishment stations. The galley was for the most part, closed for business; there was no one to cook. However, especially late at night, it was noted by several crew members that the stewards discreetly prepared sandwiches and soup for the officers in the Wardroom Pantry. Generally, for those that knew about that, it seemed best to just stick to a "whatever" type of attitude.

One morning at breakfast to the surprise of many, there was some fresh homemade bread available on the mess decks. This explained where the bread had come from for sandwiches in the Wardroom. The first class commissaryman once again had found time to make homemade bread. Thereafter, maybe a couple of times over the next several weeks, fresh homemade bread was put out on the mess decks for the crew. Other than that, the cuisine of the day for the rest of us, well, of course, was C-rations and MCIs. You could somewhat supplement your diet if you had a stocked gedunk locker, but for many, our gedunk lockers were becoming bare.

Adaptability was the name of the game. Young people put in tough situations can be impressive in how they deal with constantly changing circumstances and uncertainty. It is the power of youth and is why wars are always best left to the young to fight them. What is surprising was our morale, which was generally good. When it came to doing our jobs and responsibilities, no one closely supervised us.

Our leadership, the petty officers, chiefs, and officers, rarely, if ever, questioned any of us on task completion or accomplishment; it was just expected that we had done our jobs. I think this was key to our generally good morale. One has to remember that this was still the draft era. However, we were in a sense an all-volunteer Navy, meaning that most had volunteered to avoid being "ground pounders" in the Army or the Marine Corps. Many of the junior enlisted didn't want to be here, but here they were. In spite of that, I would say that more than 90 percent of us were determined to do a good job and were resolved to never let our shipmates down, because they were our family.

On the morning of December 17, our ship departed from our MR1 station at Point Allison shortly after 0500. Our orders from CTG 75.9 were to proceed on duties as assigned and rendezvous with the carrier battle group under the command of CTG 77.3. Out in the Gulf of Tonkin, CTG 77.3 assumed tactical control of our ship at 0810. Initially, our ship was ordered to maintain visual signaling distance, but to stay within a distance of five nautical miles from USS *Midway*. At 1020, *Midway* signaled our ship to take our station astern of her and maintain a distance of 1,500 yards (0.75 nautical miles).

Now that our ship was out at Yankee Station with the carrier battle group, we shifted to Watch Condition III. Watch rotations again went to four hours on, off eight hours. So far we had spent 22 exhausting days in Vietnam either on the gun line at MR1 or taking part in raids attacking North Vietnamese coastal defense or other targets. Operations had gone on essentially around the clock. The entire crew was exhausted. Our ship being assigned to CTG 77.3 was a welcome break.

Now that both of the ship's evaporators were operating, being able to take Navy showers was welcomed by all. The ship's supply officer promised that clean laundry was forthcoming very soon. All departments had cleaned up their respective berthing compartments and all now had their assigned racks available again to sleep in. It was now possible to get six or seven consecutive hours of sleep, which was almost a luxury. When moving about the ship, we no longer had to navigate around the stacks of empty powder cartridges (called retrograde) that had been stowed anywhere there was available space. Once again, the cooks had the galley back in full operation, turning out three meals per day, plus mid-rats. Eating C-rations to survive on was now just a memory. You could say, we were in Fat City; all was well and back to normal.

Another benefit of our ship being at Yankee Station was the fairly regular delivery of mail. At least once, or sometimes twice, each week the carrier's helicopter would come over our after deck and drop off mailbags. The crew really enjoyed these fairly regular mail calls. Once again, the importance of sequentially numbering all letters was demonstrated. For example, Jan's letters #33 and #37 might be received, and at the next mail call, I would get letters #32 and #34.

For the quartermasters, we faced one minor dilemma: how to accurately determine the actual ship's position. Now out in the Gulf of Tonkin and away from land both visually and on radar, ship navigation was challenging. The Loran "A" was useless for navigation, so the ship's position was loosely tracked by DR. Using celestial navigation was not going too well either, as every morning and evening twilight period, the sky was overcast and cloudy.

Then we found some relief from a system called the Navy Tactical Data System (NTDS), a computerized information processing system developed by the Navy for use in combat ships. It took reports from multiple sensors on different ships and collated it to produce a single unified map of the battle space. This information could then be relayed back to the ships and to the weapons operators. In Navy parlance, our ship was a non-NTDS ship. However, our ship did have the NTDS data subsystem processing equipment on board, specifically Link 14. Link 14 provided a means for NTDS units to transmit track information, identity, engagement status, track reports, and gridlock information to non-NTDS units.

Our Link 14 was installed in CIC. The navigation plotters in CIC and the quartermasters quickly learned we could find our own ship's position quickly and easily using the data provided from Link 14. The Link 14 readout would provide the aircraft carrier's latitude and longitude coordinates for the time of the data. On the data printout, our ship's NTDS identity would be in the data. The readout used a type of Cartesian X and Y coordinate system of our ship's position from the aircraft carrier. Our assumption was, "It's a damn aircraft carrier; surely they know where in the hell they are!"

On the navigation chart, first we would plot the carrier's latitude and longitude coordinates, then the X coordinate length (distance) in nautical miles would run as indicated either 000 or 180 degrees (true north or south) from the carrier. Next, the Y coordinate distance, also in nautical miles, would run as indicated either 090 or 270 degrees (true east or west) from the X coordinate. At the end point, the Y coordinate was our ship's NTDS position. How accurate was the Link 14 position data? No one could say, but for us it was an easy way to get our position, and it probably was a lot more accurate than our estimated and DR positions.

On Monday, December 18, most of the morning was spent alongside USS *Wabash* for FAS replenishment. A good share of the afternoon was spent chasing down USS *Niagara Falls* (AFS 3), a Mars-class combat stores ship. We were scheduled to have a VERTREP with *Niagara Falls* that afternoon to receive stores and supplies. The VERTREP didn't happen and was ultimately cancelled.

Our ship was ordered to take station 1,500 yards off the starboard quarter of USS *Midway* for "plane guard." A plane guard ship was tasked to recover the aircrew of planes or helicopters which might have to ditch or crash in the water during aircraft carrier flight operations. Plane guard ships were never stationed directly astern of the carrier. On board, the motor whaleboat (rescue boat) was prepared for immediate launching.

While approaching the carrier to land or following a failed landing, aircraft might ditch or crash. In that event, the plane guard ship proceeded to the approximate position of the aircraft, and their rescue boat was launched into the water to rescue the aircrew. The plane guard role could be dangerous. When conducting flight operations, aircraft carriers frequently changed their course and speed to maintain optimum take-off and landing wind conditions for their aircraft. A breakdown in situational awareness on the part of the plane guard ship's watch officer could place the ship in danger of colliding with the aircraft carrier.

On December 18, the U.S. resumed bombing north of the 20th parallel in North Vietnam under the name Linebacker II. Five Navy aircraft carriers were in the Gulf of Tonkin to launch their aircraft to participate in the bombing raids. The U.S. Navy's aircraft carriers assigned to participate in Linebacker operations were USS *Ranger* (CVA 61), USS *Enterprise* (CVN 65), USS *Saratoga* (CV 60), USS *Oriskany* (CV 34), and USS *America* (CV 66). During Linebacker II operations, aircraft sorties from the carriers re-seeded the mine fields in Haiphong Harbor and conducted concentrated strikes against surface-to-air missile and anti-aircraft artillery sites, enemy army barracks, and petroleum storage areas. Most of the Navy's tactical air attack sorties were centered in the coastal areas around Hanoi and Haiphong, focused on Haiphong naval and shipyard areas and their railroad and truck stations.

The next morning our ship was detached from USS *Midway* to go rendezvous with aircraft carrier USS *Enterprise*. Our ship was ordered to close *Enterprise* to be within visual signaling distance. At lunch, down on the mess decks, the rumors were going wild. Some were wondering about being detached from *Midway*. What did it mean for us? The question asked of me several times was, "What about Christmas in Singapore; is that off?"

The actual purpose for the rendezvous with the aircraft carrier was for the *Enterprise* to transfer by helicopter new crew members reporting on board our ship. Late that afternoon our ship was detached from USS *Enterprise* and USS *Midway* took tactical command of our ship. By 1700, our ship was at our plane guard station with *Midway*.

The next morning, we received the news that the night before, USS *Hoel* (DDG 13) and USS *Goldsborough* (DDG 20) had attacked targets at Hon La Island off the coast near to Vinh Son in North Vietnam as part of the Linebacker II operation. While conducting the combat mission, *Goldsborough* had been hit by coastal artillery fire, causing fires and a five-foot-wide hole through an upper deck. The ship had been able to continue its combat mission despite the damage and casualties. Two sailors had been killed, and six had been injured.

We would learn some days later that one of the six injured died later as a result of his wounds. Our ship had conducted night raid attacks at Hon La Island back on December 2. On board it was speculated that the NVA gunners on Hon La had either gotten lucky or someone had taught them how to shoot since we had been there.

On December 20, most of our day was spent waiting for USS *Midway* to complete her FAS replenishment with USS *Wabash*. After *Midway* completed her breakaway maneuvers with *Wabash* and was clear, then our ship went alongside *Wabash* for FAS replenishment. At about 1600, USS *Midway* finally came to a southerly course at a speed of 25 knots, beginning the passage to Singapore. Our ship was assigned to stay at a station 2,500 yards astern of *Midway*. Essentially, we would follow

Midway the passage distance of 650 nautical miles to Singapore.

For destroyers, escorting an aircraft carrier during a passage could be frustrating. Unlike destroyers, aircraft carriers didn't follow straight route legs to get from points "A" to "B" as fast as they could. No, they had to zigzag the whole damn way, still conducting flight operations while en route. A destroyer would make the passage from the Gulf of Tonkin to Singapore in about 40 hours. *Midway* would take over three damn days to cover the same distance.

On Christmas Eve, the ship arrived at the ANZUK Naval Basin, which was part of the former British Sembawang Naval Base, and docked with our starboard side to Berth 6 at about noon. The Sembawang Naval Base was located in Sembawang at the northern tip of Singapore. The British Naval Forces had withdrawn from Singapore in 1971. ANZUK was a force formed by Australia, New Zealand, and the United Kingdom to defend the Asian Pacific region.

The ship was going to be docked in Singapore for seven days. Since the dock offered Hotel services such as steam, freshwater, and electricity, the ship's boilers and engineering plant would be shut down and go to cold iron status. This made all of the snipes in engineering pretty happy since now they all could get some liberty and time off the ship in Singapore. There were a number of British, Australian, and New Zealand naval ships also docked in the basin.

The crew really needed this break. It had been 30 long and hard days since leaving Subic Bay. Except for three hours or so tied to the dock at Da Nang in Vietnam, the ship had spent all of its time underway since leaving Subic Bay. The endless days on the gun line, running Linebacker operations at night, and the daily underway replenishment evolutions had taken a toll on both the crew and the ship.

Many were excited about the prospect of going to the Bob Hope USO show on board aircraft carrier USS *Midway* the next day, Christmas. Others just wanted to get off the ship for a while, or take some time to rest and relax. As the ship went to sea and anchor detail for entering port, the list to sign up for those that wanted to go to the

Bob Hope USO show was posted outside the Ships Office. I wanted to go, but by the time the sea and anchor detail was secured and I could get below, the list had already been taken down. Only a limited number from the ship could attend the USO show, and the list was full.

I was a bit disappointed, thinking it would have been cool to actually see Bob Hope in person. Our generation had grown up watching him on television and in the movies. Besides all of his television shows and films, Bob Hope was well known for his unwavering support of the troops and the exhausting USO performance tours he had been doing since World War II.

One thing that was noteworthy about our time in Singapore was that the character of the crew had changed. The change I'm referring to had to do with any personality conflicts, friction, or tough feelings that might have existed between some crew members back in Norfolk. All of that was now gone. Everyone in the crew, officers, the chiefs, and enlisted now seemed to have a strong sense of comradeship with each other. In spite of what we had just gone through, our morale was high; you could say we had very good "esprit de corps," or team spirit. Our commanding officer, the XO, the ship's officers, and the entire crew had been battle tested, all had done their respective jobs, and had done them well. I don't think this fact had actually sunk in with anyone on board until our time in Singapore.

The ship's crew went into the four duty section rotations for our time in port. The ship was going to be on holiday routine for most our stay, which meant that except for duty days, everyone had liberty. I had duty the first day on Christmas Eve and was assigned to the afternoon watch and the mid-watch on the quarterdeck for the day. Starting with Christmas Day, I would have three full days of liberty before my next duty day.

My Christmas Day plan was to first find a phone exchange to make a call home to Jan, and after that go off base to see what fun and partying could be had. I had managed to put aside a bit of money since Subic Bay. Our pay had been tax exempt while in the combat zone, plus I had

$65 more per month of hostile fire pay, so there was a bit more spending money than normal.

In 1972, Singapore prescribed to Time Zone Description (ZD) of -7.5 hours GH, halfway between Zone Descriptions -7 G and -8 H. That made Singapore's zone time 12.5 hours ahead of the zone time in Norfolk (Eastern Standard Time), or 13.5 hours ahead of Central Standard Time. A lot of guys on the ship were planning to call their families back home for Christmas and constantly pestered any QM with questions like, "What time is it right now in Cleveland?" These types of questions were responded to with our standard answer of, "Look at your watch and subtract 13 and ½ hours of time from your watch time. Remember, depending on the time of day here, it may be the day before back home." Adding that part about the day before was too much for some guys. I often carried a small pocket notebook, so I'd just do the math for some of them on a slip of paper.

The next morning, I left the ship alone and after asking around, found the Overseas Telephone Exchange office located immediately outside the naval base main gate. But first, I had to find a currency exchange to change some of my U.S. money to Singapore currency. Once I had gotten my U.S. dollars exchanged for Singapore dollars, it was back to the telephone exchange office. In the phone exchange, I filled out the call information form for the overseas operator, prepaid for the phone call, and was given my call and phone assignment slip. Surprisingly, my wait was only about 20 minutes before my number and phone assignment were announced. It was about 1030 local time, which was about 9:00 p.m. on Christmas Eve back in Iowa.

After talking with the operator, I could hear ringing on the line, but the ringing went on and on with no answer at home. After about a dozen rings, the operator said the call would have to be terminated. I asked her to please try again, so she agreed to try. This time, after about the third ring, to my great relief, Jan answered the phone.

At that moment one has to overcome the urge to yell, "Where were you?" and instead just said, "Hello, honey, you don't know how good it is just to hear your voice." I was happy and relieved to hear that all was going well with Jan and our son. It had been over a month since we had last spoken since I'd called her from the Philippines. I had prepaid 20 minutes of phone time, which we used every last second of before saying our final "Miss you, I love you, and goodbye." I didn't know it then, but it would be six more weeks before I would be able to call her again.

Coming out of the telephone exchange, one of my snipe buddies, Matt, was sitting on a bench. I asked Matt what his plans were for the day. Matt had heard that right up the street was "The Strip," and he proposed that we go there. Matt and I began our walk down Admiralty Road. Within less than one mile we came upon an area which had a long row of shops, "makan stalls" (food stalls), and bars. The area's actual name is Sembawang Village. By that time it was around 1130, and we walked around for a while looking at the shops and food stalls.

One of the makan stalls looked like it was serving something that closely resembled fish and chips, so we ordered our lunch. The food was not bad; it was deep-fried fish and potatoes wrapped and served in newspaper. The makan stall also served ice-cold bottled Heineken beer. We sat at an outdoor table enjoying our lunch, the beer, and the mild and beautiful Singapore weather.

After 30 days of confinement to the ship, it felt to us like it probably did to someone who had just gotten out of jail. We had our freedom to move about, but were not sure what in the hell to do with our newfound freedom. As sailors, we would solve that issue in short order as the bar right next door was just opening for business.

After finishing our lunch, we immediately shifted berths over to the bar. The bar owner was setting up tables and chairs out in front, which to Matt and me looked like a good place to plant our butts. Matt proclaimed that since it was Christmas and he was a Texan, our drink of choice for the afternoon should be Southern Comfort on the rocks. I could see no reason to disagree with Matt's choice of alcoholic beverages.

We asked the bar owner if we could order a fifth of Southern Comfort with ice and glasses. He bowed and said, "Yes, yes," then went inside. The owner returned shortly with a bottle of Southern Comfort, glasses, and a bucket full of ice. The bar owner didn't return alone; his wife and two adult daughters were with him. He expressed to us that he, his wife, and daughters all wanted to wish us Merry Christmas. They chimed in together, speaking in their best English, "Merry Christmas to our American friends."

We thanked them for the warm greeting; each one of them shook our hand and bowed to us as they backed away and walked back inside the bar. We each poured ourselves a glass of Southern Comfort on the rocks and made our toasts of "Merry Christmas" to each other. The Christmas festivities were about to begin.

The afternoon slipped by as we slowly sipped our Southern Comfort and relaxed, just shooting the bull. Later in the afternoon, several more of our shipmates showed up, then a couple more guys came along, and before long we had a party going. Matt and I ordered another bottle of Southern Comfort after killing the first one.

During the afternoon, the conversation turned to our time on the gun line and the attacks on the NVA shore installations. A big part of the discussion was about the times the ship had come under counterbattery attacks from the NVA. Present for this discussion were a mixture of crew members from the engineering, operations, and weapons departments. The engineers believed it was freakier to be in the below deck engineering spaces while counterbattery rounds were exploding close aboard. One guy talked about how he could now identify with the submariners during World War II, and how they must have felt while being attacked from the surface by depth charges.

Several of the snipes talked about how when the incoming rounds exploded underwater close to the ship they could watch ship's hull heave in and out. They really couldn't describe the noises the hull made as it was stressed and strained other than to say, *"It was just f**king freaky, man."*

235

Those of us from operations and the bridge crew agreed that it was probably better to be topside. The point the snipes drove home was that at least those up topside could see the explosions and knew where the incoming rounds were falling in relation to the ship. One of the engineers commented, "At least on the bridge, you know what's going on. Down below, all we know is that we need to keep the (propeller) shafts turning and the lights on."

One of the operations guys walked through the general process from the moment the EWs detected J-band radars radiating from the NVA and J-band radar locked-on to the ship. He explained that on many occasions the ship didn't have just one J-band radar locked-on the ship, but often two and three. He explained how dangerous it could be when three J-band radars were locked-on, since the counterbattery could become very accurate.

A sonar technician explained how sonar could detect the bearing and range of incoming rounds as they splashed into the water and could report it even before the round exploded. I knew this to be true, because on many occasions on the bridge, we would hear the sonar reports come over the intercom. For example, we would hear, "Splash, 050, 250 yards," a split nanosecond just before the round detonated.

My contribution to the conversation was explaining how many times the NVA had used "bracketing shots" in trying to find the actual range to our ship. Usually the first incoming round would splash over, just beyond the ship; the second incoming round would splash under the actual range to the ship; and we counted on the third round falling one-half the distance between the first and second rounds. Our standard ship avoidance maneuvers had become weave patterns, where upon seeing the splash from the first round, we would immediately order the ship's speed to "all ahead full" or "all ahead flank" and turn the ship in the direction to the first splash.

On seeing the second splash, the ship would immediately be turned toward the direction of the second splash. The idea was that by the time the third round arrived (i.e., their kill shot), the ship would have moved out of the bracketed targeting area. Someone asked me if the maneuver was a standard naval tactic. My answer was, "I don't know."

I explained that the first time we'd used the maneuver, the XO had had the conn and had given all of the ship's speed and helm commands to execute the maneuver. After the danger was over, the XO had seemed pleased with his success and commented that he had learned about the maneuver from the movie *In Harm's Way*.

Throughout the afternoon, we all avoided the word "scared." Most tended to substitute with terms or phrases such as, "freaky," "freaked," "crazy," or "it was f**ked up!" I don't think it was a case where no one wanted to admit to ever having been scared or fearful, because I don't think any of us truly ever were. The phrase, "tense anxiousness with some apprehension" was probably more applicable. Did we have concerns and worries about returning to combat operations? Of course we did. However, I would say that with the experience we all had gained in the prior 30 days, we knew what to expect and had the confidence we could do it again. Did we want to? Probably the answer for most of us was, no! But we didn't have any choice in the matter anyway; there was no other alternative. As the late afternoon arrived and most of us were now somewhat fueled up with alcohol, the discussions turned to lighter subjects.

By nightfall, instead of getting something to eat at one of the makan stalls, we moved the party inside the bar and continued drinking and having fun. A live band was setting up inside. Suddenly, about a dozen or more bar girls arrived and began to move in with us at our tables. These women were mostly from Malaysia or Thailand, and "drop-dead gorgeous" was the best description of them. Guys were falling all over each other vying to buy the drink for their bar girl of choice. Several of the girls wanted to be clear that they were not "Boom-Boom girls," which meant they were not prostitutes.

The band began to play Deep Purple and Doors songs, and just like in the Philippines, the songs covered sounded just like the actual artists. When they played the song "The Crystal Ship" by the Doors, you would have sworn it was Jim Morrison up there singing.

Later in the evening, Matt and I were on working on our third, or it might have been our fourth, bottle of Southern Comfort. Things seemed to be going along just fine, as everyone was having a good time. Then, a group of Australian and New Zealander sailors burst in and took over the bar area. Immediately after the Aussies and New Zealanders showed up, a bunch of British guys came running in. The Brits were all in costume dressed as Native American Indians. Most of them were wearing full American Indian regalia, complete with feathered headdresses, loincloths, moccasins, the whole bit. Some had spears, a couple had bows and arrows, and they were loud. A couple of them occasionally would let out what they thought was a good rendition of the Native American war cry, yelling and shrieking loudly. By now there were probably about twenty or more guys from *Rich* in the bar.

The general hellraising from the combined Aussie, New Zealand, and British group was starting to piss a couple of our guys off. I think the real issue was that some of the bar girls had left our tables and moved over to the bar area. A sensible person would have seen where this situation was headed, but drunken sailors have never been known for being sensible.

For a while everyone had some unity in the bar when the band played Deep Purple's "Smoke on the Water." For the part of the song's lyrics that went, "Smoke on the water, a fire in the sky," almost everyone sang along. Apparently, this particular song resonated with everyone. On the ship, some had tried to convince the XO that "Smoke on the Water" should be the ship's breakaway song during underway replenishments. By tradition, Navy ships played their chosen breakaway song as the ship went to ahead flank speed to quickly and smartly move away from the replenishment ship after breaking the replenishment rig. Many in our crew liked the song, because for us, being off the coast of Vietnam everyday involved lots of gun smoke on the water and at night, fire in the sky.

In talking with several of the Australians and New Zealanders, all of them were stationed on board either the Royal Australian Navy (RAN) or Royal New Zealand Navy (RNZN) frigates homeported in Singapore. All of them had completed tours on their respective ships on the Vietnam gun line and had participated in various Linebacker operations. They felt much the same about Deep Purple's song "Smoke on the Water" as we did.

Later, I got up from our table and headed to the back of the bar outside to the W.C. area, which had a long urinal trough and a commode. While I was standing at the urinal, a tall New Zealander walked in and took a position on my right side at the urinal. As I was pissing, the guy asked me, "Where you from in the States, Yank?" I told him I was from the Midwest, farm country. Next, he said, "You know, Yank; for a man, you have big tits," then reached over and grabbed a fleshy area of my right chest, squeezed hard, and let go.

I didn't say anything to him or even react to what he had done. I finished pissing, and as I was zipping up my jeans, I realized the nearly empty bottle of Southern Comfort was still in my left hand. From my mother's side of the family, I had inherited the Northern European long torso with a large ribcage, and my barrel chest was a trait from my dad's side of the family. I had always been a little sensitive about my build and large chest size. What the New Zealander had done, both through his comment and action, really pissed me off.

Turning to leave, the New Zealander blocked my path, and said, "Now where do you think you're going, mate?" I didn't say anything. Suddenly, and to my own surprise, I was swinging that nearly empty Southern Comfort bottle, hitting the guy hard along his right temple and smashing the bottle to pieces. Next, I grabbed him by the throat and punched him in the face with a good hard right.

I have to give the guy credit, as he went down, he muttered, "You shouldn't have done that, Yank." I turned and walked back toward the bar.

There was a hallway leading from the W.C. back to the bar, and one of the bar girls who had been setting at our table rushed up to me and said to me several times, "You no fight. You no fight. You come back tomorrow night!" Loud bangs and yelling were coming from the bar area. I could see the band members quickly moving their instruments and equipment off the stage. I headed into the bar area and, holy shit, there was a full-on brawl in progress. I saw Matt fighting with two guys and other guys from our crew were fighting, so I jumped in. The whole thing was crazy, tables and chairs broken as bodies slammed into them. My strategy was to punch anyone I could while trying to wade through the fight, looking to help any shipmate in need.

I was aware of taking some good hits in the head and body, but fortunately, alcohol combined with adrenaline tends to mask pain in the heat of the moment. There were a bunch of guys fighting behind the bar, when suddenly the whole damn bar toppled over and crashed onto the floor. Christ, even some of the light fixtures had been ripped out of the ceiling. The fight suddenly ended when most of the Aussies, New Zealanders, and the Brits held up their hands, laughing, and one of them yelled several times, "Yanks, that's enough; it was just good fun."

Looking around the bar, it was in total shambles; it looked like a bomb had gone off in the place. One of the Aussies stepped out and proclaimed that the bar was now closed and we all should find a new bar. Then he invited "the Yanks" to come along with them and have the next drink on them. The bar owner, along with his wife and daughters, appeared from somewhere. To my surprise, they didn't seem upset or angry over their now-wrecked bar. The bar owner and his family lined up by the door, and as each person filed by, the bar owner and his wife wished each of them a "Merry Christmas."

I noticed there was a small cardboard box on a table by the door that each person was putting money in as he exited the bar. All of us from USS *Rich* followed suit and stuffed whatever spare Singaporean money we had in the box on our way out. What a surreal evening it had been so far. However, the night was not yet done for me.

We all went down the road together to Nelson's Bar, where we engaged in some extensive drinking.

While I was sitting at a table, the New Zealander from the earlier altercation in the W.C. walked up carrying two drinks. He sat down, then slid one of the glasses over to me and said, "Yank, thought I'd buy you a drink. That was a good move you put on me; no hard feelings."

I held up the glass of whatever it was and said, "Cheers." The drink tasted like some type of sour mash type whiskey; it was awful, but I didn't want to show it. I asked him, "What is this?"

He told me it was a type of Scotch whiskey made in New Zealand. After a few more rounds, around midnight, I was not feeling too well. The previous 12 or more hours of Southern Comfort and drinking who knows what else, combined with no food and the big fight, all was catching up to me. Plus, my head and other body parts were starting to throb with pain. At some point, I must have just passed out.

From this point on, I have very little memory of what happened. Later, I had some recollections of being helped to walk to other bars, and some memories of being awake several times. Each time, there was a full glass of something in front of me in some bar or another. One time, someone had given me a lit cigar. That's the balance of my memories for the remainder of that night.

Returning to consciousness was confusing, as I couldn't quite figure out exactly where I was. I was laid out in a bed or something. For a while, I couldn't even decide if I was even alive or not. Suddenly, a voice in the dim light said, "Hey, man, you're awake. How do you feel?

Squinting my eyes, I saw the face of one of my buddies slowly come into focus. I asked him, "Where am I?"

He replied, "You're on the ship in your rack, dumbass." Then he told me that a van had pulled up to the ship's gangway at about 0500 that morning and some guys had sat me down on the dock and left. The quarterdeck watch had helped me get on board and down to the berthing compartment. Apparently, they had also helped me with getting my shoes and clothes off and got me into my rack.

I asked my buddy what the time was. I couldn't believe it when he told me it was just after 2000. I had been asleep for almost 15 hours.

With my buddy's help, I got out of my rack, grabbed my douche kit, and went up to the after head. After stripping down, I got in one of the shower stalls and took a long, hot Hollywood shower. Coming out of the shower, I went up to one of the sinks. My reflection in the mirror showed that my face wasn't too bad, a couple of bruises on my cheeks, a cut above my right eye with some swelling. Someone, my guess was the corpsman, had put a steri-strip on the cut above my eye.

Looking in the mirror at the rest of my body, there were too many bruises to count. There were bruises peppered all around on my chest, stomach, upper and lower back, on both upper thighs, and even on my butt cheeks. I looked like someone who had taken a severe ass whipping. Obviously, more damage had been done during the bar brawl than I'd realized. At that moment, I made the decision to swear off ever drinking Southern Comfort again. That was one decision I have stuck to in life.

I went back to my rack and lay down. It took a long time to find a halfway comfortable position before going back to sleep. The next day was still a liberty day for me, so after breakfast, I swung by sickbay to see about getting something for my pain. The junior corpsman (doc) was in sickbay; as I entered, he smiled and asked how I was doing.

I told him that I was generally okay, but was wondering if I could get some Motrin or something for the pain. He handed me a packet of Motrin and told me that I hadn't been the only one looking for pain relief that morning. Apparently, the day after Christmas Day, several other crew members had arrived back on board in similar conditions to mine.

A couple of guys in the berthing compartment were talking about renting a taxi to go check out the downtown areas of Singapore. They asked me if I wanted to go with them, and I readily agreed. With time, effort, but not without some pain, I managed to get dressed and ready to go. Looking back at those days, the power my young body possessed in its ability to heal was impressive. With the combined effects from a lot of sleep, some food, and Motrin, I was essentially ready to go again.

I hate to say it, but my Christmas Day antics had served a good purpose. I couldn't remember the last time I'd felt as relaxed and stress free as I did that day. It had been a great stress relieving exercise in spite of the physical pain.

Outside the naval base main gate on Admiralty Road, we found a taxi driver who agreed to take us to the downtown area of Singapore. The distance from Sembawang Village to the downtown area was about 29 kilometers/18 miles and the drive took close to 40 minutes. The trip turned out to be kind of a bust. The downtown area had been already overrun by the sailors off USS *Midway*. A crew size of 4,300 was typical for USS *Midway*'s class of aircraft carrier. Just imagine any mid-sized city where 3,000 plus sailors or more all arrive at about the same time. It wasn't pretty.

We decided within an hour to find a taxi to take us back to Sembawang Village. We spent the rest of the day looking at the sights. That evening we hit several bars and did some moderate drinking. I decided I would limit my drinking that night and conserve my energy since I had duty the next day.

Some of our bar conversations turned to the topic of the Linebacker II operations back in Vietnam. What news we'd had on the operations, as always, seemed focused on the Air Force B-52 bombing and the Navy's bombing campaign launched from the aircraft carriers at Yankee Station. The fact that USS *Goldsborough* had been hit in combat action by NVA coastal artillery fire told us that the destroyers attached to Task Unit 71.1.1 were probably involved in executing the same type of night raid attacks on coastal targets as our ship had done earlier in the month.

The ship was scheduled to depart Singapore on the morning of New Year's Eve—Sunday, December 31. After my duty day on Thursday, that left me Friday and Saturday to get off the ship as much as possible before we departed. The orders for the ship were to proceed back to Subic Bay for one day to refuel and to refit the ship, then proceed to Vietnam for duty back at Yankee Station and MR1, the gun line. The word on the ship was that this time we would be going back and would be staying in Vietnam probably for the duration. How long would the *duration* be, and what did it mean for our ship and crew? Nobody seemed able to say.

We had seen in the news that the peace talks in Paris between the U.S., the South Vietnamese, and North Vietnamese had collapsed in mid-December, and we knew that Operation Linebacker II had started back in Vietnam. At least for now, all the news sources indicated that for the immediate future it was not known if the North Vietnamese were willing to continue negotiating any type of peace agreement.

By now, the crew had established its favorite bars or watering holes in Sembawang Village. The preference for most was to spend what time remained in Singapore just lying low, relaxing, and enjoying the live bar bands. A number of guys had settled in by pairing up with the Malaysian and Thai bar girls to take best advantage of the temporary but pleasant companionship they provided. The hard partying and heavy drinking was over. Now, it was more about wringing the best we could from every remaining hour until it was our time to leave.

On Sunday at 1100, the ship got underway from the dock at the ANZUK Naval Basin and proceeded outbound into the waters of the Singapore Strait. It took a little more than an hour to make the passage around the northeastern coast and eastern coast of Singapore Island. Then the ship was back in the Western Pacific Ocean. By early afternoon, the ship completed the scheduled rendezvous with USS *Midway* and took our assigned station off the carrier's stern. Our Christmas break was over, and we would bring in the New Year of 1973 while underway, bound for Subic Bay.

Upon leaving Singapore, USS *Midway* and our ship were actually scheduled to first divert further south to cross the equator (0 degrees latitude), then proceed back north. Singapore is at latitude coordinate 1º 17.4' N, about 77 miles north of the equator. For whatever reason, the trip to the equator was canceled and after we kept our rendezvous with USS *Midway*, she set a northbound passage speed of 25 knots.

Many in the crew were disappointed at the lost opportunity to become a "Shellback" and having to remain in the "Pollywogs" status.

A "Trusty Shellback" was a sailor who had previously crossed the line (equator) and had been initiated. Shellbacks had to prove they were true Shellbacks, so they always kept their Shellback certificate or wallet card with them, attesting to their Shellback status. The Trusty Shellbacks were disappointed at the lost opportunity to initiate the Pollywogs during the "Crossing the Line" ceremony and initiation. There seemed to be some sense of urgency for our ships, or at least USS *Midway*, to get back to the Gulf of Tonkin.

The ship arrived back at the Subic Bay Naval Base late afternoon on January 2. We moored port-side-to outboard of USS *Tucker* (DD 875). Some of the crew not in the duty section were allowed liberty that evening, but their liberty expired on board at midnight. Surprisingly, not many bothered to go ashore. Most of the evening through early the following morning was spent topping off the ship with freshwater and refueling from an alongside oil barge.

That same night, personnel from the Subic Bay weapons department and our weapons crew changed out all four 5-inch gun barrels on mounts 51 and 52. The 5-inch/38 caliber bore was rated to fire 2,000 rounds before needing replacement. We had far, far, exceeded that in December. At 0900 the next morning, we got the ship underway from Subic Bay and proceeded out into the South China Sea. The orders for our ship were to rendezvous with USS *Midway* and escort her to Yankee Station.

At 2313 that night, our ship caught up with USS *Midway*. *Midway*'s base course was 270 degrees, speed 22 knots. She assigned our ship to take station two miles astern of her. The next morning, *Midway* gave our ship permission to steam independently while we affected several engineering repairs. By early afternoon, with our engineering repairs completed, we regained station with *Midway*. Once again, our ship was put on plane guard duty off *Midway*'s starboard quarter at 1,500 yards.

The second day out of Subic Bay, we hit really bad weather. High winds and big seas had the ship rolling and pitching heavily. That morning at breakfast, one of the new crew members that had checked on board the ship in Subic Bay sat next to me. He was a fireman in the engineman rating fresh out of "A" school, and this was his first time at sea. He asked me if it was always this rough of a ride. I explained to him that destroyers rolled and pitched a lot. He began to tell me that he had spent the night watching the forward emergency fire pump, which was on the line because the main fire pump was down.

He added, "The seas were so damn rough in the forward part of the ship as it was coming out of the water, and the fire pump kept losing suction. That's all I did all night long, shutting down the pump every time it lost suction and restarting it to get suction again." I smiled and told him there were a lot of things on board that had to be nursed along to keep them working. Then he asked, "You live in after berthing, right?" I told him that I did.

Next, he asked, "Is it normal for water to be sloshing around on the deck in there all the time?" I remember telling him that, yes, that was normal. He shook his head and said, "I guess if this is destroyer life, I'll just have to get used to it."

Our ship stayed with USS *Midway*, primarily providing plane guard during flight operations. Escorting *Midway* and plane guard duties became the routine for the next several days until 0920 on the morning of January 6, when the bridge crew and the lookouts sighted an aircraft launching from the carrier's flight deck and crashing into the sea. We immediately passed the word throughout the ship to "man the recovery detail." The captain arrived on the bridge and took the conn.

Midway helicopters conducted the primary search with our ship assisting. At 0928, eight minutes after the crash, the helicopter marked a position in the water with a floating smoke signal marking an area of aircraft debris. The commander of task group (CTG) 77.3 ordered our ship to recover as much of the debris as possible. For nearly an hour and a half, our deck and rescue boat crews worked, using grappling hooks and line.

At about 1130, one of Midway's helicopters arrived over our deck to load all recovered aircraft debris. The crashed aircraft was an A-7B Corsair II. The pilot had ejected from the airplane but had been killed.

During that night, we saw a message that the radioman brought up to the bridge about an explosion on board USS *Henry B. Wilson* (DDG 7) while operating off the coast from Saigon in South Vietnam. USS *Wilson* was the same ship we had worked with during the night raid attacks in North Vietnam in December. Two sailors had been injured from a premature shell explosion in Mount 51. The explosion had destroyed about one foot of the gun barrel on one of her 5-inch/54 caliber guns. What had happened on board USS *Wilson* had been one of our major concerns in mid-December when our 5-inch/38 caliber guns began had begun experiencing frequent foul bore casualties.

The next several weeks, the routine turned to serving as plane guard ship for USS *Midway* during her flight operations and completing underway replenishment at sea for FAS or to take on stores about every third day. Escorting aircraft carriers burned a lot of fuel. Destroyers as escorting and plane guard ships were constantly changing course and speed to stay on the assigned station. To intercept other ships often required speeds in excess of 18 knots, and in some cases staying at speed in excess of 25 knots just to keep up. Those types of higher speeds served to suck down fuel and boiler feed water fast.

During this time I took the advancement examination for the rate of QM3. Being at Watch Condition III, with our watch rotations now back to four hours on and off eight hours, gave me more time to study and prepare for the examination. The advancement examinations were administered on the mess decks. Everyone's advancement examinations had to be mailed to the Bureau of Naval Personnel in Washington, D.C., for grading and promotion selections. It would take at least two or three months before any of us would know the results.

On January 11, another combat action occurred involving USS *Cochrane* (DDG 21), USS *McCaffery* (DD 860), and USS *Turner Joy* (DD 951) near Vinh, North Vietnam, about 100 miles north of the DMZ. This action, The Battle of Brandon Bay, for the three destroyers was to conduct a coordinated strike from seaward at high speed, with a large number of Air Force B-52s dropping about 900 tons of bombs, followed by an attack from Air Force and Navy fighter-bombers. The goal of the attack was to hit NVA troop staging areas and petroleum storage sites in the vicinity of Vinh.

USS *Midway* and other aircraft carriers launched their fighter-bombers for the attack starting at 1900. In this attack, all of the destroyers came under heavy NVA counterbattery. The three ships later estimated that there were well over forty different NVA coastal gun emplacements firing 5-inch projectiles or larger on them at one time. The NVA counterbattery after the destroyer attacks became so intense that after taking the brunt of the NVA counterbattery, the surface strike commander ordered the high-speed retirement of USS *Cochrane* and USS *McCaffrey*. *Turner Joy* was ordered to stay behind long enough to cover the other ships with her 5-inch/54 caliber guns that could put out a rate of fire of 40 rounds per minute.

I recall this attack in part because of the over pressure shockwave that hit our ship from the B-52s dropping their bombs essentially all at once in the target area. Our ship was offshore about 12 to 15 nautical miles out, and the blast shockwaves as they overtook us started with humming sounds from vibrating steel, then built until rattling began and actually shook the entire ship. The early evening sky to our northwest repeatedly lit up with brilliant white and yellow high intensity light flashes from the exploding bombs.

There had to have been direct hits on the petroleum or ammunition storage sites. One massive explosion after another went on for close to 30 minutes. Just before each loud explosive boom could be heard, orange and yellow high intensity light flashes jetted upward into the evening skies. Someone on the bridge asked out loud, "Did someone drop a goddamn nuke?"

Throughout the attack, blast pressures kept up the continuous harmonic buzzing and rattling noises throughout the ship. To this day, anytime there are thunderstorms with severe lightning and thunder, I can't help but stay outdoors as long as possible while correlating the lightning flashes and load cracks of thunder to this attack. It's not the same as the spectacle of that night, but it's very close to the sound of war.

Many in the crew were becoming more optimistic about our immediate future and were okay with the idea of staying out at Yankee Station. One comment heard on the mess decks summed up how many in the crew were feeling: "This plane guarding shit beats the hell out of getting our ass shot at every other goddamn night."

In the interim period since the ship had last been on the gun line in mid-December, we had received a considerable number of new crew members on board. You could detect looks of disbelief on the new crew members' faces as guys would sometimes recount our earlier experiences on the gun line or during Linebacker operations. My thought was that if we did go back, they would just have to see it for themselves, then they would believe it. I hoped we wouldn't, but as it turned out, we went back.

The next morning at 1113 on January 20, our ship was ordered to detach from USS *Midway* and CTG 77.3 and report to CTG 75.9. We were to proceed to the area of MR1 at Point Allison, back on the gun line. I guess the 7th Fleet staff had decided our ship had been having it too good for too long. It was our turn back in the barrel.

After detaching from USS *Midway*, the ship was brought around to a new course of 265 degrees (west), speed 25 knots. Apparently, we were going to race ourselves in covering the distance back to MR1. At 1600 that afternoon, we checked in with the NGLO and the ANGLICO Marine spotter. We shifted back into Watch Condition II, with watch rotations six hours on, then six hours off.

Less than 30 minutes later, our ship was providing gunfire support on targets in several areas located just south of the DMZ. The now-familiar area between the Cua Viet River and the DMZ seemed to be the hot area once again. The conditions here had remained the same; it was like we had never left.

Now back on the gun line, the tempo of gunfire support missions was reduced from what it had been in December. For the next day or so, our ship was only firing 50 to 90 rounds per six hour watch rotations, which was much less than we were accustomed to. During the mid-watch on January 22, we fired 160 HE rounds into target areas inland of the sand dunes north of the Cua Viet River, just to the south of the DMZ. During this gun fire mission, we did get six or seven rounds of counterbattery fire from NVA positions, but none of the incoming salvos were closer than maybe 400 or 450 yards.

These NVA shore battery positions appeared to be located about two miles north of the DMZ at a coastal point of land called Cap Lai, also known as Mui Lai. However, it seemed almost as if they really didn't want to kill us, or they were just piss-poor gunners. The counterbattery fire coming from Cap Lai was not big-gun HE projectiles such as we had experienced elsewhere. Here, the counterbattery splashes were much smaller and closer together. We guessed the NVA was firing anti-aircraft cannons at us, definitely not much bigger than 40 millimeters. The ship stayed at Watch Condition II and did not go to GQ stations.

One of the new crew members on watch asked me, "Are they really shooting at us?"

I replied, "Yes, but it's really no big deal."

I could just make out the guy's face in the low light; he was looking at me in kind of a weird way when he said, "Man, you're crazy."

The next afternoon, I was working at doing some cleaning out on the port bridge wing. It was a warm afternoon with partly cloudy skies. Even in moderate temperatures, working while wearing the hot, bulky flak jacket was a pain. It had been the standing order for some time that anyone on the weather decks while the ship was near the shore had to wear a flak jacket at all times. I decided to stop working for a while and took a smoke break.

Gazing at the beach on the ship's port side and just offshore from the beach, I could see some long bamboo poles sticking up out of the water. In the past, our assumption about these poles had been that the Vietnamese fisherman used them to set and secure their near-shore fishing nets. The ship was at slow speed of about 4 to 5 knots. As the ship moved along the beach, I noticed two longer than usual bamboo poles sticking up out of the water. One was close to the beach and the other one was farther out in the water. As our ship moved along, the two long bamboo poles lined up with each other forming a natural range, which also lined them up with the ship. And that was when it happened.

From the beach area south of Cap Lai, came repeated *"BOFF, BOFF … BOFF, BOFF"* sounds. On the water between the shore and the ship, I could see twin small geysers of water as fired rounds impacted the water. I opened the port bridge wing door and began to tell the OOD we were being fired on from shore. He was already aware of the situation and was ordering the lee helmsman to increase the ship's speed to 20 knots. I realized that the NVA or Viet Cong were using anti-aircraft or some other type of cannons to fire on us.

Another set of *"BOFF, BOFF … BOFF, BOFF"* sounds came, then the successive small twin impact geysers appeared, each time getting closer in range. The cannon gunners were walking each salvo out to us and with each salvo getting closer to the ship. After the last of the *"BOFF, BOFF … BOFF, BOFF"* sounds, the set of impact geysers appeared very close to the ship, but just off the stern on the port quarter as the ship was moving away.

It was at that moment when the sensation of déjá vu came over me. I realized that what had just happened was pretty damn close to the dreams I'd had back when the ship was en route from Guam. Except that in reality, when it had actually happened, I hadn't died.

We deduced that the long bamboo poles were being used by the gunners on shore. When the ship had lined up with the bamboo poles out in the water, the NVA gunner had the bearing line up to the ship all set. All they had to do was to walk out each set of salvos in finding the range to the ship; actually a pretty clever, cheap, but thankfully fairly ineffective gunfire control system.

The next night's mid-watch events were similar to the night before. We fired 96 HE rounds into target areas inland on spotted targets both north and south of the DMZ. Twice, the spotter requested we fire illumination rounds over the target areas before resuming the gun fire missions. Twice during the watch we got counterbattery fire from the NVA positions near Cap Lai. Again, most of the incoming salvos fell well short of or well over the range to our ship. As with the night before, the ship stayed at Watch Condition II and did not go to GQ stations.

The next morning, on January 24, we got word that the day before the North Vietnamese had returned to the peace talks in Paris and had agreed to sign a cease-fire agreement. According to the terms of the agreement all hostilities were to end, effective midnight, Greenwich Mean Time on January 27. For us, the cease fire would begin at 0800 local time on January 28, in four more days. After lunch, we began to wonder if the cease-fire agreement was actually real or not. Between noon and midnight, we fired 258 more HE rounds onto designated targets, both north and south of the DMZ.

The tempo of NGLO and Marine spotter calls for gunfire support missions increased throughout the day. For some stupid reason some of us had thought that with a signed cease-fire agreement, we would just slide nice and easy to the cease-fire deadline date and time. Apparently, that was not going to be the case. By the mid-watch, some of us had realized it was going to be ugly right up to the very end. Others began to express doubt about the cease-fire. Several guys asked, "Could this cease-fire stuff just be bullshit?"

During my next watch, the mid-watch on January 25, we fired 120 HE rounds on the same general target areas we had been pounding on for the two previous days. At about 0400 the lookouts reported splashes in the water astern of us at about 500 yards. Sonar was reporting bearing and ranges to more counterbattery fire as the rounds splashed in the water. Since the counterbattery was not a direct or immediate threat to the ship, we had no intention of returning their fire. Just like the previous times, we stayed in Watch Condition II and didn't bother going to GQ stations.

Finally, January 28 arrived. On the mid-watch, we brought the new day in with an attack on Highway 1 in the Quang Tri province. The NVA was pouring truckloads of troops, artillery, and armored vehicles down the highway south of the DMZ. We moved our ship near shore to an area of shallow water just north of the Cua Viet River entrance in order to increase the effective range of our guns inland. Between 0030 and 0630, we fired 303 HE rounds onto spotted targets along the highway. The Marine spotter reports came frequently over the radio with feedback on the effect our gunfire was having in stopping the NVA movements.

The call for cease fire came at 0630, but within three minutes, the spotter was back on the radio with more targets. We commenced fire again at 0633. We kept firing on targets until cease fire was called at 0745. We had shot another 150 HE rounds between 0633 and 0745, 15 minutes before the cease fire agreement went into effect at 0800, then it was all over. At 0747, the captain ordered the ship to come around to a new course of 125 degrees, speed 15 knots. Our ship began to move away from the coast of Vietnam.

During much of the time since the ship had left Subic Bay, the traditional striking of the ship's bell on the hour and half hour had been dispensed with. The BMOW on watch that morning, a third class petty officer, approached the OOD at 30 seconds before 0800 wearing a crisp, clean white hat.

He came to attention while rendering a hand salute to the OOD and made the following formal and traditional request, "Officer of the deck, request permission to strike eight bells on time, sir."

The lieutenant, who was the OOD, smiled broadly, returned the BMOW's salute, and replied, "Very well, Boatswain Mate. Permission granted to strike eight bells on time."

With that, the BMOW walked to the 1MC intercom, turned on the switches for all of the amplified speakers throughout the ship, then took the bell's clapper in hand as he watched the second hand on the bridge clock. The moment the clock's second hand came to the 12-hour position indicating 0800, the BMOW began the strikes on the bell, "*Ding, Ding... Ding, Ding... Ding, Ding... Ding, Ding.*" Immediately following the bell strikes, he made the traditional, customary, and routine 0800 voice announcement over the 1MC: "Now turn to. Commence ship's work."

What the boatswain mate had accomplished by following naval tradition and custom was to communicate throughout the ship that our war was over and the cease fire was in effect. I don't believe there could have been any finer way of marking this huge occasion than with the boatswain mate's simple act of "striking eight bells."

The orders for the ship were to move out to a waiting station offshore and rendezvous with USS *Horne* (DLG 30). En route to the waiting station, we received a helicopter over our deck from the aircraft carrier USS *Ranger* (CVA 61) delivering mail to our ship. I have never forgotten the mail call from that day. I got a Christmas care package from my older sister back in Illinois, sent on December 5, so it had taken a little less than eight weeks to reach me.

Down in the chart room, I shared the contents of my package with my shipmates. All the cookies in the package were broken, but no matter, we ate every crumb. In the package was also a small smorgasbord of crackers, cheese, and meat spreads, candy, and other various snack foods. The timing of the package's arrival could not have been any better; it gave us a reason to celebrate that our war was over. Whatever my shipmates didn't want from the package was earmarked to go to my gedunk locker.

It may be hard for some to understand, but when our ship was on the gun line, with hours and hours each night spent at GQ stations carrying out the night raids and attacks, plus the ever-constant rearming and refueling operations, there were two things in extremely short supply. One was sleep, the other was food. During combat operations, most maybe got one meal per day, time permitting. That was why care packages such as the one my sister sent me were so valuable and important. It wasn't really about the food; it was more about the momentary feeling of comfort and comradeship.

Our celebration was short-lived. Within a short time, the refueling detail was called away. It was time for me to get back on the helm. The rest of the day would be spent going alongside for a VERTREP with USS *Mount Hood*, then onto USS *Ponchatoula* (AO 148) for a FAS, and later, another VERTREP with USS *San Jose*. By late afternoon, our ship was refueled, rearmed, and had replenished its stores. We made our rendezvous with USS *Horne* late afternoon at the waiting station area. Most of the U.S. 7th Fleet ships had pulled away from the coast of Vietnam to a number of offshore waiting stations.

Relief came to the crew in the form of the ship shifting to Watch Condition III, the normal watch rotations of four hours on and off eight hours. The ship's routine was coming back to normal, and as always for many of us, we were appreciative that we got our racks back in our berthing compartments. Once again, we had our racks back to sleep in.

The purpose was to have the fleet poised at various waiting stations in the event that the cease fire didn't hold or if it was decided it was necessary to move the fleet back in. Our ship's waiting station was about 50 nautical miles out in the Gulf of Tonkin, almost due east of Dong Hoi, North Vietnam. The war wasn't really over yet; unfortunately, more Americans were still going to die.

The time at the waiting station area with USS *Horne* was spent essentially patrolling the area running along 25 nautical mile legs, staying roughly parallel to the North Vietnam coastline. Several times our ship would proceed away from *Horne* to go investigate suspicious small craft that had either been sighted visually or by radar. Each time the small craft turned out to be innocent Vietnamese fishing vessels.

During the mid-watch on Tuesday, January 30, our ship was maintaining our station staying between 4,000 and 10,000 yards ahead of USS *Horne*. Just after 0200, CIC reported to the bridge that there had been a mid-air collision between two Navy F-4 Phantom Jets in our immediate vicinity. At 0210, our ship called away and stationed the recovery detail. Based on CIC's recommendations, we maneuvered the ship to the position where CIC estimated the downed aircraft should be.

At 0240, we had visual sight of the first pilot in the water, and the watch officer in CIC was in communication with the pilot over his survival radio. We kept the pilot illuminated with a searchlight just forward of the ship's port beam about 20 to 30 yards from the ship.

The USS *Horne* was over a mile away, in the process of rescuing another pilot from the water. Our ship called *Horne*, requesting permission to carry out the rescue of the pilot. There was a sense of astonishment by many on the bridge when *Horne* called back denying our request and telling us to standby the pilot until they could arrive and affect the rescue. We marked the pilot's position with floating life ring buoys with attached rescue strobe lights. *Horne* ordered our ship to clear the position.

We lost radio contact with the pilot as we cleared away to allow *Horne* to make her approach to the downed pilot's position in the water. It took *Horne* over 20 minutes to make it to our position and carry out the pilot's rescue. At 0300, the unit commander on USS *Horne* ordered our ship to stay clear of the area and to standby. At 0330, our ship was ordered to stay within a distance of 5,000 yards from USS *Horne*. Finally, at around 0440 *Horne* called us with a position for our ship to proceed to and begin running search patterns in conducting search and rescue efforts for the other two downed air crewmen.

The F-4J Phantom had two-man aircrews, the pilot and a flight officer. The other F-4J aircrew hadn't been located yet. The two jets had been returning to USS *Ranger* (CVA 61) from a barrier combat patrol mission over the Gulf of Tonkin when, about 90 miles from USS *Ranger*, a mid-air collision had occurred between the two aircraft. At 0505, after arriving at the commence search point, our ship began the maneuvers, carrying out an "Expanding Square" search pattern.

The Expanding Square search pattern is where the ship starts the pattern at a constant search speed and after running each set search leg distance, the ship turns 90 degrees, runs the same search leg distance, then makes the next turn of 90 degrees. The turns of 90 degrees are continued at the end of each search leg. If the pattern could be viewed from above while tracing the ship's track, it would create at the end of every fourth turn a square shape.

As the ship runs the pattern, the search leg distance is increased at every third leg. Thus, when the ship has searched one square the next square will be of an expanded size from the previous one. The track spacing between each successive square is equal to the increase in the distance of every third search leg.

Our ship, along with USS *Horne*, conducted search patterns for the remainder of the day, searching for the other two air crewmen. Later in the afternoon, USS *Ramsey* (DEG 2) joined up and participated with our ships in executing various search patterns. At 1910 that evening, USS *Horne* detached our ship to steam independently for the night. The search for the other two F-4 air crewmen was being called off. Later, we learned we had been searching for Lieutenant James Duensing, the F-4's pilot, and his flight officer, Lieutenant Junior Grade Roy Haviland. These two airmen are officially listed as Missing in Action (MIA); neither was ever found. The two F-4J Phantom jets were the last Navy aircraft lost during the Vietnam War.

On January 31, reports from American military advisers in the countryside of South Vietnam reported the following: *"Cease fire or no, operations are continuing much as before and with the support of daily air strikes and heavy artillery barrages they (the South Vietnamese military forces) have finally begun to roll the Viet Cong back. More Vietnamese Air Force tactical air strikes were flown in Lam Dong in the three days after the cease fire than had been flown in the previous six months."*

I guess the content of the report was to give the impression that now, after the cease fire, the South Vietnamese military appeared to be able to prosecute their own war against North Vietnam without our help.

In company with USS *Horne*, our ships were slowly heading further and further toward the southeast, away from the Vietnam mainland. On Wednesday, January 31, we learned what our near-term fate would be. Our ship would rendezvous with USS *Shasta* (AE 33) for STREAM high-line ammunition on-load, then to USS *Milwaukee* (AOR 2) for an FAS replenishment.

Below decks, the rumors were running rampant. The question from many generally was, "If the war is over, why all the rearming?" If anyone including the captain knew the answer, they weren't talking. However, the question did get answered right in the middle of the FAS operation with USS *Milwaukee*.

The XO came on the bridge with a piece of paper in his hand and went out to the port bridge wing to speak with the captain. After a discussion, the XO came into the bridge; he was actually smiling as he walked over to the ship's 1MC intercom and picked up the microphone. Then he said, "Attention on the *Rich*, this is the XO. I am informing you that on completion of the FAS with USS *Milwaukee*, our ship is detached from CTG 75.9 and we are to proceed independently on duties assigned to the port of Hong Kong for a 10-day port visit."

Judging from the smiles of happiness on everyone's face on the bridge, you would have thought the XO had just said he was going to give everyone a million dollars each.

Later, we learned there was more in the naval message than just the port visit to Hong Kong. After Hong Kong, the ship was to proceed to Yokosuka, Japan, for a seven-day maintenance and ship repair period. Then we were to depart Yokosuka, Japan, on February 17 for the passage to San Diego, CA. From San Diego, via the Panama Canal, the ship was projected to arrive back in Norfolk on or about March 23, 1973. Now that was the kind of news everyone wanted to hear.

For those of us on board USS *Rich*, our war was over. None of us could say for certain how many, but we knew our shooting onto targets both in North and South Vietnam had killed the enemy. This also meant we had killed a considerable number of human beings. There is a certain kind of mental disconnect to this type of killing, I guess because it's not up close and personal killing. We often couldn't see the actual moment when our form of death was delivered; we could only hear about it from the spotter over the radio with descriptions of the results from our shooting accuracy.

None of us ever discussed any of this between ourselves; we all knew what we were doing. There was no need or good reason to discuss it. The subject has always been just left alone, at least outwardly and verbally. In writing of this story, it is the first time in over 45 years that I have discussed or told about my experiences on board USS *Rich* during her deployment to Vietnam. I have no answer to the question of why I have never talked about or discussed it before now. That's just the way it is.

9. HEADED TOWARD PLANET EARTH

Just because combat operations had ended, the deployment obviously would continue for the ship and our crew. There were still almost 12,000 miles of the earth's surface between us and Norfolk. Yes, most of the crew was pumped about going to Hong Kong. The ship was also in need of numerous repairs, which would get completed in Japan. The effects of combat operations in Vietnam had not been kind to the ship. There were a number of engineering issues that had been caused by the many operations carried out at flank speed bells.

The ship also had some superstructure and hull issues. Some damage was minor, some more significant. Most of the hull issues had been principally caused by blast pressures from the close aboard underwater explosions from counterbattery. Even though we were only four months into our deployment, many in the crew just wanted to go home.

Our ship departed from an area east of Yankee Station on February 1, on the mid-watch bound for Hong Kong. The passage plan distance from the ship's departure point to Hong Kong was only about 650 nautical miles, so at a speed of 16 knots, it would take us just a little over 40 hours of steaming to be at the approaches to Hong Kong Island. Early morning on February 3, the ship began its approach to the Toi

Islands southwest of Hong Kong Island. This was before the International Convention on International Regulations for the Preventing of Collisions at Sea had been amended, adding vessel "traffic separation schemes" with respective inbound and outbound vessel traffic lanes through major waterways.

As our ship got closer to the southern channel entrance leading into Hong Kong, there were hundreds of ships, fishing vessels, and sampans everywhere, coming from every direction. It was going to be a busy and challenging morning for navigation and ship control by the bridge crew to get the ship safely into Hong Kong and Victoria Harbor.

I had taken the QMOW navigation watch at 0345 that morning. As our ship approached the area of the Toi Islands that morning, I got another lesson in radar navigation. Coming from seaward, the navigational challenge is always to get more accurate fix positions of the ship. It is a transition from open-ocean, not so accurate electronic navigation and DR, to more accurate piloting navigation with visual compass bearings to navigation aids and radar navigation. That day, the weather was chilly and the sky was heavily overcast with thick and low dense clouds. The challenge was to correlate the DR positions with radar ranges to islands and other land features.

That morning, I was principally using radar bearings and ranges to the outer islands and correlating the radar images to the islands on the navigation chart. Several radar fixes in a row showed our ship to be well away from our DR position. With that information, I made a course change recommendation to the OOD, which he acted on and ordered the helmsman to make the course change. Several minutes later, I took another round of radar ranges to points on the different islands. This time the radar fix showed the ship back closer to our original DR position. Something was very wrong.

I quickly found the error; the earlier images on the radar's display, taken to be the islands, had actually been radar images of low altitude clouds. Clouds with their high water vapor content are dense, and next to metals, water is the next best reflecting surface of radar radio waves.

I quickly reconfirmed the ship's actual position and made the recommendation to the OOD with the correct course to steer. It was a valuable lesson in ship navigation for me, reminding me to always look for a second independent source of navigation information or data to either confirm or dismiss the accuracy of the first obtained navigation information or data.

Hong Kong Harbor lies between the north side of Hong Kong Island and off the coast of southern China in the South China Sea. It is one of the most perfect natural harbors in the world.

Our ship made up to a mooring buoy outside of the main shipping channel in Victoria Harbor at 0900 that morning. Since the ship was moored to an anchored buoy and not to a dock, the engineering plant was going to have stay lit-off. The ship's crew would be in the three section duty rotations while in Hong Kong. Other than on-duty days, it would be holiday routine for the crew.

Once the ship was moored, from the bridge we could stop and take in the view of Hong Kong and Kowloon. In 1973, Hong Kong was still a British Crown possession. The view of Hong Kong from the harbor looked like walls of tall skyscraper buildings in front of a backdrop of taller, steep mountains. To go ashore in Hong Kong from the ship would require water taxis that would run continuously day and night. Kowloon was an urban area in Hong Kong comprising the Kowloon Peninsula and New Kowloon. The only way to reach Kowloon from Hong Kong Island was to take a ferry boat across from Victoria Harbor.

My duty section had the duty for the first day in Hong Kong. I was on the first quarterdeck watch until noon. Just before noon, a sampan came alongside the ship and tied up at the bottom of the ship's accommodation ladder. A small older Chinese woman, standing no more than 4 feet 6 inches tall, came up the ladder and, once on the quarterdeck, said her name was Mary Soo. Mary Soo then demanded to speak with the ship's first lieutenant. I didn't realize it at that moment, but we had just met the famous Hong Kong Mary Soo.

We asked Mary Soo to wait, and the officer of the watch sent me to go find the first lieutenant. I found the first lieutenant in the Wardroom and told him a Chinese woman named Mary Soo was on the quarterdeck and wanted to see him. The first lieutenant acted as if I had just told him there was a three-star admiral asking for him on the quarterdeck. I followed him out of the Wardroom as he rushed to the quarterdeck to meet Mary Soo.

Mary Soo was on board to make a deal to paint the entire exterior of the ship. Navy regulations prohibited paying foreign nationals in cash for work accomplished on the ship, but other ways of compensating workers like Mary Soo were easily found. Since a good part of the crew would be ashore every day on liberty, most of the prepared food in the galley would go to waste. This was where Mary Soo came in. Her deal was to paint the ship in exchange for all of the ship's leftover food. The first lieutenant quickly made the deal with Mary Soo.

After the deal was completed, within an hour, a small fleet of sampans arrived alongside the ship, and a small army of mostly women filed on board to start painting. The ship provided the paint, and Mary Soo's crew did the work. Mary's crew of mostly young Asian women would paint the ship's sides from small sampans. To apply the paint, they used old cloth rags instead of paint brushes or rollers. After breakfast, lunch, and dinner, women from Mary Soo's group came on board and were allowed to go to the galley to collect the food leftovers.

No one really knew how old Mary Soo was. One of the boatswain mates said that as far as he knew, she had been painting Navy ships calling on Hong Kong for decades. The story as we heard it was that Mary Soo served the food in a restaurant she owned and only recruited orphans to work on her crews. She used the profits from her restaurant to pay her workers. Recruited young female orphans were sworn not to engage in prostitution or to date sailors, and if they were caught doing either, Mary Soo would immediately fire them.

Late the next morning, I got on the water taxi to the fleet landing dock with a couple of my buddies, and from there, we headed to downtown Hong Kong. Our first stop was at one of the major hotels where a number of crew members had rented rooms. Off the hotel's main lobby area were a number of high-end shops and stores. Most of the shops were selling expensive jewelry, ivory carvings, gold, and brass ornaments.

While passing through the lobby, we saw some of the ship's officers sitting in the lobby with their wives. There was that class hierarchy again, where they could afford to have their wives or girlfriends fly over to meet them in Hong Kong. I was bit surprised, because to my knowledge, we'd had pretty short notification about our port visit to Hong Kong. I expressed this surprise to one of my buddies, who was a radioman. He told me that on the night we'd received the message directing our ship to Hong Kong, the radioman had been told to find a MARS operator so some of the officers and crew could call home.

MARS is the military affiliated radio system. The ship initiates MARS by attempting to call, then making contact over high-frequency radio with a stateside MARS operator. MARS operators usually are volunteer HAM (amateur radio) radio operators, who will then place a long-distance collect phone call. My buddy continued by saying that he thought most of the officers had made MARS calls that night. He added, "I never told you about this, right?"

I told him, "No problem, my lips are sealed."

Generally, MARS calls were reserved for when a service member had received notification from the American Red Cross or some other similar agency about serious family emergencies. Typically, at the commanding officer's discretion, the ship would try to make a MARS phone call if the service member desired to call home.

To me, this was another example of the obvious and distinct divide between the quality of life for the enlisted sailors as compared to the officers. The on-board climate and subculture always seemed to be that it was an officer's right to be self-serving and generally look out for his own self-welfare first. To be fair, this culture was reflective of the prevalent hierarchical order at the time, where many officers were still taught somewhere during the commissioning process that enlisted personnel were members of a lesser order than themselves. Most of us came to understand this culture, but that didn't mean we agreed with it; we had just learned to accept it.

The main reason we'd gone to the hotel was that they had an international telephone exchange. My first priority was to make my phone call to Jan. This phone exchange was different; here, you paid for the international long distance call after the phone call was completed. The phone booths were almost luxurious. They were large, air-conditioned, and equipped with comfortable chairs. After filling out the call request form and turning it in, the wait began. After about an hour, my waiting number was announced. I was a bit concerned about the time of the call since back home the time would be the night before, after 11:00 p.m.

After several rings, I heard Jan say "hello." I had written her that we had left Vietnam, but that letter had been sent only four days before. I told her we were in Hong Kong. Her reply was that she had been wondering where I was. She knew the war had ended, but had had no idea where our ship was. She seemed relieved and told me that she had been worrying about what was going on and where I might be. It had been six weeks since we had last spoken when I had called her on Christmas Day from Singapore.

The big piece of news she didn't know about yet was that the ship was headed home. After she heard my news, she immediately said, "Well, I've got to start making plans to get back to Norfolk before you get home." I told her I'd call from Japan with any updates or changes to the schedule and gave her the dates we would be in Japan. After about 30 minutes, my budget for the phone call was tapped out. We said our goodbyes, then hung up. I always felt much, much, better after talking with Jan.

After my phone call, I caught up with my buddies. Every street was lined with shops, restaurants, night clubs, and bars. We ate lunch at a street-side lunch shop and by mid-afternoon, we felt the sun was far enough past the yardarm to partake in some alcoholic refreshment. We found a bar that looked interesting and went in. Inside the bar, it was dark; loud music was playing; and Chinese and Asian women were everywhere. I thought we had time warped from mid-afternoon to midnight.

The price for our drinks seemed reasonable, so we decided we had found an adequate watering hole for the afternoon. As for the bar girls, it was the same scenario as in the Philippines and Singapore: "Buy me a drink, Joe?" However, the bar girls here had a bit more class. They would actually ask, "What is your name?"

I noted one unique thing about Hong Kong. There seemed to be buildings under construction everywhere you looked. Attached all around the perimeter of each building were scaffolding structures spanning from the ground to the highest parts of the structure, looking like giant jungle gyms. The curious thing was the scaffolding material, constructed all from bamboo poles lashed together; no steel such as we were accustomed to seeing back home. Chinese construction workers could be seen scrambling and climbing around on the bamboo scaffolding high up on the buildings.

One evening in a bar, I commented to a British fella about all the tall buildings in Hong Kong and all the new ones being built. He smiled and pointed his finger upward as he replied, "In Hong Kong there is very little land between the harbor and the mountain; the only other option is to build vertically."

I didn't do too much of anything while in Hong Kong other than going out for a couple nights of drinking and partying, mainly because my money situation was tight. Almost all of my pay went home to Jan. Upon arrival in Hong Kong, I did have some extra money saved from tax exemption and hostile fire pay, so I decided to send my extra money home by postal money order. However, because the ship was going to be there for 10 days, I could demand my price and get it for standing other people's duty. My rate was $60 per day, so for the 10 days in Hong Kong, I had three duty days of my own, then took standby duty on three other days, and voilà, I made $180.

Soon, our departure date arrived. At 1200 on February 13, we broke off our anchor chain from the mooring buoy, got underway, and steamed out of Victoria Harbor back out into the South China Sea. The passage plan distance from Hong Kong to Yokosuka, Japan, was 1,545 nautical miles. The Yokosuka Naval Base was located on Japan's main island of Honshu. At our planned transit speed, it would take less than four days to make the passage to Japan.

The trip to Japan went smoothly and without much bad weather. Early morning on February 17, our ship began the approach to Tokyo Bay. Just before sunrise, Mount Fuji became visible just off our port bow while the ship was still over 45 nautical miles out at sea. Mount Fuji is about 50 miles west of Yokosuka and is the highest mountain in Japan with the elevation of its peak at 12,389 feet.

The Yokosuka Naval Base is about 11 miles south of Yokohama, located on a peninsula in the southwestern section of Tokyo Bay. At 0900, our ship moored at Berth 6 on Sherman Pier at the Yokosuka Naval Base. The naval basin waterfront was packed with docked 7th Fleet ships homeported in Yokosuka. A lot of other destroyers in the same status as our ship were undergoing preparations before starting their homeward passages across the Pacific Ocean to their respective home ports in the United States.

Within an hour after docking, workers and crews from the Yokosuka Naval Shipyard and Repair facility were swarming all over the ship. One of the major engineering problems that needed to be solved was that we had been constantly taking on seawater through both the rudder posts packing and the propeller shafts packing glands. The packing had been blown out from all the concussions from the ship firing on the gun line and close underwater explosions. These areas of damage meant the bilge pumps had also been worked a lot in keeping the ingress of seawater under control.

The yard workers came and went on the ship around the clock. They spent several days on the shrapnel holes welding small- to medium-sized steel plates over the damaged areas. As they were completed by the shipyard workers, the crew painted over the repaired areas and patches.

I learned that for years, Navy ships coming from Yankee Station or the Vietnam gun line had been sent to Yokosuka to be patched up and repaired before the ships were sent back stateside to their home ports. In part, the Yokosuka stop was necessary because the ships needed the repair and maintenance. The other reason, told to me by someone I considered reliable, was that the Navy did not want to send its ships home with visual battle damage or in an obviously rundown condition for families of the crew and the news media to see.

On our second day in Japan, I was able to call home and speak with Jan. Besides wanting to talk with her, I wanted to keep her updated on the ship's schedule and to check in with her as to when she planned to fly back to Norfolk. To my surprise, she had already received the money order from Hong Kong. I explained to her that after the ship left Japan on our scheduled departure date of February 5, it would be at least March 8, before the ship would arrive in San Diego, which would be our next opportunity to talk again. After hanging up the phone, it hit me: in just 33 more days, I would be home.

I went out into town for one or two nights, just to get off the ship. The closest sections of Yokosuka were outside of the main gate from the naval base. After crossing Yokosuka Highway and Dobuita Street there was street after street of shops, bars, nightclubs, and restaurants, the normal fare of what I had found so far in Asia. On the ship, we had been briefed to establish the actual cost of the meal before ordering in bars that also served food. Some bars in Yokosuka were notorious for grossly overcharging sailors for their meal, then demanding full payment. If the sailor balked at the high prices, the bar would call the Navy shore patrol (SP) or the Yokosuka Police.

This actually happened to a group of us during our first night in town at one of the bars that also had a restaurant. We found the place, which seemed to be kind of off the beaten path down a long, narrow side street. After entering, we found we were the only Americans in the place, which really didn't bother or concern us. We all followed the advice we had been given and checked with the waitress to ensure the actual cost for our meals would be the same as stated on the menu. Sure enough, after eating, when the check came for the table, the payment amount on the check had been tripled from the amount it should have been. Several of us argued with who we assumed was the manager, an elderly Japanese woman, about the high charges on the check.

It wasn't long before two 6-foot tall plus Navy shore patrolmen were standing at our table. One of the SPs was a really big and tall first class petty officer boatswain mate. He calmly explained to us that it would be best to just pay the bill and be on our way. Several of us tried to tell the SPs how the place was overcharging us. The big SP, in a stern command voice said, "Just pay the bill and let's go."

We followed his demand and paid the bill. Outside of the restaurant, the SPs pulled us aside and told us to get out of that part of the town as the local communist agitators were active that night. One of the SPs explained that in that part of town, it was common for the communist agitators to look for U.S. sailors like us to either beat up or kill if they could. We decided that it probably would be wise to follow the SP's advice, so we left for the other sections of town where they said it would be safer.

During the daytime, we made the rounds to other ships in Yokosuka, bumming any supplies we could get. We needed supplies badly, and there were some navigation charts we needed for the passage home. The normal stuff was in short supply as well: pens, pencils, deck logbooks, weather observation sheets, and different types of record books. One resupply method was to go from ship to ship to speak with each QM gang and ask or beg for whatever you thought you could get them to give you.

"Hey, man, you wanna swap?" That was the question we heard on ship after ship homeported in Yokosuka. As we made our rounds bumming supplies at each ship's quarterdeck, we would ask to speak with the duty QM. After the duty QM would arrive at the quarterdeck, we would describe what supplies we were looking for and ask for what they could spare. If the duty QM agreed, he would escort us up to the bridge. On almost every ship, while walking along the main deck, guy after guy would ask, "What ship are you on and what's your home port?"

Our reply was always, "The USS *Rich* out of Norfolk."

Then would come the standard question, "Hey, man, you wanna swap?"

My reply was always, "No, thanks."

The Navy today still has the Exchanges of Duty (SWAPS) program. In order for two sailors to SWAP duty assignments, they have to be of identical rate and rating, serving in the same type duty. Either way, based on what I had seen of Japan so far, I wasn't interested. After being asked about a dozen times, "Hey, man, you wanna swap?" the fact that so many had asked told me life might not be that good on ships homeported in Japan.

The day before we were scheduled to depart Yokosuka, I noticed that USS *Cone* (DD 866) had docked that morning at a berth ahead of our ship. USS *Cone* was my friend Al's ship from MM "A" school. That afternoon, I went over to *Cone* and asked the quarterdeck watch if they could page or send word for Al. Just minutes after Al's name was called over the 1MC, my friend came out of the after watertight door on the port side and walked toward the quarterdeck. When Al saw me, he truly was surprised.

We headed down to *Cone*'s mess decks to talk. In talking with him, I learned his ship had arrived on the gun line about two weeks after we had. He discussed how his ship had participated in the Linebacker II operations in late December and explained how his ship had spent a lot of time in what he called "a very hostile environment." Except for a brief break on Christmas Day, his ship had conducted two or three strike missions every night. We talked about the experience of receiving counterbattery fire from the NVA shore batteries.

Al expressed much the same as our snipes had that, "Down in the hole, the underwater shell explosions will freak you out." He mentioned that just before midnight on New Year's Eve in 1972 the *Cone* had fired the last round of surface ordnance for the 7th Fleet. *Cone's* condition was much like our ship with some superficial damage from shrapnel, but no significant damage suffered by the ship. I had hoped that we could go out that night for a couple of drinks, but Al had the duty and couldn't get anyone to standby for him.

After explaining how my transition from the MM rating to the QM rating had transpired, Al said, "Man, you are lucky; at least on here, being a snipe really sucks." I noted throughout our talk that even though he said nothing specific, my friend was miserable. I often thought of him as having more experience than myself, since he'd already had one year in the Navy when we'd met back at "A" school. But his time in the fleet and experience was the same as mine, and I could understand his dilemma.

A couple of snipes on my ship who'd come onboard about the same time as me constantly reminded me of how lucky I was to be "up in the fresh air." I felt bad for my friend and it was tough to see someone who usually was upbeat and positive feeling so down about his circumstances. Before ending my visit, we exchanged mailing addresses and telephone numbers, with the promise to look each other up some day. I said goodbye to my friend and went back to my ship.

The next morning, at 0715 local time, we got underway from the berth at Sherman Pier and departed the port of Yokosuka. The passage plan distance from Yokosuka to San Diego was 4,865 nautical miles. Our passage plan was to follow a modified Great Circle route taking our ship into the higher latitudes of the northern Pacific Ocean. A rendezvous with a Navy fleet oiler was to take place about mid-passage for underway replenishment FAS, well north of the Midway Islands.

Within a day after departure from Japan, the skies began to cloud over and the weather turned cold. The cold northwest winds whipped up sea waves of substantial height. As the ship headed east-northeast, we had following seas generally on the port quarter. Following seas make it harder to steer a good course, as the waves slammed into the stern causing the ship to yaw from side to side as it surfed down the face of each wave into the next trough.

The weather also made the use of celestial navigation nearly impossible. Every morning and evening twilight period, the skies were overcast with full cloud cover, obscuring the stars and planets. That limited fix positioning navigation to Loran "A." Obtaining fixes of the ship's positions by Loran "A" was getting harder to obtain each day due to atmospheric or weather conditions. So essentially, navigation for the passage was coming down to DR positions.

At some point on February 28, the ship once again crossed the International Date Line, moving us from east longitude into west longitude. At least now the ship was in the correct hemisphere, the western hemisphere. To us, this was much the same as a spacecraft entering the earth's atmosphere on returning back to earth from outer space. We were making progress in getting back to "the world." The weather remained much the same day after day, with not much sun and a lot of clouds, wind, and waves.

Late afternoon on March 1, we made the rendezvous with the Navy fleet-oiler ship. I don't recall the name of the ship, but it was a welcome sight. All of the QMs were a little antsy about what the actual position of the ship was since we had been navigating across the Pacific Ocean mainly by dead reckoning. I was the underway replenishment helmsman and wouldn't be at the navigation plot.

I made the suggestion to one of the QMs that while we were alongside we should ask the oiler for its position coordinates. He asked the signalman if they could signalman-to-signalman using Semaphore, and ask the oiler's QMs for their latitude and longitude coordinates. Sometime later one of the signalmen came down to the bridge and gave the QM a piece of paper with latitude and longitude coordinates written on it. The QM immediately plotted the oiler's coordinates on the chart and smiled. He came over to me at the helm station and said, "Shoot, we're only off from their position by about three miles, not bad."

We had been dead reckoning the ship's position for the better part of five days. Assuming the oiler's position was somewhat accurate, being only three miles different from their position was actually pretty damn good. After about three hours alongside the oiler, our ship made the breakaway and cleared the oiler. The ship's course was set to take us to San Diego from our new and latest fix position, courtesy of the Navy fleet-oiler. We still had over 2,650 nautical miles to go to San Diego.

As the ship traveled further east, the weather slowly improved each day. Morning and evening twilights were still disappointing as the amount of cloud cover foiled our attempts to get fixes from observations of the navigational stars or planets. On several different days, I managed to get morning sun shots for a single line of position (LOP) that we combined with sun observations taken at Local Apparent Noon, which, when reduced, yields the ship's latitude LOP.

Advancing the earlier morning sun LOP along the ship's course line for the dead reckoned distance onto the Local Apparent Noon's latitude LOP, where the two LOPs intersected or crossed, formed a "running fix position." In celestial navigation jargon, we called this the "noon" position. Our running fixes showed that our DR position was still good, but we would update our DR positions each time from the latest running fix position.

On Thursday, March 8, during the morning watch, our ship began its approach to San Diego. I had the 0400 to 0800 watch that morning. As we approached the Southern California coastline, eventually we made radar land fall. Now it was possible to get more precise fix positions of the ship plotted on the chart using radar ranges and bearings taken to coastal features. After several consistent radar fixes, I determined the ship was only several miles north of where it should be. I showed my navigation plot to the OOD, and he agreed that we should turn to a more southerly course.

We essentially sailed parallel to the coastline for about three miles before picking up Point Loma on radar and sighting the Point Loma Lighthouse. At 1000, the ship went to sea and anchor detail for entering San Diego. Having used just dead reckoning navigation for about 90 percent of the Pacific Ocean crossing, I was happy with how close we had actually come to hitting our planned point of arrival.

Entering San Diego Bay requires that a ship approach from the south. When entering the bay, Point Loma is on the port side of the ship, or the west side of the channel. North Island is on the ship's starboard side, or the east side of the channel. Ships must steam inbound between Point Loma and North Island, then sail around the northern side of North Island. After clearing North Island, the ship needs to change course to the south as it enters into San Diego Bay. The San Diego Naval Base piers are on the east side of the bay. It was a fairly short and easy transit from Point Loma to the docks at the naval base.

The ship docked at Pier 6 at 1030, we were back in the United States, even if it was California. The first order of business for the ship was a freshwater washdown to remove all of the salt from the ship. Refueling the ship, receiving supplies, and loading stores all were on the schedule of events for the next day. We would be in San Diego for three days over the weekend before the ship would leave on Monday, bound next for the Panama Canal.

I had duty the first day in San Diego. Now being back in a U.S. port, there were rows of telephone booths at the head of the pier. That evening, the duty section leader gave me permission to leave the ship to go make a phone call. My phone call, of course, was to my wife, Jan. At the phone booth, it was almost a luxury to just dial "0" to speak with the operator and place my collect call home, and not have to go through the telephone exchange rigmarole of making an international call.

Within moments, Jan and I were speaking. I mainly wanted to tell her the ship's estimated time of arrival in Norfolk, which now was scheduled for 0900 local time, March 23. She told me that she had flight reservations for her and our son to fly back to Norfolk the following week, and her brother Joe would pick them up at the airport. She had left our car at Joe's home in Virginia Beach, so she would spend the first night at Joe's house before going home to our apartment in Norfolk. After the typical long goodbyes, we hung up. Once again after hanging up the phone, I mentally counted the days to go; there were 14 days and a wake up.

The next day was a busy one for the crew loading supplies, stores, and fueling the ship. Saturday and Sunday were to be holiday routine for the crew. On Friday night, several of my buddies and I walked out the South 32nd Street gate from the San Diego Naval Base into San Diego. Just off base near Main Street was The Strip with the Fleet clubs, stores, and bars. We bypassed The Strip and headed up to National Avenue, where we had heard there were some good bars and clubs.

The first bar we walked into was almost as if we had flashed back to Olongapo. The place was filled with pretty Filipino women. My friends were shaking their heads up and down and smiling, and one of my buddies said, "All right, this place looks good." The difference was, none of us heard the standard, "Buy me a drink, Joe?" These women acted more like American women, where the guy had to approach the woman, not the other way around. Also, their English was much better. All in all, they were still very friendly.

The night turned into a barhopping exercise, going from place to place. After a few beers at each bar, we would move on. Around midnight, we found ourselves back at the first bar where we'd started the night. Several of my buddies were a bit disappointed to find that most of the women were now focusing on sailors from the base or other ships. The tables, booths, and the dance floor were all busy with paired up women and sailors. Having learned by now that these types of situations were formulas for trouble, I made my excuses to my buddies, left the bar, and started the walk back to the ship. I didn't need any trouble at this point, as my focus was on just getting home.

I went out the next night again just to hit the bars in San Diego and to get off the ship. The outcome was pretty much the same routine as the night before and ended the same for me, walking back to the ship alone. I had duty the next day on Sunday, so it seemed prudent to conserve my energy. This line of thinking came with a realization about myself: *Damn. Maybe I'm starting to grow up?*

On arrival in Norfolk, the ship was scheduled to have the customary period of 30 days called "standdown." The post deployment standdown allowed up to one half of the crew to take up to 15 days of leave and upon the first group's return from leave, the other half of the crew could take their leave. Who got leave in the first leave period depended upon how early one got his leave request approved. The XO had already put out the word that no standdown leave requests would be accepted until after the ship had left San Diego.

Sunday, during my duty day, I submitted my "request chit," hoping my leave request would be in the first cut. As an inducement to get my request approved, I only requested 10 days of leave instead of 15 like everyone else would. It was a tactic based on the advice from one of our old salts.

The next morning at 0800, the ship got underway from Pier 6 and backed out into the channel. Once the ship was fair in the channel, ahead bells were rung up on the main engines and we began the reverse trip through San Diego Bay, outbound back to sea. After passing Point Loma on the starboard side, some guys on deck let out some whoops and hollers, celebrating the start of our final legs of the trip home.

Once the ship was clear of the outbound fairway channel, we rang up on the engine order telegraph turns for the passage's planned SOA of 16 knots. We were on our way, but it was still a long way to go. Including the Panama Canal transit, the distance was 4,426 nautical miles from San Diego to Norfolk. The passage plan distance from San Diego to the Rodman Naval Station in the Canal Zone was 2,516 nautical miles.

The passage to the Panama Canal from San Diego was a fairly easy one. Speaking from the navigation perspective, the weather conditions were great. The days were sunny with partly cloudy skies. The morning and evening twilight periods were clear, which allowed for good star observations and good resultant star fix positions. The good weather gave me and the other QMs more opportunities to become better celestial navigators. Even the Loran "A" receiver was behaving well, giving good Time Difference (TD) readouts that resulted in Loran TD LOPs that closely matched our DR position and the celestial fix positions.

Everyone seemed to be in a good mood, and why not? We were on a smooth ocean passage and Vietnam was behind us, with the Panama Canal and home ahead of us. Oh, and I also had found out that my standdown leave request had been approved. I would have 10 days of leave upon our arrival in Norfolk. Life once again seemed good.

After several days, the ship was well south of the Baja Peninsula and had entered the Eastern Pacific Ocean. The clear, pristine seawater here seemed to have attracted pods of sperm and blue whales. It became almost routine to see whale spouts around the ship. Other marine life was abundant in numbers and frequently seen throughout the day. Schools of porpoise and mahi-mahi (dolphin fish) running alongside the ship were common. On several occasions, different species of large sea turtles were spotted near the ship. One fish species that was always present and needed to be cleared off the decks every morning was the flying fish.

After more than six days at sea, the ship entered into the Gulf of Panama during the mid-watch on March 18. We began our final approach to the Panama Canal Zone during late morning. The sea and anchor detail was set at noon for entering port and passed under Pan-American Bridge at about 1230. By 1300, the ship was moored at the Rodman Naval station dock. A fuel barge came alongside about an hour after docking and the ship began to take on fuel for the final leg home. The plan was for the ship to stay overnight at Rodman, getting underway the next morning for the northward Panama Canal Transit. We were getting closer all the time. After the canal transit, only one final leg of the journey would remain.

The crew was granted liberty later that afternoon and for the evening, with liberty expiring for everyone on board at midnight. There was a vendor selling cold beer at the head of the dock, so a number of us sat in the shade of some avocado trees, drinking ice-cold Balboa beers until dinnertime. The only guys who seemed interested in going to Panama City for the night were the single guys.

Many opted to either go to the naval station's enlisted club or just stayed on board. Later, after one of the other QMs and I had finished re-checking the completed Passage Plan for the route from Cristobal to Norfolk, we decided some good American beer as a nightcap was in order. After changing into civilian clothes, we headed off the ship and started the walk across the naval station to the enlisted club. Part of the walk to the enlisted club took you along a road with dense jungle on one side of the road. At night, there was very little lighting along parts of the road, so it was pretty dark in some areas.

All kinds of noises and racket began to come from the jungle. The noise actually was the loudest damn incessant hoots and howls either of us had ever heard. The volume of the hoots and howls would go down, then would come back up. At times, the howling was so loud we could barely speak to each other without yelling. We soon realized we were probably hearing howler monkeys. At the club, we asked the bartender about it.

She smiled and said, "Yes, they do that sometimes at night." For the Panamanians, apparently it was just another routine night.

The next morning, the sea and anchor detail for getting underway was set at 0830. The Panama Canal Pilot arrived at the ship at 0850. At 0900, we took in our mooring lines and got underway from the docks at the Rodman Naval Station. We backed the ship out into the main channel, ahead bells were rung up on the main engines, and we began the northbound passage in the canal to the first locks, the Miraflores Locks. I really can't say I remember that much about the northbound Panama Canal transit.

That afternoon, we disembarked the Panama Canal Pilot after

getting out of the Gatun Locks on the Caribbean side of the canal. Our ship proceeded north into Limon Bay and we cleared the Cristobal breakwater at close to 1800. We secured from the sea and anchor detail and set the normal underway watch sections. The ship was brought to the course to steer, which would keep us on our first planned route leg. We had 1,860 nautical miles to go. Only four more days of steaming and it would be over.

Late on March 20, a "North Atlantic High Seas and High Winds Advisory" came in by radio message from the Navy's Fleet Weather Central in Norfolk. A late winter storm, a northeaster (nor'easter), was off the U.S. Atlantic coast. Nor'easters are different from tropical cyclones in that the low-pressure system develops from cold air masses coming down from Canada, mixing with warm air masses and warm tropical water brought northward on the Atlantic's Gulf Stream current.

The nor'easter's cold-core low pressure centers can get very intense; this is what makes them different from tropical cyclones, which have warm-core low pressure centers. As they develop into a full-blown storm, they generally track in a northward direction. The result is the same with dense clouds, heavy rains. These Atlantic storms can contain very strong and persistent winds, which rotate in a counterclockwise rotation around the storm's center, the same as a tropical cyclone.

Nor'easters often create strong winds and high sea state conditions off the coast of Cape Hatteras and the North Carolina Outer Banks before moving north along the Atlantic coast. The storm's position and track was located right smackdab along our intended route to Norfolk. March 20, was also the date of the vernal equinox, the first day of spring, so technically, this storm was an early spring versus a late winter storm. The captain and XO decided it would best to increase our SOA from 21 knots to 26 knots in order to arrive off the North Carolina coast and the Outer Banks sooner than planned, in the event we would have to slow our speed due to bad weather or high seas.

By late afternoon Wednesday, March 21, the ship had made it the through the Windward Passage and was on a northwest heading moving toward the Florida Strait. The ship began the northward passage through the Florida Strait during the mid-watch, and by midmorning the ship was off the coast of central Florida. That afternoon, northwest winds began to pick up and significant sea waves began rolling in from the north off the ship's port bow. The ship's ordered speed was still at 26 knots.

Throughout the evening hours, the winds and seas seemed to stay fairly consistent without indications of building up so far. The ship was actually about 11 hours ahead of schedule at this point due to the excess 5 knots of speed over the planned SOA. It was looking like we would actually have to slow our speed soon to stay on our originally planned ETA in Norfolk.

Starting with the mid-watch on March 22, the weather began deteriorating as we started to encounter strong thunderstorms and heavy rains. The wind speed and sea wave height were increasing in between each round of thunderstorms. The ship began its normal heavy rolling and pitching in the seas. At the speed of 26 knots, the ship's bow and hull were pounding into each wave, causing the entire ship to lurch, shudder, and shake with each impact. About midway through the watch, the captain called the OOD and ordered him to slow our speed to 18 knots to see if that would reduce the pounding and improve the ride. The speed reduction did lessen the pounding, but did nothing to reduce the ship's rolling and pitching.

By morning, the captain was forced to reduce our ordered speed even further to 16 knots. The ship had caught up to the nor'easter, now off the coast of South Carolina. By the time I came on watch for the 1200 to 1600, our speed had been slowed to 14 knots. The winds were now gusting to 70 to 80 knots, and the wave heights were 35 to 40 feet. The winds were now from the north-northeast just off the starboard bow. The waves being driven by the wind were coming from the same direction. As each wave hit, the ship's bow, the forward deck, and the superstructure would disappear into the body of the wave. The ship shuddered and made groaning noises as the upward acting forces of buoyancy caused the ship's hull to rise out of each wave and into the next wave trough.

That afternoon, over the span of three hourly Loran "A" fix positions, our estimated actual speed over the ground was only about 5 knots. In other words, the force from the wind and seas were causing the ship to lose 9 knots of speed, which also meant we had only made 15 nautical miles over the ground in those same three hours. The hours we had in hand of being ahead of schedule were starting to slip way.

Below decks that evening, in spite of the bad weather and the heavy rolling of the ship, everyone was in high spirits. A lot of guys already had their bags packed, ready for our scheduled arrival the next day. At dinner that night, several guys asked if we would still be able to make the ETA to Norfolk. I told them maybe. After dinner, I hit my rack to try and get some sleep before the mid-watch. As always, it was really tough to sleep whenever the ship was in heavy weather.

I finally gave up on sleeping around 2100 and got up. Hardly anyone was sleeping anyway because most everyone in the crew, including me, had varying degrees of "channel fever." Get-Home-Itis was the same thing as channel fever; you were feeling anxious and getting impatient about getting home. Anyone who has ever gone on long ocean voyages has experienced channel fever.

That night, upon arriving on the bridge to take the mid-watch, I found the XO, Janson, and the captain all at the chart table, huddled over the navigation chart. On speaking with the QM, he told me that they were trying to figure out what our new ETA would be to Norfolk. The captain decided to file a revised ETA of noon versus our original ETA of 0900 to Norfolk. The revised ETA in part was based on a weather forecast indicating an improvement in the weather off Cape Hatteras. The forecast also predicted storm movement farther north throughout the night. The ship had only been making about 7 knots of speed over the ground for the past several hours.

The weather during the mid-watch improved some. The winds were now only gusting to around 50 knots. It was too dark to estimate the height of the waves, but judging from the pounding, rolling, and pitching of the ship, the waves were still obviously significant in height. Our ordered speed had been reduced to 12 knots. The captain's "Night Orders" to the OOD and the bridge watch were to increase speed as soon as the OOD deemed it safe to do so. Well, the conditions ended up staying so rough that the OOD decided it was best to stay at the ordered speed of 12 knots throughout the watch.

After the 0400 to 0800 sections relieved the watch, I hit my rack for a couple hours of sleep, getting back up at 0600. I knew the sun would just be coming up, and to satisfy my channel fever, I wanted to get up to the bridge to see what the weather conditions looked like. Getting to the bridge about 15 minutes later, looking out the bridge windows, I could see the big sea waves still coming. I guessed the noon ETA was probably out of the question. This bitch of a storm was not going to let go of us yet.

I checked the navigation plot, and we were doing a bit better now, making almost 9 knots good over the ground at an ordered speed of 14 knots. It was going to be a long, long day. At 0800, the captain filed a revised ETA of 1630 that afternoon at the Chesapeake Bay entrance, and the final ETA at the Naval Station D&S Piers for 1800.

Finally, by noon, the weather conditions were starting to improve. The winds were now gusting at 25 to 35 knots, but the sea wave heights were reducing. The sun began shining through breaks in the clouds every so often as well. Things were starting to look up. More importantly, we were now making about 12 knots over the ground, a big improvement.

At 1630, the sea and anchor detail was set for entering port. I had just enough time after getting off the 1200-1600 watch to get below in order to shave, take a fast shower, and change into my dress blue uniform for entering port. Finally, at 1715, our ship was passing the Cape Henry Lighthouse on our port side as the ship slowed to take the pilot boat alongside and for the Pilot to board the ship. The ship entered into Thimble Shoals Channel, beginning the inbound trip through the southern part of Chesapeake Bay, and ultimately to the Naval Station's D&S Piers.

An hour later, our ship began the final approach to Pier 23. We were to moor with our port side to dockside. I was the port bearing taker, so I could see what looked like several hundred people on the pier waiting for the ship's arrival. I scanned the crowd on the dock looking for Jan, but couldn't spot her anywhere. I knew she had to be there, but I just couldn't locate her in the crowd. The ship moored at 1830, the Pilot departed the ship; and we secured from the sea and anchor detail. It was finally, finally over; we had made it.

Before we could go below, the bridge equipment all had to be stowed away and secured. Between me and the other QMs, that took like three minutes. My next job was to go find Jan. I could see the gangway from the port bridge wing and people were coming up, filing on board. The gangway and quarterdeck were set up on the helicopter flight deck, which was the largest open deck area on the ship. I worked my way aft to the flight deck, and on getting there it was packed with people. The deck lights had been turned on, illuminating the decks, as the sun had already set and it was getting dark.

I began to move through the crowd looking for Jan. I finally spotted her through the crowd about 15 feet away; she was carrying our son in her arms, but she was turning away from me, looking around. I got close enough to where by reaching over at least one other person, I was able to tap her on the shoulder in an attempt to get her attention. I'll never forget, she turned, looked at me, and turned away as if she didn't recognize me.

Next, I heard a loud but familiar voice, "Jan, that's him; it's George." It was my brother-in-law, Joe. He tapped Jan on the shoulder and got her attention while pointing at me. Within a moment, we were in each other's arms with our son jammed between us. For me, now it was really over.

I was happy to see that Joe had come with Jan and our son to meet the ship. I learned from Joe that they had been waiting all day, since about 0830 that morning, and it hadn't been until around noon that a naval officer had showed up to notify everyone that the ship had been delayed due to bad weather. I left Jan with Joe while I went back below to the Ships Office to get my leave papers. On looking at my leave papers, my leave start time and date of 0900, March 23, had been lined through and retyped to read 0700, March 24. The PN told me the XO had directed them to change everyone's leave start dates to the next day.

Next I went to the berthing compartment to pick up my bags and gear, then back up to the quarterdeck area to find Jan and Joe. Going down the gangway onto the pier and walking to Joe's car parked out in the huge lot at the D&S Piers for me was one big blur. I barely remember the drive home, until we pulled up in Joe's car at the front of our apartment around 8:00 p.m.

Shortly after we got inside, Joe said his goodbyes. I thanked him for being such a help to Jan while I was gone; he just smiled as he closed our front door and left. I looked around our apartment, then at Jan, then at our son, who was asleep. I was here on my home planet, Planet Earth. What do you suppose my first order of business was?

I took a very long, very hot Hollywood shower. I wanted the smell of the ship off me. I wanted to feel like a normal human being again. I had 10 days of leave ahead of me to forget about everything. For now, my focus could be on the two people that mattered more to me than anyone else in the world, my wife and son.

A deployment homecoming experience for a married couple is somewhat of a honeymoon period. There is time to catch up on each other's experiences while separated. In some respects, it's about getting to know each other all over again. Our son was now 15 months old and he had changed a lot in my absence. For one, he could walk really well on his own, and he walked a lot. At times, he would try to talk and jabber a lot. Whenever I looked at him, he always gave me his big, broad smile. I wasn't sure if he knew me or even understood that I had been gone. But that really didn't matter to me; we were back together as a family. For Jan and me, I think the biggest thing was that the unknowns for us from before the deployment were now in the past; they were history.

My leave was soon over, and it was time to check back on board. I went back to the ship on the morning of April 3. The atmosphere on board was laidback and relaxed. The ship's engineering plant status was cold iron; all Hotel services were coming from the pier. During the standdown, the crew was split into three in port duty sections. With over one-third of the crew on leave, the ship would stay in three duty sections until the end of the standdown period. Other than the necessary ship's work of cleaning and equipment maintenance, except for the daily fire drill for the duty sections, other activities were kept to a minimum.

In port, everyone had to report onboard by 0700 and the workday started at 0730. It was actually a good time. Except for on duty days, once whatever work needed to be done was complete, we could leave and go home, usually not later than 1300 or 1400, so the workdays were short.

About mid-April, still during the standdown period, the advancement and promotion list arrived on board. My name was on the list as having been selected for promotion to paygrade E-4, third class petty officer, Quartermaster rating. I was to be promoted to QM3, effective July 1, 1973. The raise in base pay from E-3 to E-4 was meager, about $14 a month. It did represent an increase of my Basic Allowance for Quarters by $16 a month; my sea pay stayed the same at $13 a month. So cumulatively, I would realize a gross gain in income of just over $30 a month.

This amount doesn't seem like much of an increase in pay, does it? Well, $30 in 1973 is equivalent to $165 today. Promotion in the military is obviously more than just about pay. It's also about taking on more duties and responsibilities, plus the perks of a little bit of prestige, and recognition for past hard work, and yes, a little pride.

The ship got back into the swing of things on April 24, which was the end of the 30-day standdown period. At that point, the crew went into the normal four in port duty sections, which meant we could now go home after the workday three out of every four nights. Within a week after the standdown ended, the ship began a series of engineering inspections and hull surveys. The inspectors and surveyors were finding problems in both the engineering plant and had some concerns about the integrity of the underwater portions of the ship's hull and hull openings.

These problems were not unexpected, considering the pounding and stress the old ship had been put through during the deployment. It was decided that the ship would begin an extended intermediate maintenance and upkeep period to fix and repair many of the issues. To many in the crew this was good news of sorts; it meant not getting the ship underway for at least several more months.

I believe it was in late May when the commanding officer was to conduct a personnel inspection of the entire crew and there would be an awards ceremony held after the personnel inspection. The uniform of the day for the personnel inspection was dress whites. The day of the personnel inspection came, and it was held on the pier in an area large enough to accommodate the entire crew lined up in ranks organized by each department. Near the inspection area, there was a small stage, podium, and microphone. The commander of the destroyer squadron and some other senior officers would be attending the ship's awards ceremony.

After the captain's personnel inspection of the ship's crew, the crew was kept in ranks at "parade rest." The squadron commander and other officers arrived and were greeted by the captain and XO. The captain, along with the squadron commander, took to the stage to begin the ceremony. The XO took the stage, and speaking over the microphone, gave the command, "Ship's company, attention."

The squadron commander, captain, and the other officers took to the stage. The squadron commander moved to the podium, and the XO gave the command, "Ship's company, parade rest." The squadron commander now at the podium began to make his remarks about the ship and the ship's accomplishments and performance during our deployment.

Next, the captain took to the podium and made his remarks. Then the awards ceremony began, first by the XO calling out each individual's rank and name, calling those receiving an award to fall out of ranks and to fall in front and center. Soon, all those to receive awards were lined up in a row, front and center to the stage.

Many of us in ranks were exchanging questioning glances with each other. A look of dismay was on some faces, and on some faces there were outward looks of disgust. The reason for this was that the only members of the crew receiving any recognition or awards that day were the ship's officers and one chief petty officer. The chief was the first class commissaryman, since promoted to chief, who had made the homemade bread for the crew back in Vietnam. First the department heads, all lieutenants, received citations read by the captain and were awarded Navy Commendations and other medals by the squadron commander. Next, citations were read for the junior officers and they received various medals or awards.

Last, the citation was read by the captain for the chief commissaryman about how all his hard work in making the homemade bread had contributed to the high morale of the crew. I can't say for sure, but I believe the chief was awarded a Letter of Commendation. A small number of the enlisted crew members were ordered to come front and center. This small group of crew members mainly received Letters of Appreciation. Shortly after that, the squadron commander, along with the captain and other senior officers, went on board the ship.

After all had been "bonged" on board with the ship's bell by the quarterdeck watch, the XO took to the stage and gave the command, "Ship's company, dismissed." That was it; the dog and pony show ended. Once on board, down in the berthing compartment, comments heard were along the lines of "What a crock of bullshit," or "That was just f**ked up." I was somewhat satisfied in my realization that others thought much the same as I about what had just happened.

Apparently, most of the ship's crew members below the rank of E-6 were not deserving of any higher recognition. The hard work, dedication, and for some I knew about, almost superhuman efforts that had ensured our objectives were achieved in combat operations did not count for much. As I have pointed out, what happened that day is just a summation of the naval culture during those times. You could say this about the command and the officers we served under on board USS *Rich*: "They used us well."

EPILOGUE: LIFE BEYOND USS *RICH*

I have shared some details from approximately four years of my life, from teenager to young man. These four years represent only about six percent out the total years I have lived so far, but they shaped the footprint from which the rest of my life was launched. I included some of my life experience as a teenager to hopefully help give younger readers a bit of perspective on rural life in the 1960s. Some readers from my generation may enjoy reminiscing on this period of innocence, evolution, and change. It was a period void of smart phones, the internet, color TV, cable TV, 24-hour news cycle, social media, and the microwave oven.

A much simpler time, and I would advocate calling it a much better time. Patriotism didn't need to be taught to us; it was instilled into our spirit and nature from every aspect of our lives and upbringing. However, the national and international events playing out at that time and how our elected and appointed leaders behaved brought about change. As some of our political leaders' behavior and actions became publicly known, it created a tiny crack of public distrust. This crack later grew into a fracture of distrust and suspicion between the people and our own government, particularly among young people.

The U.S. Navy in 1971 to 1973, which I have written about, was a much different military organization from what it's evolved into today. However, at least on board warships, the focus of leadership hasn't changed; it has to be on mission accomplishment, but the thinking on what is a leader and leadership has changed. Most, but not all, of the leaders on USS *Rich*, were what some leadership experts would probably categorize as "self-serving leaders" or "bosses." Sailors obeyed them, but they didn't follow them. There were a few who did lead by example and did care about their sailors, and as a result, their sailors did follow them.

Some current or former naval officers might wholly disagree with my descriptions of some officers serving on *Rich* and their demeanor. My intent was to go back over 45 years to try and remember my views and perspective through the eyes of a sailor at 20 years old, living and working in the lower levels of the shipboard hierarchy. Something the average naval officer has never done or experienced.

Since Vietnam, except for one day of action in the Persian Gulf in April of 1988, U.S. Navy ships have not been in any sort of kinetic combat gun-to-gun battles or missile-to-missile battles. For the Navy destroyers in Vietnam, gun-to-gun battles happened frequently. The intent of these actions was to suppress whenever possible North Vietnamese threats to the air campaigns or to prevent build-ups and incursions by NVA troops in their attempts to move farther south.

USS *Rich* was awarded her third campaign star (formerly called "battle star") for the Cease Fire Campaign in 1972 and 1973. Everyone in the crew was awarded the Combat Action Ribbon and the Vietnam Service Medal. The Combat Action is a ribbon-only award; it is not a medal or metal badge. After the WESTPAC/Vietnam deployment, the ship was back to normal Atlantic Fleet operations by the early summer months of 1973. In September, the ship was transferred to Philadelphia, PA, first for an extensive overhaul and shipyard period at the Philadelphia Naval Shipyard. After the shipyard period, the ship transferred to a destroyer squadron, designated for the training of Naval Reserve crews. The ship's new home port became Philadelphia.

On April 30, 1975, Saigon surrendered to the North Vietnamese, a little over two years after the cease-fire agreement took effect. By this time, President Ford was in office, and his administration planned the complete evacuation of American presence in South Vietnam. Our ambassador in South Vietnam was in denial that Saigon was about to fall to the communists and refused to start any evacuation efforts of friendly Vietnamese until it was too late. This led to the debacle many watched on television of the desperate South Vietnamese people fleeing their own country ahead of the communist onslaught.

I stayed with the ship until October of 1975, when, as a second class petty officer (QM2), I reenlisted for new orders to a special boat unit, coastal-river division, at the Great Lakes Naval Station, principally operating on Lake Michigan. Less than a year after reporting to Coastal-River Division 21, the unit was decommissioned. The QM Rating Detailer in Washington talked me into taking a shore tour as a Navy recruiter in Chicago, Illinois. During the fall months of 1976, after recruiting school and training, I was assigned to my first recruiting office located in one of Chicago's suburbs. Over the next three years, I was assigned to various recruiting offices in the Chicago suburbs and later to the inner city areas.

It was there in Chicago that Navy and other military recruiters faced severe anti-military reactions, which at times included violence. For some recruiters, finding themselves in uniform on the wrong Chicago streets didn't end well. The factions from the liberal antiwar movements were still alive and active in Chicago. Now, some of these factions had morphed into carrying out anti-military and anti-American activities. It was here where on several occasions, members of the public walked up to me and spit in my face, simply because I was in uniform. While walking along the streets of Chicago, we became accustomed to people yelling obscenities or calling us names such as "fascists" or "baby killers."

I would never call the people who did these things Americans, for they were not. These people hated us; they were vicious, and somehow very twisted in what they thought America should be. After about two years on the streets of Chicago, I lost count of how many times people pulled guns or knives on me so I would know they were armed in their attempts to threaten me.

Several of our recruiting offices were the recipients of pipe bombings. These pipe bombing attacks on our offices were courtesy of the Armed Forces of National Liberation (FALN), a Puerto Rican terrorist organization.

This was the post-Vietnam Era I knew and experienced. Somehow, I survived my three-year tour in that environment and moved on. To me, it was time spent in another war zone, except it was Chicago instead of some far away shithole. It was as if our country was still trying to tear itself apart.

In late 1977, I learned of my old ship meeting her end. In July, Rich had been in a collision with USS *Calossahatchee* (AO 98) during an underway replenishment. The old destroyer suffered a casualty in her steering control just as she was breaking away from *Calossahatchee*. The steering casualty caused the ship to steer into the path of *Calossahatchee*, resulting in her being hit fourteen times by the Cimarron-class oiler. My old ship suffered significant and serious damage to her superstructure and main deck areas, and her port side hull was penetrated numerous times below the waterline. Despite the damage, Rich was able to steam under her own power to the naval station at Mayport, Florida. In Mayport, initial repairs were completed and the ship was then able to steam back to her home port in Philadelphia.

Several months after the collision, the Navy's in-service (INSERV) inspection of the ship determined the ship was too badly damaged to justify the cost of repairs, and it was recommended the ship be stricken. On December 15, 1977, at 0911, USS *Rich* was officially decommissioned in Philadelphia. Later, in 1979, the ship was broken up as scrap. A tough ship, manned for 31 years by tough crews, met a tough end to her life.

I never really considered myself a combat veteran after Vietnam, though technically I guess I am. I know a lot of my friends and buddies from USS *Rich* don't see themselves as combat veterans either. After all, no one on our ship was killed or wounded in combat, and to be a combat veteran you had to experience that, right? Our ship didn't suffer massive and disabling battle damage, and to be a combat veteran you had to experience that, right? We didn't have to fight every action with small arms while employing ground tactics against the enemy, and to be a combat veteran you had to experience that, right? There were no grand gestures made by the public in welcoming us home, and to be a combat or war veteran you had to experience that, right? In our psyche, we just didn't fit the narrative that many of us thought we knew and understood pertaining to combat veterans. We didn't fit in that mold.

I'm not a thin-skinned person. If I ever was, the first two years in the Navy took that away from me. My Vietnam experience never seemed like a topic I cared to speak about. It was easier to keep it to myself. If my wife reads this story, she will learn of many experiences that I have never discussed, even with her. Family members from the Midwest have never seemed to care enough to ask about my time in Vietnam, which I'm actually fine with.

However, over the years, there have been many articles published and television shows aired on topics from the Vietnam War. The story of the Navy destroyers in Vietnam and the part they played is never told. Why has there been no coverage of the action on the gun lines or the strike missions? Maybe the stories weren't seen to be glamorous or gory enough? That's why I felt this story needed to be told.

The actions our crew were put through were not unique from any other destroyer sent to Vietnam. All destroyer crews went through the grinds and challenges that are described in many parts of this story. If the war had continued, the cycle for our ship would have continued with rotations of roughly three weeks on the gun line and carrying out strike missions followed by three weeks or so out at Yankee Station. I think naval commanders understood that for a destroyer, 18 to 21 days of continuous combat operations were the outer limit of crew endurance and stamina.

The crew of USS *Rich* was young. We represented a minuscule splinter group from our generation. We took on or accepted the burden of military service. We were a group of young men who transformed into a unified, efficient, and deadly fighting team. We took part in bringing a long, unpopular, and viciously fought war to a close. As our generation retires or moves into retirement, we will soon wither away and die off. Once that happens, the sub-subspecies of our generation who served and fought in Vietnam will be extinct from our planet, the likes of which will never be seen again.

GLOSSARY OF TERMS AND ACRONYMS

AE - Navy ship class designation for Fleet Ammunition Replenishment ships.

AFS - Navy ship class designation for Fleet Combat Stores ships.

AO - Navy ship class designation for Fleet Oiler Replenishment ships.

AOR - Navy ship class designation for Fleet Replenishment Oilers.

A-7 Corsair - Aircraft carrier-capable subsonic light attack aircraft. The Corsair II initially entered service with the United States Navy (USN) during the Vietnam War.

Boatswain Mate of the Watch (BMOW) - An enlisted assistant to the officer of the deck (OOD) during underway watches. The BMOW must see that all deck watch stations are manned with qualified personnel and all watchstanders in previous watch sections are relieved. The BMOW must verify that every person in the watch has been properly instructed and trained. A BMOW must be a qualified helmsman and supervises the helmsman if senior to the QMOW.

Chaff - A radar countermeasure in which ships launch spread a cloud of small, thin pieces of aluminum, metallized glass fiber, or plastic, which either appears as a cluster of primary targets on radar screens or swamps the screen with multiple returns. A short-range mortar operated from in CIC launches chaff or infrared decoys from naval vessels.

Combat Information Center (CIC) - Most of the warfighting functions are handled from the ship's Combat Information Center (CIC). In peacetime steaming, CIC acts as the electronic "eyes and ears" of the ship, advising the bridge team how to navigate and maneuver safely and serving as a backup to make sure everything is being done safely. In alert situations and combat, CIC takes the lead, with the bridge team maneuvering the ship, communicating to the crew, and ensuring all stations are manned and ready.

Conn or Conning Officer - An officer responsible for instructing the helmsman on the course to steer. While performing this duty, the officer is said to have the conn.

Danger Close - The term "danger close" is used when fire support is directed close to friendly forces.

DD - Navy ship class designation for destroyers.

DDG - Navy ship class designation for guided missile destroyers.

DE - Navy ship class designation for destroyer escort. The DE designation for these ships was changed to FF or fast frigate in 1975.

DEG - Navy ship class designation for destroyer escort, guided missile.

DLG – Navy ship class designation for destroyer leader, guided missiles.

Department Head - As the representative of the commanding officer, the department head is responsible for and reports to the CO about all matters that affect his or her department. That includes administrative matters, the operational readiness of the department, and the general condition of equipment.

Division Officer - Division officers are responsible to act as assistants in general to department heads.

Engine Order Telegraph (EOT) - Two telegraph units and alarms must be installed, one on the bridge and one in the engine room. The order is given by moving the bridge unit's handle to the desired position on the dial face. This sends an electrical signal to the EOT placed in the engine room whose pointer acquires a position according to the signal given from the bridge. An audible alarm sounds at both ends. Accordingly, the watchkeeping engineer acknowledges the order by moving the handle of the engine room EOT to the required position and takes necessary action. This sends an electrical signal to the bridge EOT unit, causing its pointer to acquire the respective position.

Electronic Warfare (EW) - Examples of offensive electronic warfare include radio jamming (flooding a frequency with another transmission, for instance) or radar jamming (degrading radar signals through the introduction of deceptive decoys or "noise" that renders the device useless). Defense measures employ many of the same principles used in offensive electronic warfare.

Executive Officer (XO) - The executive officer (XO) is the aide or executive to the commanding officer. The XO is usually the next ranking line officer aboard ship and is the direct representative of the commanding officer in maintaining the general efficiency of the ship. The XO's responsibilities include the command's assigned personnel. With the help of department heads, the XO arranges and coordinates all ship's work, drills, exercises, and policing and inspecting the ship.

F-4 Phantom - Aircraft carrier-capable tandem two-seat, twin-engine, all-weather, long-range supersonic jet interceptor and fighter-bomber originally developed for the United States Navy by McDonnell Aircraft.

Fueling at Sea (FAS) - In fueling at sea (FAS), fuel is pumped from the delivering ship to the receiving ship. Typically, the STREAM rig is utilized for FAS operations.

Gun Target Line - An imaginary straight line from gun to target. Usually determined as a true bearing direction from the ship to the target both on the bridge and CIC, then corrected to the gun's actual shipboard position as part of the firing solution.

Helmsman - The helmsman is a qualified steersman who steers courses prescribed by the conning officer.

Junior Officer of the Deck (JOOD) - The junior officer of the deck (JOOD) is the principal assistant to the OOD. Anyone making routine reports to the OOD normally makes them through the JOOD. The JOOD often has the conn and serves as the conning officer during routine underway bridge watches. JOODs are the ship's division officers from different departments.

Lee Helmsman - The lee helmsman who stands watch at the engine order telegraph (EOT) on the bridge rings up the conning officer's orders to the engine room, making sure all bells are correctly answered.

Lookout - The lookout watch, mans assigned lookout stations and performs duties as prescribed in the ship's lookout instructions. They are under the direct supervision of the BMOW and OOD.

Main Control - The forward engine room (B-2) also called Main Control. The throttleman in Main Control operates the main engine throttles in response to orders received from the bridge on the EOT. Each engine room controls its own throttles. The After Engine Room (B-4) is subordinate to Main Control in the forward engine room.

Messenger of the Watch (MOOW) - The messenger of the watch stands the watch on the bridge (under way) and the quarterdeck (in-port). The MOOW delivers messages, answers telephones, and carries out such duties as the OOD may direct. Messengers need to be familiar with various departments of the ship and ship's company. The underway messenger is normally assigned from the weapons/deck department.

Officer of the Deck (OOD) - The officer of the deck (OOD) is in charge of the ship and is responsible to the commanding officer (CO) for the safe and proper operation of the ship or station. That includes navigation, ship handling, communications, routine tests and inspections, reports, supervision of the watch, and carrying out the plan of the day (POD). The OOD typically is one of the ship's department heads, usually a lieutenant.

Scuttlebutt - The origin of the word "scuttlebutt," which is nautical parlance for a rumor, comes from a combination of "scuttle," to make a hole in the ship's hull and thereby causing her to sink, and "butt," a cask or hogshead used in the days of wooden ships to hold drinking water. Even in today's Navy, a drinking fountain is still referred to as the scuttlebutt.

Semaphore - The Semaphore signaling system is an alphabet signaling system based on the waving of a pair of hand-held flags or arms in a particular pattern. The arms or flags are extended, in various positions representing each letter of the alphabet.

Sound-powered Telephone - Sound-powered phones operate using voice power and require no batteries or external electrical power source. Sound-powered telephone circuits are hardwired aboard ship to connect all primary and auxiliary spaces or operating stations.

Standard Tensioned Replenishment Alongside Method (STREAM) – A transfer rig utilizes a tensioned wire highline suspended between two ships. The exact type of STREAM rig is dependent on the kind of cargo. In all rigs, cargo to be transferred is connected to a trolley, which rides on the highline. The trolley is moved between the ships by inhaul and outhaul winches located on the delivery ship.

Styx Missile - Anti-ship missiles are guided missiles that are designed for use against ships and large boats.

Terrier Missile - A two-stage medium-range naval surface-to-air missile (SAM).

Quartermaster of the Watch (QMOW) - The QMOW is an enlisted assistant to the OOD while under way (and in-port on certain classes of ships). The QMOW assists the OOD in navigational matters and maintains the ship's deck log. Additional duties include reporting and recording weather changes and executing required ship's navigational lighting changes. The QMOW, who must be a qualified helmsman, supervises the helmsman if senior to the BMOW.

Underway Replenishment (UNREP)- A method the Navy uses for transferring fuel, ammunition, and stores from one ship to another while underway.

Vertical Replenishment (VERTREP) - The transfer of cargo between ships using helicopters. VERTREP is often used to supplement connected replenishment.

1MC - This is the general announcing system, over which word can be passed to every space in the ship. The ship's alarm system is tied into it as well. Transmitters are located on the bridge, quarterdeck, and damage control central/central control station; additional transmitters may be located at other points on the ship.

21MC – Captain's command intercom. It differs from the 1MC system in that it provides two-way communications. Each unit has a number of selector switches. To talk to one or more stations, you position the proper switches and operate the PRESS-TO-TALK switch.

ABOUT THE AUTHOR

George Trowbridge served over 20 years in the U.S. Navy, and retired from active service in 1992 as a Master Chief Petty Officer, Quartermaster with the Surface Warfare (SW) designation. He served at sea in five different destroyers or frigates and on coastal-river fast patrol boats, including the *USS Rich*. George completed seven overseas deployments, starting with Vietnam and ending with Desert Shield/Desert Storm. His shore tours were as a Navy recruiter in the Chicago metro area and later as a navigation instructor at the Navy's Officer Candidate School.

After retiring from the Navy, George sailed for several years as a Merchant Marine Officer on board various commercial merchant vessels. His experiences working on board merchant vessels prompted him to become a training provider for the maritime industry. George has founded two maritime training institutions and has managed two other similar institutions in the Gulf of Mexico region.

George and his wife Janice live in Largo, Florida. He recently semi-retired, but still teaches marine technologies and ship navigation training courses part-time.

Made in the USA
Monee, IL
24 August 2021

76398144R10174